Bound to Act

Bound to Act

MODELS OF ACTION,
DRAMAS OF INACTION

Valeria Wagner

STANFORD UNIVERSITY PRESS
STANFORD, CALIFORNIA

Stanford University Press
Stanford, California
© 1999 by the Board of Trustees of the
Leland Stanford Junior University
Printed in the United States of America

CIP data appear at the end of the book

In memory of Bill Readings,
dear friend, teacher, and colleague

☞ Acknowledgments

This book was originally a doctoral dissertation presented in 1996 at the University of Geneva, under the direction of Professor Richard Waswo. I began writing it in 1993 while I was a visiting student at the Comparative Literature Department of the University of Montreal, on a scholarship granted by the International Council for Canadian Studies. Work on the dissertation continued in Geneva, where I was a doctoral student and taught in the English Department. The revision into book form was completed in 1998, at which time I was in Argentina doing research on a grant from the *Fonds National Suisse de la Recherche Scientifique*, which kindly afforded me time to dedicate to this project.

Bill Readings commented on my first doctoral scribbles with his characteristic generosity, giving impetus to this project. Richard Waswo's critical enthusiasm has been invaluable to this work, from its uncertain beginnings to this definite end. The infallible comments of Wlad Godzich consistently made their way into both thesis and book, as have those, albeit somewhat distorted, of Pete De Bolla, whose teaching marked my student years. Eric Méchoulan and Johanne Villeneuve have been sympathetic readers of chapters 3 and 4, respectively. Equally sympathetic were the readers of my doctoral dissertation, Peter Hughes, Wolfgang Iser, and Patrizia Lombardo, all of whose comments I did my best to integrate into this book. More critical, and rightly so, were the students with whom I experimented with various approaches to the question of action in literature. They helped me to identify inadequacies in my analysis.

Saba Bahar and George Varsos have been significant figures throughout, shaping my reflections in innumerable ways. George Varsos, in particular, has been an interested and interesting reader and critic of all my work, as well as my personal consultant in Greek. Jean-Jacques Bonvin, Susan Bruce, Christophe Cupelin, Anne Labarthe, Christopher Mikton, Beatriz Moral, Alejandro Moreira, Eric Noël, Simone Oettli, and Dominic Rainsford have kept the horizon of my concerns open and lively.

During the last stage of the revision I was surrounded by Andean mountains and friends—Anne Buholzer, Fabiana Imola, Fernando Krichmar, Diego Moreira, Nicolas Roman, Valentina Salvi, Javi Sánchez, Coco, Rita, and Julio. Back in the city, Peter Kahn and Armando Poratti helped me through various tribulations related to, respectively, the English language and the pagination of Aristotle's texts.

Both my immediate and extended family gave me their unconditional—and very practical—support: Daniel, Susana, and Paula Wagner; Herminia and Adriana Petruzzi; Alvaro and Marcela Díaz; Laura, Marina, and Irene Tettamanti; Fernando Ramírez; Aurelio and Guillermo Narvaja. I am grateful to them all, as I am to both identified and unspecified teachers, colleagues, friends, and students.

Special thanks to Neil Hertz, who encouraged me to submit the manuscript for publication.

V.W.

☞ Contents

Bound to Act

ᗘ Introduction

> It is beyond doubt that the capacity to act is the most dangerous of all human abilities and possibilities.
>
> Hannah Arendt

> Mere movements of the body—these are all the actions there are.
>
> Donald Davidson

Men of action

In one of the "eight exercises in political thought" published under the suggestive title *Between Past and Future*, Hannah Arendt suggests that "it would be adequate for the world we have come to live in to define man as being capable of action."[1] Arendt's definition both evokes and contrasts with previous instances of man's self-interpretation, all of which, she reminds us, privileged a given human capacity above others. In Greek classical antiquity, man's defining traits were his "supreme" capacity for speech and for political activity; Rome and medieval philosophy understood man as the *animal rationale*; in early modernity "man was thought of primarily as *homo faber*"; and in the nineteenth century "man was interpreted as an *animal laborans*." In the twentieth century, now that "for the first time in our history," as Arendt claims, "the human capacity for action has begun to dominate all others" (CH, p. 62) and "seems to have become the center of all other human capabili-

---

[1] Hannah Arendt, "The Concept of History," p. 63; henceforth referred to as CH.

ties" (CH, p. 63), it would be time that man begin to understand himself primarily as a *man of action*. According to Arendt's understanding of "the world we have come to live in," however, this has failed to happen: There is a time lag between contemporary man's self-understanding and the actual predominance of his capacity for action. Action has become man's defining trait, but man has not yet fully grasped his condition as a *man of action*. And this lack of self-understanding is dangerous, Arendt warns us, because, although action has always been "the most dangerous of all human abilities and possibilities . . . the self-created risks mankind faces today have never been faced before" (CH, p. 63).

Schematically, Arendt's argument is that, understood as the capacity to start new processes, action is inherently dangerous because unpredictability is its inevitable corollary. This is not too worrisome as long as human action is restricted to human affairs, for then its consequences are limited and can be politically manageable. But today, she argues, the field of action has expanded to the point of engulfing the natural limits that once contained it:

The moment we started natural processes of our own—and splitting the atom is precisely such a man-made natural process—we not only increased our power over nature . . . but for the first time have taken nature into the human world as such and obliterated the defensive boundaries between natural elements and the human artifice by which all previous civilizations were hedged in. (CH, p. 60)

The obliteration of these extrahuman "defensive boundaries" implies, ultimately, that in principle everything is within reach of human action: "All the processes of the earth and the universe have revealed themselves either as man-made or as potentially man-made"—and to an extent that they devour "the solid objectivity of the given" (CH, p. 89). And the absorption of the given—whether natural or historical—into the horizon of possibility and potentiality of human action inevitably affects the political realm, finding its extreme expression in "the totalitarian phenomenon," which, Arendt argues, "is based . . . on the conviction that everything is possible—and not just permitted, morally or otherwise" (ibid.): "Totalitarian systems tend to demonstrate that action can be based on any hypothesis and that, in the course of consistently guided action, the particular hypothesis will become true, will become actual, factual reality" (CH, p. 87). In light of the all-pervasiveness and apparently endless potentiality of human action, to think that contemporary man is defined by this "supreme" capacity is not only to describe him in those terms but also, and more urgently, to raise the question of what he can—and should—do with his potential for action. In other words, to understand man as being, fundamentally, an agent, is to set it as a task for him to act upon his decisive capacity for action and to contain it within human bounds.

"Man" as the species, however, upon which bears Arendt's diagnostic of "the world we have come to live in," should not be confused with men, its members. Indeed, while the human capacity for action may well be proper to the species, the task of enacting this capacity and of acting upon it can be handled only by particular human beings. And if there seems to be no limit to what the species can do, the actions of individual men have a much more limited scope. It is so much more limited, in fact, that the eminent philosopher of action Donald Davidson goes as far as to argue that "we never do more than move our bodies: the rest is up to nature."[2] Extreme and provocative as it is—and we will return to it below—Davidson's claim has the advantage of taking the perspective of individual agents with respect to action. What emerges is that what the species might view as the incorporation of nature into human artifice its individual members interpret as the exact reverse. It is actions, for them, that take on a natural character as soon as they are enacted, instead of nature's becoming an extension of human artifice by man's acting into it. The field of human artifice is thus reduced from all of nature to particular bodies, so that the endless potentiality of man's capacity for action is grasped by individual men as "mere movements" of their bodies. Needless to say, herein resides the dangers Arendt warns against, for it was ultimately with "mere movements of the body" that the atom was

[2]Donald Davidson, "Agency," p. 59.

split; and it is, again, mere movements of the body that make atom bombs explode. In other words, we do all with mere movements of the body, but they are not all that is done—and it is this crucial transition that contemporary man, or rather, men, seem unable to fully grasp.

This brief confrontation between the political philosopher's and the philosopher of action's views draws a paradoxical portrait of our contemporary man of action: at once omnipotent and impotent; capable of all yet in control of nothing; creator of new worlds that are beyond his grasp; supreme actor yet mere spectator. But if we consider the apparent "splitting" of contemporary man as two conceptually distinct "stages" of action instead of as two coexisting traits of agents, the paradox, if not the problem, dissolves. In a more detailed discussion of action, Arendt herself draws our attention to "the curious fact" that

both the Greek and the Latin language possess two verbs to designate what we uniformly call "to act." The two Greek words are *arkhein*: to begin, to lead, and, finally, to rule; and *prattein*: to carry something through. The corresponding Latin verbs are *agere*: to set something in motion; and *gerere*, which is hard to translate and somehow means the enduring and supporting continuation of past acts.[3]

The carrying through of something or the supporting continuation of past acts foregrounds the properly political dimension of action, for, as Arendt observes, "only with the help of others could the . . . beginner . . . really act, . . . carry through whatever he started to do" (WIF, p. 166). Indeed, although human action in general is "a strictly political phenomenon" (CH, p. 61), it is its interactive dimension that necessarily presupposes a public and politically organized space. In other words, whereas the capacity to begin something new can be conceived in nonpolitical terms and can thus be attributed to man as a species, the continuation or carrying through of what has begun can be attributed only to politically related human beings.

Contemporary man's difficulty with integrating these two con-

---

[3]"What Is Freedom?" p. 165; henceforth referred to as WIF.

ceptual moments of action can be conveyed by portraying him double-faced: *homo agens* on one side and *homo gerens* on the other, the two faces looking in opposite directions and unable to evaluate each other. These two faces would never meet in the same individual, but each could appreciate a version of the other, seen in other individuals, and be thus integrated in the public space of the political. As Arendt develops throughout her work, however, the realm of the political, the common "space of appearances where [men] could act" (WIF, p. 154)—as it was first conceived by the Greeks—is precisely that which contemporary mass societies have "lost."[4] Whether or not the Greeks ever "had" it is not, here, to the point, although Arendt's appeal to the *topos* of loss to frame her account of "the world we have come to live in" should not go unmentioned. But in fact it is clear that in Arendt's analysis the Greek polis functions more as a conceptual than as a historical reference, and more precisely as the political model grounding the "old truism" that "the *raison d'être* of politics is freedom" and that "freedom is primarily experienced in action" (WIF, p. 151).[5] In opposition to this understanding of politics as the space where freedom is exercised in action, the contemporary and dominating liberal credo is that "politics is compatible with freedom only insofar as it guarantees a possible freedom *from* politics" (WIF, p. 149, her emphasis). If Arendt's observations are correct, then, the impotence of contemporary men with respect to their own acts—"mere bodily movements"—should come as no surprise, for the space is missing

[4]"For a mass-society is nothing more than that kind of organized living which automatically establishes itself among human beings who are still related to one another but have lost the world once common to all of them" (CH, p. 90).

[5]"To use the word 'political' in the sense of the Greek *polis* is neither arbitrary nor far-fetched. . . . [T]he very word, which in all European languages still derives from the historically unique organization of the Greek city-state, echo the experiences of the community which first discovered the essence and the realm of the political. It is indeed difficult and even misleading to talk about politics . . . without drawing to some extent upon the experiences of Greek and Roman antiquity, and this for no other reason than that men have never, either before or after, thought so highly of political activity and bestowed so much dignity upon its realm" (WIF, p. 154).

where their capacity for action could be exercised and exerted in turn upon the capacity itself.

There is no need to delve deeper into Arendt's argument to note, with her, that the political is not experienced today as a "space of appearances where men could act." Indeed, not only is the political perceived as an *inaccessible* space, impervious to citizens' interventions, but there is, moreover, very little faith in political action in general. Nothing we can do seems capable of changing the course of events; political action is perceived as ultimately useless, without influence in a world governed by autonomous political and economic laws. This disenchantment with political action is pervasive enough to have been exploited for commercial purposes, as is apparent in a series of advertisements reported in an article published in 1994 in *Le Monde Diplomatique*.[6] The ads presuppose citizens' discontent with the political establishment and present their power of acquisition as a remedy to political impotence: Thus Opel tells us that "there's more to life than what the government has to offer" (*Il n'y a pas que l'offre gouvernementale dans la vie*); Peugeot incites us to "join their movement" (*Réjoignez notre mouvement*); and the Parisian bookshop FNAC, claiming to be "an agitator since 1954," invites us to obtain their "party card" (*Parce que la FNAC prend parti pour vous, prenez la carte*). Here, buying both replaces political action and ensures an immediate and infallible, albeit metaphorical, inscription of the citizen in a collectivity. The goods purchased are the means of access to an alternative political space or organization in which the capacity for action can be exercised and actions can be carried through to their end. For, indeed, how could the act of buying, as an act, fail, or exceed the purchaser's control?[7]

[6]Emmanuel Soucher and Yves Jeanneret, "Manipuler les idées et les désirs. Publicité et politique: le mélange des genres doit être clairement dénoncé."

[7]Although the staging of the buyer in a political scenario conveys a certain political reality, because it correctly places the site of power in the economic realm, it is clear that the political power "acquired" in buying a Peugeot does not compare to that possessed by those who own the trademark Peugeot. The collapse of the economic and the political in advertisements is consequently not

A commercial for the detergent Skip Power, reported in the same article, makes a more revealing use of the metaphor of buying as political action. The authors of the article stress the timing of the advertisement, which coincided with the beginning of the 1995 presidential campaign in France—a campaign that apparently took place in an atmosphere of "suspicion and corruption." It is in this context that Skip Power invites us to wash our dirty clothes:[8] "Difficult spots (*taches*): seize the power!—With Skip Power you eliminate more difficult spots (*taches*) from the outset (*du premier coup*)." "Clearly," the authors conclude, "for clean politics, let us vote for a detergent from the first round! What remains is political action reduced to the elimination of spots." This reduction is in fact double, for the commercial relies heavily on the pun on the word *tache*—"spot"—and *tâche*—"task." The difficult spots are thus the "spots" of political corruption as well as the political tasks that governments fail to accomplish, and they will both be eliminated when the buyers "take over" the situation (*prenez le pouvoir*—"seize the power") with Skip Power. In this manner the political task is converted to one that is mundane and feasible, a task that all citizens and consumers are capable of carrying out. As the authors of the article point out, this conversion from political to daily task eliminates the former, so that the commercial ultimately exempts the consumer from his or her tasks as a citizen. But in the meantime, the consumer has been offered—at a low price—what very few discourses today can offer: a direct connection between a daily and a political task; a bridge between individual and political spheres of action.

The connection that Skip Power offers, of course, is a disconnection. As its name suggests, this miraculous washing powder skips both the problem and the solution to the problem that the advertisement seized upon to win the consumer's sympathy. The problem

---

a gesture of denunciation or of exhortation to revolt and seize the economy. Rather, the identification of the consumer with the political activist clearly exploits the citizen's sense that political action is in itself impossible.

[8]In French, as in English, to wash one's dirty clothes in public is to exhibit one's problems or to expose one's discrediting secrets.

was that citizens are suspicious of the ongoing political campaign, they have no faith in the political establishment, and they feel impotent, unable to cross the divide between what they can do and what should be done. By collapsing political action into a daily task, Skip Power metaphorically enables citizens to skip from their individual to political spheres of action, thus seemingly restoring their capacity to carry through political tasks—represented by the dirty clothes. But Skip Power also offers consumers the power to *skip the act*—that selfsame daily, accessible task that was to be converted into consequent political action. The clothes will be washed effortlessly, "*du premier coup*"—no scrubbing, no sweating, no failure. In other words, the actual carrying through of the task is reduced to the sheer potential of carrying it through: Skip Power sells "portable" political action that fits within a daily gesture. We could thus conclude, paraphrasing Davidson, that consumers never do more than move their bodies—the rest is up to Skip Power.

The mark of action

From this brief incursion into the advertising industry it would seem that it is not only political action in its restricted sense—militancy, political activism, participation in a political party, and so forth—that is under question; contemporary "men of action" are ill at ease with action in general.[9] This can be verified through a discussion of Davidson's essay on "Agency," in which he sets out to show that "there is a fairly definite subclass of events which are actions" (p. 44)—in itself a sign that the notion of action does not go without saying, as it needs laborious argumentation to be demarcated from what simply happens.[10] More significantly, in order

[9]This of course makes sense if we grant, with Arendt, that human action is always "strictly speaking a political phenomenon" (CH, p. 61) and that the political is the "space of appearances where men could act" (WIF, p. 166).

[10]The extent to which individual agents can be said to be able to act is a recurrent concern in Davidson's work—in his essay "Intending," for instance, he is bent on explaining "the possibility of autonomous action in a world of causality" (p. 88).

to "save" the subclass of actions from being engulfed into the class of events, Davidson purports to establish the extent to which an individual's actions can be said to be his own: "What events in the life of a person reveal agency; what are his deeds and his doings in contrast to mere happenings in his history; *what is the mark that distinguishes his actions?*" (p. 43; my emphasis). It is individual agency, then, that is ultimately at stake, as if we needed to find out what it consists in, or to confirm that it does, after all, "exist."

We saw that Davidson's eventual conclusion, which, he announces, "may come with a shock of surprise," is that "we never do more than move our bodies: the rest is up to nature" (p. 59). "Disappointment" may be a better term to describe his readers' reaction to this reduction of action to bodily movements, for while it comes as no surprise that we always move our bodies when we act—that bodily movements are a moment of all our acts—it is hard to be content with the idea that this is all we do, particularly in a context that promised a distinction between actions and events. But Davidson is adamant: "There are no further actions [than bodily movements], *only* further descriptions" (p. 61; my emphasis). When "we" build a dam, then—and Davidson grants that it does happen—we should say, to be precise, that we move our bodies and the dam is built—the transition from one to the other, we might add, is but a "Skip Power effect."

Let us trace Davidson's argument to see what leads him to rely on bodily movements as the mark of agency. His initial move, we saw, was to consider the question of the difference between actions and events with respect to individuals, emphasizing their agency over their actions. The criterion of differentiation between actions and events is thus the origin of the former as opposed to their consequences—not the results of the actions but the fact that someone does them. This is because all other points in the chain of actions can be analyzed in terms of what Davidson calls "ordinary event causality." Hence, in one of his examples, Davidson manages to hurt someone's feelings by denigrating his necktie (p. 48), and although what Davidson says causes the hurt, Davidson himself does not cause what he says. Here, although Davidson is responsible for the effect of his words, he himself does, without mediation of event causality, only the saying. The saying, moreover, is the only stage of the incident that Davidson cannot deny he is the agent of, for although he may not say what he says with the intention of hurting the person's feelings, whatever he says he says intentionally (no one said it in his stead; he was not physically compelled to move his mouth in such a way as to say it; and so on). Causality intervenes between Davidson's act (saying something unpleasant) and its effect (hurting someone's feelings), but not between Davidson and his act: He speaks intentionally and is neither "caused" to say what he says, nor does he himself cause his saying.[11]

If there is a first attribution of agency that cannot be explained by recourse to event causality (and on which event causality in fact depends), then there must be actions "corresponding" to this first attribution of agency, actions that can be satisfactorily distinguished from events. It thus becomes necessary for Davidson to delimit the field of an agent's actions in function of this "primary" agency, for which he coins the term "primitive actions": These are acts that "cannot be analyzed in terms of their causal relations to acts of the same agent" (p. 49). They must consequently be actions "we do not do by doing something else" (p. 59). They must be actions "before" they have effects, or in spite of their effects. This condition leads Davidson to conclude, first, that "all primitive actions are bodily movements" (p. 49), and then, that all actions are primitive actions.[12]

Bodily movements resist causal analysis because, as Davidson convincingly argues, agents cannot be said to cause them.[13] From

[11]This is not to say that Davidson is not responsible for his act: "Event causality can spread responsibility for an action to the consequences of an action" (p. 49). The point is that event causality concerns "the effects and not the causes of action" (p. 53). As far as intentionality is concerned, it would seem that at this level of analysis it can be defined only in terms of its not being causality.

[12]Davidson specifies that bodily movements must be interpreted "generously" enough to "encompass such 'movements' as standing fast, and mental acts like deciding and computing" (p. 49).

[13]It does not make sense, for example, to postulate a previous act that causes

this perspective, they are something we do not do by doing something else. But they are also, as Davidson realizes, something we do *in* doing something else—we do not just "move"; we dance, point at something, do gymnastics, and so on. In other words, although bodily movements can be considered as means to an end, it is hard to consider them as an end in themselves.[14] When Davidson moves his fingers to tie his shoelaces, he does not first move his fingers and then tie his shoelaces; neither does he tell himself, "I am going to move my fingers, which will cause my shoelaces to be tied." In order for bodily movements to qualify as primitive actions, however, they must be distinguishable from their effects— there must be an end *to* them, if not *in* them. Thus Davidson acknowledges that "unless the agent himself is aware of what he is doing with his body alone, unless he can conceive his movements as an event physically separate from whatever else takes place, his bodily movements cannot be his actions" (p. 51). He argues, however, that for this to be the case it is enough that there be "*some* description of the movement under which [the agent] knows that he makes it": "So, if I tie my shoelaces, here is a description of my movements: I move my body in just the way *required to* tie my shoelaces" (p. 51; my emphasis).[15]

---

the act of moving my finger. For, although "it may be true that I cause my finger to move by contracting certain muscles," "doing something that causes my finger to move does not cause me to move my finger; it *is* moving my finger" (pp. 49–50).

[14]Only for an observer could Davidson's action of tying his shoelaces be satisfactorily described as "the action of moving his fingers," but then the observer in question, we feel, would be lacking information, or would be interested, for example, in the suppleness of the joints of the agent's fingers. When *I* tie my shoelaces, I do not tell myself that I move my fingers—the movement of my fingers is secondary to what they do, to the point that it appears to be, rather than the means to the end, a side effect of the end.

[15]What makes this description sound either redundant or incomplete is that it is obviously the transcription of a demonstration, collapsing a question and an answer such as: "How do you tie your shoelaces?—Look, I tie them like *this*." What cannot be conveyed in this description is the gesture of reference to the bodily movements—that is, the fact that showing the action (or how the action is done) is tantamount to performing the "required" bodily movements.

In Davidson's argument, what makes this description sufficient to establish the status of action of bodily movements is the relationship of necessity between moving one's body in just such a way and the result of tying one's shoelaces, which Davidson manipulates in favor of his argument. For the requirement in question is mutual but not symmetrical: I move my fingers this way because I am tying my shoelaces; but I can tie my shoelaces because I am moving my fingers this way. Or, it is the prospect of tying my shoelaces that determines the movement of my fingers, puts "an end" to them in particularizing them as *these* movements, but it is the movement of the fingers that makes possible the tying of the shoelaces. Once it is established that bodily movements are the condition of possibility of "tying my shoelaces," Davidson can isolate the finiteness or definition that the prospect of tying my shoelaces grants the movement of my fingers: The prospect establishes the "thisness" of the bodily movements so that these can be considered as a separate event, and the "whatness" of the prospect can be ignored. This reasoning allows Davidson to consider the movement of the fingers as the cause of the tying of the shoelaces, which suffices, in his view, to grant bodily movements the status of action: "What was needed was not a description that did not mention the effect, but a description that *fitted the cause*" (pp. 51–52; my emphasis).

Bodily movements can be said to be primitive actions, then, because they are causes without being themselves caused, and their causal function concludes them as separate events, ending in themselves.[16] But this implies that primitive actions are defined as

[16]As Professor Michèle Le Doeuff suggested to me, Davidson's reflections on agency could be inscribed within a tradition of reaction against an overemphasis on final causes—hence in his argument the centrality of final causes in accounts of action is relativized, as they have a purely descriptive function with respect to primitive actions and serve the purpose of asserting the causal status of bodily movements over the events that ensue from them. But Davidson does not turn to efficient causes to account for actions in his turning away from final causes. An efficient cause would already be more than a primitive action in Davidson's argument, for it implies a relation to an object that the self-reflexivity of bodily movements defended by Davidson excludes. It seems to me that given Davidson's stress on the "present" of primitive actions, on their

much in terms of their dissociability from their consequences as in terms of their immediacy to the agent—for bodily movements are, after all, temporally and spatially "contemporaneous" to the agent; they constitute the "present tense" of actions in the ordinary sense. Accordingly, Davidson's thesis that bodily movements are the actions that genuinely bear the agent's mark raises the question of the agent's relation to "other actions . . . those actions in describing which we go beyond mere movements of the body and dwell on the consequences, on what the agent has wrought in the world beyond his skin" (p. 55). In other words, how can the field of agency be enlarged while preserving the agent's mark on his actions? The answer is that it cannot, for, if the agent's agency is fundamentally restricted to his body, it is hard to explain "how the movement of the hand is related to the action of tying one's laces" and "how the action of tying one's laces is related to one's laces being tied" (p. 55). Hence Davidson's strategy is, in his own words, "to collapse all actions into the primitive" (p. 61), so that there is no relation to other actions, because there are no other actions.

To make this point Davidson appeals once again to the distinction between an event and its consequence, arguing that to describe an event with reference to its consequence is not to include the consequence of the event in the event itself.[17] Thus, if the queen kills the king by pouring poison in his ear with a movement of her hand, the consequence of her act is that the king is dead—the movement of her hand causes his death—but his death is not included in her action, in

---

unmediated relation to the agent and their function as medium for other actions, bodily movements correspond to the "material cause" of actions. This is to say that "complex" actions appear at this stage of Davidson's argument to be "made" of bodily movements, in the manner in which a chair is made of wood. Regardless of the shape of the chair, the wood remains a piece of wood, which can be considered as such independently of its other uses (and can consequently end up in the fire). It would appear, then, that Davidson's stress on the mark of agency leads him to an aesthetic perspective on action (see chapter 5 for a discussion of aesthetic "views" of action).

[17]What is at stake here is the distinction between description and event: "being attempted and being known to occur are not characteristics of events, but of events as described or conceived in one way or another" (p. 60).

the sense that it does not "conclude" it. His death is not the temporal end of her action, although it certainly is its objective.[18] The queen, then, "does" the killing, not the death—and the killing in question does not differ from the movement of the queen's hand, because the actual killing does not take more time than the movement (p. 58). Here Davidson's argument is that, although the description of the action may refer to its consequence, it does not lengthen the time of the action: The actual event is self-identical according to temporal criteria.[19] And it is this temporal "identity" of actions and bodily movements that finally implies, in Davidson's argument, that the latter are what *there is* in actions: "Mere movements of the body— these are all the actions there *are*" (p. 59; my emphasis).

What we have at the end of Davidson's search for the mark of individual agency is, ultimately, the individual agent. Indeed, abstracted from descriptions and from duration, bodily movements are but a display of mere presence, of sheer being there. This ontological reduction of action to being is in a sense inherent to the model of action that tacitly shapes Davidson's concerns and that presupposes that there must be a direct relationship between an agent and his actions, so that whatever he does, he does (as it

---

[18]His death, in fact, may not even "belong" to the temporal stretch of her action, for it may take place weeks after she actually pours the poison. What might suggest a confusion between the act of killing and the death is that they may be simultaneous—as the queen pours the poison, the king dies. But here the example of death can be exploited in favor of Davidson's argument, albeit without his agreement. For although it can be said that the death occurs *at* the same time as the act of killing that causes it, it certainly cannot be said that the death takes place *in* the same time as the action. After all, death is a departure from temporality, it is not within reach in the time of the living.

[19]Here's another example: "hitting the bull's eye is not more than doing something that causes the bull's eye to be hit, and this, given the right conditions, including a weapon in hand, I can do by holding my arms in a certain position and moving my trigger finger" (p. 60). We have, first, the exclusion of the consequence from the event itself, although it refers to the consequence; then, given this distinction, the reduction by temporal identification of hitting the bull's eye to moving the trigger finger. The fact that hitting the bull's eye could have been done differently ("this I *can* do by . . . ") shows that the basic criterion for the reduction of "complex" to "primitive" actions is temporal.

were) in "one piece"—hence Davidson's interest in those actions "we do not do by doing something else." We are familiar with this model of "direct action" through the image of the archer as the paradigmatic agent and the arrow reaching its target as the paradigm of action.[20] The agent aims at his target and shoots the arrow: According to the requirements of direct action, his action must be one, and conclude when the arrow reaches the target. The trajectory of the arrow thus represents the unity of the action. To consider the agent's action as "whole" through this spatial metaphor, however, raises the issue of the time zero of the act, and of the infinite divisibility of the intermediary stages between its beginning and its end. In other words, analyzed according to this spatial metaphor, the arrow may never reach its end, for its trajectory can always be further decomposed in time and space.[21] In Davidson's argument this pitfall is avoided, because the unity of action is based on its immediate realization—bodily movements are after all actions we do at once, and not just without the mediation of other actions. Davidson, in short, brings the target home: The distance the arrow of action must travel is nil; the target is ultimately the here and now of bodily movements. These are direct and they never miss the mark, but their beginning is their end.

The sounds of action

Taking up Arendt's double definition of action, we could say that the main problem with Davidson's search for the mark of individ-

[20]This image resurfaces in contemporary texts slightly transformed by time: The archer becomes a gunman, and often the target is someone, killing being one of the recurrent examples in philosophy of action. The attraction of killing as the paradigmatic action might be explained by the fact that it effectively stops interaction—the individual "threatening" one's property over one's actions simply disappears. It is, in short, a very final act; there seems to be an extremely definite temporal end to it, coinciding with the end (as objective) of the action.

[21]This, of course, is Zeno's paradox. With respect to the place of bodily movements in this model, they would have to be considered as prior to "the rest," or as a "slice" of the action.

ual agency is that it leads him to sever action in the sense of *arkhein* or *agere* from action in the sense of *prattein* or *gerere*. That is, in order to keep the individual agent at the origin of his actions and in direct connection with them, Davidson must dissociate action as the beginning of a new process from action as the carrying through of a project. The agent thus retains his capacity for action—his bodily movements—and hence his status of origin of actions, but he lacks a legitimate connection to what his bodily movements begin. In Davidson's argument the gulf between these two dimensions of action is effected by the dissociation of actions from their descriptions, following the imperative of showing that "there is a relation between a person and an event, when it is his action, *that is independent of how the terms of the relation are described*" (p. 61; my emphasis). To be sure, Davidson acknowledges our need to recur to descriptions of our actions, but for him these are, as we saw, only descriptions: "If I move the earth, this *sounds* like more than moving my body. The argument shows *it is not*" (fn. 20).[22] Here "I move the earth" is "but" the sound of my silent movements, which *are*. With regard to their silent being, the sound of my description is not "more," and, we could almost add, is no more.[23] For although moving the earth is moving my body, the converse is not true—bodily movements can not only be described in a number of different ways but could also turn out to be a variety of actions having no connection to "moving the earth."[24]

But if Davidson can do without the "content" of the descriptions of actions, he cannot do without a descriptive moment, how-

[22]This comment should obviously be read as an indirect rebuke to would-be heroes and megalomaniacs. It is probably also addressed to "metaphysical" traditions of reading, for which meaning is something "hidden." Davidson's insistence on the uniqueness of the event in spite of the multiplicity of descriptions implies that, on the contrary, meaning is fully exposed: Whatever they "sound" like, our actions are *all there* (or here) in our bodily movements.

[23]Davidson would object to this "description" of his argument—but then it is only a description.

[24]Thus the conversion of bodily movements into "moving the earth" is left up to magic (Skip Power) once again.

ever minimal, in his construction of "primitive actions," upon which he then collapses all other actions. When he says, for instance, that he moves his fingers "in just the way required" to tie his laces, he is relying on a deictic moment of action: The required way is, ultimately, *this* way, which is "pointed at" in the performance of the act, although it remains at the "fringes" of the description. It does not, however, remain at the fringes of language, for deictics, in the properly linguistic form of self-referentiality, are constitutive of language as an act. We have known this since Saussure "discovered" that language does not refer directly to "the world" but refers "first" to itself.[25] This formal priority of the self-referential moments of language over its referential function can be the source of great anxiety when taken too literally as a priority, for it can then seem as if language remained closed upon itself and did not refer at all to the "outer world"—much in the same way that, in Davidson's account, bodily movements seem to enclose action within the agent's skin.[26] The analogy here is not abusive because the isolation of the constitutive moments of both language

[25]Language refers to itself in Saussure's sense that signs relate to each other differentially, within language, and thus refer only "indirectly" to concepts. But language also refers to itself in Benveniste's sense that there is a deictic moment in all utterances that closes language onto itself. Thus Benveniste wonders: "What then is the 'reality' to which *I* or *you* refers? It is solely a 'reality of discourse,' and this is a very peculiar thing" ("La nature des pronoms," p. 252).

[26]Davidson, I should stress, does not argue that bodily movements are temporally prior to actions in the ordinary sense. He does, however, isolate bodily movements on the basis of their formal priority over their articulation through time. The extent to which this priority is only formal is apparent in the examples Davidson uses to discuss bodily movements as "separate physical events from the rest." These are mainly the examples of speaking and of tying one's shoelaces, two activities that mark the beginning of children's autonomy. Teaching children these activities certainly involves highlighting the bodily movements necessary to articulate specific words and handle laces. To emphasize the "required" bodily movements we do things like exaggerate and amplify them, which demands a certain extent of analytical deconstruction of the actions that are being taught. In other words, we must *construct* bodily movements as separate from the action they partake in, and often do this by presenting them as prior to the action under explanation.

and action on the basis of their formal priority over (respectively) their self-referential and transitive dimension has the same results: not only the isolation of speakers within language and of agents within movements but also the evacuation of the communicative function of language and of the interactive dimension of action.

The nature of this formal priority has received considerable attention in the case of language, and can consequently enlighten that of action, of which it is, after all, but a subclass.[27] Following Paul de Man's understanding of language, this problematic priority can be formulated such that language refers to "the world" (that is, to something outside of itself) because it refers to itself through deictics. Developing de Man's point, Wlad Godzich argues that self-referentiality actually constitutes the point of "contact" of language with the physical world:[28]

> Deictics do refer: they refer to the fact that language has taken place and that it is something that takes place, that it is even something that offers resistance. . . . [D]eictics are the means by which language makes itself into *something that takes place and something that can be referred to*, and it is from this inaugural act of reference that all other forms of reference will flow. It is, in the terminology that de Man uses, the resistance of language to language that grounds all other forms of resistance. To language, all of the real is fungible but itself, and the resistance that language opposes to itself—which may take the form of troping— establishes the reality of language to language, which then constructs all other forms of reference upon this fundamental model. (pp. xvi–xvii)

The referential function of language is here dependent on the condition of there being language's recognition of itself (self-referentiality). Such recognition is effected by the deictics, which, by referring language to language, mark the grounding of language in the physical world, in the here and now of its occurrence. Deictics thereby point out that language is "external" to itself, that it partakes linguistically of a nonlinguistic realm that it can interiorize at all other referential moments other than the one at which it refers

[27]Here I am enlarging, without any pretense of rigor, Davidson's classification of actions as a subclass of events.

[28]Wlad Godzich, *Foreword* to Paul de Man's *The Resistance to Theory*.

to itself. The inability of language to interiorize itself is what Godzich, with de Man, terms language's resistance to itself.[29]

Self-reference, then, is necessary for the constitution of language as language that refers. In Godzich's terms, this act of reference is "inaugural," for it roots language in the physical world as
an act that takes place in time. But the time in which language is
inaugurated—the deictic moment—is not the same as that of the
temporal continuity that language articulates. The time of the inauguration is the time of the pronoun "I," when I speak, the time
of the taking place of the utterance. I can then refer to the moment
"I" spoke, or to the dam "I" built; this corresponds to the articulation through time of what takes place. The inaugural act, instead,
constitutes the moment that permits endurance and opposes resistance—it is, in short, the here and now of the present tense in
which language takes place. Taking up Heidegger's terms, Godzich clarifies: "The taking place of language . . . is its ontological dimension, whereas the type of reference that takes place within the
space opened up by the inaugural act of language's taking place is
the ontic" (note 18). Our problematic "formal priority" is located in
this formulation in the articulation between the two different "taking places" of language, one of which is the taking place of itself,
the self-appointment of language to place and in time, the other
being the activity of language through time and in space—that is,
its referring beyond itself. In Heidegger's terms, the ontological is
the realm of "Being," the ontic that of "being." The term "being"
denotes a sense of time and space, and therefore of the condition-
ing of the physical in time and space. The ontological, or "Being,"
is the condition of possibility of the ontic, "being." If "being" is the
deployment through time, "Being" is the possibility of such deployment in time, the fact that it is possible that this very fact occurs.

[29]The fact that language resists itself allows us "into" language, but also
locks us out of it. Resistance, Godzich explains, is the measure of the physical
world's exteriority to ourselves. Similarly, language's resistance to itself is the
measure not only of its exteriority to itself but also to us.

The ontological, however, is not itself possible without its grounding of the ontic—possibilities are nothing in themselves; there are no abstract occurrences. Hence it makes no sense to consider Being independently of being. It is the deployment of language through time that manifests its taking place in time, the ontic that raises the issue of the ontological. The converse is only possible, which is to say, impossible—even the formulation "impossible as yet" is improper in the context, for with respect to the ontological there are no other moments. The ontological cannot be referred to and does not refer—it does not "exist" outside its founding of the ontic; it is "contiguous" if not continuous, to what it founds. Following the same logic, Davidson's bodily movements may well be considered the fundament, or condition, of possibility, of actions in the ordinary sense—which sense involves the impulse toward other moments that cannot be collapsed into the present of the here and now of bodily movements—but they need to be understood in terms of the ontic dimension they deploy, for without it, there is no taking place at all. In other words, we never just move our bodies: We do something that implies our bodily movements, but these emerge only in the impulse to carry something through, simple as it may be. Such an impulse necessarily involves language, although, as we will see, in ways more complicated than just descriptions. For action and language are mutually imbedded, to the point that we could say that language, in its referential function, represents the ontic dimension of actions while action, at its intransitive moment, constitutes the ontological dimension of language. Davidson's collapse of descriptions into a single referent, bodily movements, amounts to silencing language to its deictic moment and freezing action into a permanent moment of Being. Hence I think that we could say that moving the earth is more than moving my body—what is *more* is the articulation of my movements through time, which allows me to say and do what is possible, as opposed to being content with the idea that action is only possible.

Dramas of inaction

Let us contrast once again the political philosopher's and the philosopher of action's views to account for their different characterizations of action, the defining trait of contemporary man.[30] Both distinguish, albeit not in the same terms, between the ontological and the ontic dimensions of action. In Arendt's argument these are respectively action as a beginning (*arkhein, agere*) and as the carrying through of what is begun (*prattein, gerere*); in Davidson's they correspond to mere movements of the body and to "complex" actions—that is, those actions that we do by doing something else. It is with respect to the relationship between these two dimensions of action, as beginning and as carrying through, that their accounts part ways. The point of their departure can in fact be located in their understanding of action as a beginning, and even more precisely in their treatment of the notion of "beginning."

For Arendt, we saw, action as the capacity to begin processes is proper to human beings. This means, schematically, that through human agency new things come into the world that were not there before. In order for this capacity to be actualized, agents have to act—that is, carry through some enterprise within a horizon of interaction with others. Accordingly Arendt adopts the Greek comparison of political action—for action is, recall, always political for her—with the performing arts, "where the accomplishment lies in the performance itself" (WIF, p. 153). Whatever human agency begins, then, begins in action—we begin processes, in short, by carrying something through.[31] It should be stressed here that the issue

---

[30]The differences in Arendt's and Davidson's accounts of action can of course be attributed to their respective philosophical specializations, which define different horizons of concern. But certain trends of political philosophy provide accounts of action more similar to Davidson's than to Arendt's, while some thinkers have conceived of action in interactive terms similar to Arendt's.

[31]Arendt further contrasts political action with the creative arts: "Political institutions, no matter how well or badly designed, depend for continued existence upon acting men; their conservation is achieved by the same means that brought them into being. Independent existence marks the work of art as a

of the beginning of actions is not under consideration in Arendt's discussion, and that she asks the agent neither to be at the origin of his actions nor to leave his personal imprint on them. Quite on the contrary, Arendt argues that

> [h]uman action, projected into a web of relationships where many and opposing ends are pursued, almost never fulfills its original intention; *no act can ever be recognized by its author* with the same happy certainty with which a piece of work of any kind can be recognized. Whoever begins to act must know that he has started something whose end he can never foretell, if only because his deed has already changed everything and made it even more unpredictable. (CH, p. 85; my emphasis)

What deserves our attention, then, is *what actions begin*, not who begins them, and hence whatever takes place after the agent has begun to act. This might in turn require further action for the agent to "keep up," as it were, with what his actions began, but he should never expect to do more than "force things in a certain direction, and even of this he can never be sure" (CH, p. 60). But this uncertainty does not imply that things should be left "up to nature"; rather, it turns the attempt to direct them into men's proper task as agents.

The model of "direct" action underlying Davidson's text could almost be read as an intentional reversal of Arendt's understanding of action. Its fundamental premise is already unwittingly in conflict with Arendt's, for, instead of postulating action as the defining trait of human beings, it is human beings who function as the defining feature of actions with respect to other events. Indeed, for Davidson an event is an action if it bears an agent's mark, if it "belongs" to him, and the agent's property of his actions is in turn determined by whether he can be said to have been at their origin. It is thus the beginning of actions that holds Davidson's attention, instead of what begins with them and continues in their wake. As a result, in Davidson's model agents are capable only of beginning their actions but not of carrying them through. This does not mean,

---

product of making; utter dependence upon further acts to keep it in existence marks the state as a product of action" (WIF, p. 153).

concretely, that nothing happens beyond bodily movements, but it does mean that whatever exceeds their field cannot be conceptualized as action and in relation to agents. In other words, things still happen, but, according to this model, we do not do them—they are done, and this beyond the scope of our agency. Men's capacity for action, dramatized in Davidson's "mere movements of the body," can thus never be fully actualized *as action*. It persists instead as a capacity imbedded in agents' bodies and marking them as the site of beginning and ending of their own activity.

The problem with Davidson's account of the relationship between individual agents and actions is not, I should stress, that it is wrong—there is clearly a sense in which "we never do more than move our bodies." The problem is that Davidson's account dismisses precisely what is most consequent in action: that we do not just act but do specific things, and carry through specific projects that have more or less predictable ramifications, which it is vital to keep within the scope of further interventions. There is, as a result, not much we can do with Davidson's formulation of action, and in that sense it is a disabling conceptualization. It demotes instead of promotes the practical dimension of actions (action as *prattein* or *gerere*), ultimately confirming the predominant disenchantment with political action. Indeed, were agents to proceed according to the belief that all they ever do is move their bodies, then they would really "carry through" little more than that (but a lot more would be likely to happen, and most probably for the worse). This is not to say that readers conclude Davidson's essay on "Agency" with the firmly acquired disbelief in their ability to tie their shoelaces, or with the hope that nature will effectively take care of their dinner provided they move their bodies adequately. But, as will become apparent throughout this book, the model of action that can be disengaged from Davidson's account is not without antecedents. It is in fact an extreme, almost comic version of a family of models of action that ultimately question the possibility for action, and that have found multiple expressions in literature and philosophy at least since the Renaissance, at which time Hamlet, who is still famous for not doing what he says he will do, emerged as a paradigmatic figure of the "man of inaction." These models, I contend, have not only shaped our understanding of man as defined in terms of action but are also responsible, as far as models can be responsible, for men's perplexity with respect to action.

To emphasize the role of conceptualizations of action with respect to their enactment implies neither that "in reality" it is always possible to act nor that there are no circumstances under which given courses of action are not practicable. It does imply, however, that favorable conditions are not sufficient for action: It is also necessary to envisage its possibility. This is precisely the purpose that models serve. They have a demonstrative function with respect to what they are a model of and for. Hence their eminently dramatic quality: Models do not explain, they show, through stagings of different sorts and degrees.[32] Whether the model is an example, a pattern, an ideal, a copy, or an image, it is by definition followed, in the very different senses of "imitated" or "taken as a guide for." It is thus that models can be productive of or at least conducive to action—and that they can consequently turn out to be unproductive and conducive to nothing. The latter is the case with the different philosophical and literary versions of the model of direct action of which I have made Davidson the representative. This book traces the vicissitudes of agents that attempt to act according to its basic precepts.

Because the texts under scrutiny cover a large historical period, and because they are mostly discussed in chronological order, my inquiry may seem to be historical. I should stress, therefore, that it is not. The argument may read like a story, but it is not a history. It does assume that conceptualizations of action and of its relation to agents are subject to historical change, as are, paraphrasing Arendt, all "the constellations" that order the relationship between the different human capabilities (CH, p. 62). It presupposes, in particular, that the classical model of action had to undergo a ma-

---

[32]Hence, also, my choice of the term "model" over "conceptualization" or "representation," which do not convey the same sense of an expected *performance*.

jor reversal in order to accommodate the emerging notion of the subject, and it traces some of the movements and implications of the ensuing reconfiguration of agent and action. I draw evidence of this reversal from Marlowe's *Doctor Faustus* and Shakespeare's *Hamlet*, two plays that announce and dramatize a transition from the model according to which agents are an effect of and marked by their actions to the model we are now familiar with, and that posits agents at the origin of actions, defining them.

Needless to say, such a transition could never take place at once or be isolated in a single event, as it is in fact a shift within our interpretative "constellations." This shift, moreover, appears unresolved, often dramatized as a confrontation between an idealized "Greek" model of action that either reveals the shortcomings of the agent-centered model of action or threatens the rule of the agent that the texts attempt to formalize. But whether manifest in transition or in conflict, all the modern texts under consideration—from *Hamlet* to the *Philosophical Investigations* or Baudrillard's essays on the Gulf War—address a tension between two models of action and dramatize it in the agent's difficulty to act. The sheer persistence of such tension throughout history requires, in a sense, a nonhistorical or, at least, a nonhistoricist approach to it, as it suggests that, if it is not independent of specific historical contexts, it is at least conflictive enough to have outlasted them all.

Given the nature of the problem that this book sets out to delimit, it should not be surprising that most of the texts discussed are plays. Drama, after all, is directly concerned with the category of action through its formal investment in performance and acting, and it is bound to deploy onstage the models of action that it draws upon, if only because there is no narrator to mediate between characters and their actions. Thus, should there be tensions between what is said and what is done, they are ultimately problematized, and may even be resolved, in terms of the latter: In drama characters are by definition effects of their actions, although in modern drama the reverse must appear to be the case onstage. In other words, the transition from the "Greek" to the agent-centered models of action is to a certain extent a preoccupation inherent to modern drama, its dramatization part and parcel of the performance. In the plays I discuss this is not apparent only in the explicit references to Aeschylus and Aristotle, who come to represent the "Greek" model of action, but is significantly highlighted also in the motif of the protagonists' difficulty to actually begin their actions. This makes sense considering that characters are always already acting according to one of the models of action in which they partake but are only at the point of their beginning in the other. It is thus appropriate that their predicament should crystallize in the moment of the *passage à l'acte*, the moment, as it were, of their "stepping" into action on the stage. And from the perspective of this study it is particularly appropriate and significant that their predicament should be formulated in these terms, because the moment of the *passage à l'acte* is ultimately the temporal expression of the conceptual gap between the capacity for action and the ability to carry it through.

The other genre that this study bears upon is philosophy, at first sight a less propitious field for the problematization of models of action. But philosophy has its own difficulties with the issue of the *passage à l'acte*, in the guise of the thorny distinction between theory and practice. This distinction could be said to have been inherited from the classical scenario for philosophy, according to which philosophers withdraw from the stage of action in order to engage in the activity of contemplation, exchanging their status as agents for that of spectators. In this scenario the philosopher becomes the privileged spectator of others' actions, and philosophy itself becomes, as it were, the "other" of drama, the privileged scene for its audience.[33] As a result, however, the breach between agents and actions is exacerbated, for they do not coincide on the same stage. Alternately, it is action that disappears, fully identified to the agents that display it to the spectator's eyes. As I argue in chapter 3, either of these consequences is desirable in view of the enforcement of agent-centered models of action, but both are ob-

---

[33]See chapter 5 for a discussion of Nietzsche's treatment of the relationship between drama and philosophy in *The Birth of Tragedy*.

jects of virulent critique for philosophers bent on returning philosophy to "the active" world, as is the case with Nietzsche and Bakhtin, or attempting to redefine action for agents, as is most prominently the case with Wittgenstein. The latter, in fact, addresses the issue of the unconceptualized moment between theory and praxis not only theoretically—that is, by referring to it—but also practically, by arguing through examples that stage the coincidence of both. Wittgenstein's philosophical style thus takes fully into account the intimacy between drama and philosophy as well as their common generic concerns.

I wish to add a few comments here pertaining to the gender of pronouns. The reader will already have noticed the generic use of the masculine pronoun to refer to subjects and agents and should be warned that this will be consistently the case throughout, in strict observance of the gender of the protagonists of the texts under discussion, be they literary or philosophical. Indeed, the main characters of the studied plays are male, as are quite conspicuously Locke's subjects, Nietzsche's actors and spectators, Bakhtin's "I," "you," and "the other," and Wittgenstein's staged speakers. As for Baudrillard's *La Guerre du Golfe n'a pas eu lieu*, although it does not make an issue of the subject, it seems to set male agents as a referent when it compares the spectators of the Gulf War to an audience watching a striptease—not an activity from which women are excluded but certainly an activity largely targeted to "boys." In contrast, the background of Baudrillard's text, Giraudoux's play *The Trojan War Will Not Take Place*, overtly deals with the issue of male-centered narratives. Finally, Jean-François Lyotard, we will see, clearly stages "Man" as the endangered hero of evolution in his essay "The Wall, the Gulf, and the Sun: A Fable."

I have remained faithful to the authors' usage because I think that it would be neither appropriate nor useful to "correct" the male-centeredness it foregrounds. The subjects and agents in question throughout the discussion may well be abstract entities, but they remain gendered abstractions, difficult to dissociate from prevailing power structures. Nor was I ready to grant that the use of the male pronoun be in fact "neutered" by its function in models that are capable of influencing male and female agents alike. This is doubtless true but does not suffice to account for the systematic association of models of (in)action to the male gender. To argue that the models of action I discuss can apply to or affect only male subjects would obviously be hardly sustainable, but, as Wittgenstein's work demonstrates, theory and example are difficult to dissociate—examples are not only that to which a theory applies but also that which determine a theory. Having taken the texts under scrutiny literally, then, this study is peopled with male characters, a population I consciously reinforced by refraining from considering texts that could dramatize models of action featuring women. In so doing, however, my intention has not been to exclude the female gender from models of action but rather to spare them the drama of inaction that has captured men's imaginations for so long.

Finally, regarding translations: They are my own unless otherwise stated.

1 ⟢ Of Proud Audacious Deeds

Still but a man

In the prologue of *Doctor Faustus*, the chorus introduces the play
with the statement of what it will *not* be about:

> Not marching in the fields of Trasimene
> Where Mars did mate the warlike Carthagens,
> Nor sporting in the dalliance of love
> In courts of kings where state is overturn'd,
> Nor in the pomp of proud audacious deeds
> Intends our muse to vaunt his heavenly verse .
> (Prol., 1–6)[1]

Such a warning to an audience who would already have been familiar with the subject matter of the play may seem superfluous,
unless we understand it as the announcement of a generic novelty
in *Doctor Faustus*, be it with regard to Marlowe's previous plays or
in comparison to those usually staged at the time. More specifically, what is being announced in these first lines is a change in the
genre of the action the public is about to witness—not warlike, not
amorous, not political, not, in general, proud audacious deeds.
Faustus's, however, is not a puny story; it corresponds to the general description of what the Muse does not intend to write about—
his compact with the Devil is, to say the least, a proud and auda-

---

[1] I will be referring to John D. Jump's edition of Marlowe's play. He bases the
text mainly on the version first published in 1616 (B-version), but also draws
from that published in 1604 (A-version).

cious deed, in the two senses of the term. Thus it is not in the scope or range of the staged action that the announced generic change resides. It is, rather, the reconfiguration of the relationship between agents and actions that justifies Marlowe's claims to novelty, as it is stipulated in Faustus's "deed of gift."

Faustus's "audacious deed" follows his realization, in the course of his opening speech, that all other activities fail to raise him above his merely human condition. However much he may excel in the various "arts" he reviews—philosophy, physics, law—he remains "but Faustus, and a man" (i. 24), with limited horizons of action. He cannot "make men to live eternally / Or being dead raise them to life again" (i. 25–26). Divinity is disappointing for similar reasons, because not only can men not aspire to equal Jesus' deeds but what is more they cannot overcome their fundamental human condition of sinners: "If we say that we have no sin, we deceive ourselves, and the truth is not in us" (i. 40–41), Faustus reminds himself, quoting I John 1:8. Only magic seems capable of enabling Faustus to surpass himself as he desires, as it promises a dominion stretching "as far as doth *the mind* of man" (i. 60; my emphasis), and hence always in the measure of his imagination and expectations. Accordingly the first clause of the "deed of gift" Faustus writes at Lucifer's demand is "that Faustus may be a spirit in form and substance" (v. 96), a condition that should allow him to exceed the limits set by his corporeality to the extent of being able to transform himself according to his own "self-conceit" (Prol. 20).

In view of Faustus's desire to surpass his merely human condition, and of the price he is ready to pay for it—body and soul—the four remaining clauses of the compact may seem strangely inconsequential. Indeed, instead of demanding superhuman powers for himself, Faustus demands that "Mephostophilis shall be his servant and at his command"; that he "shall do for him and bring him whatsoever"; "that he shall be in his chamber or house invisible"; and "that he shall appear to the said John Faustus at all times in what form or shape soever he please" (v. 97–104). In other words, Faustus requests the services of a powerful servant, completely at his disposal and capable of doing everything for him, in his stead. He wants to be a supermaster, not a superagent: He interprets the magic power he longs for as the power to command others to do what he desires.[2] Having the power to command such a powerful servant, Faustus is effectively able to overcome the concrete limitations of his body and to enlarge the boundaries of the possible. But this broadening of the horizon of possibility of his actions is accompanied by the dissociation of himself from the actions he commands. Faustus's acts are henceforth decrees, their actual performance being delegated to others. And herein resides the novelty in Marlowe's play: It stages a shift from deed as act to deed as compact, figuring the relationship between agent and action in terms of government rather than in terms of performance.

That Faustus's desire to be more than a man should take the form of a reformulation of the relationship between men and their actions should not go without saying. It can be understood with respect to the two "men" Faustus rejects in his opening speech—namely, man as defined in Aristotle's works (in which Faustus is at first ready to "live and die" [i. 5]) and man as defined in the New Testament.[3] The former frames from the outset Faustus's review of the different activities he might "profess," which he considers in terms of their specific ends, echoing the beginning of *The Nicomachean Ethics*: "The end

[2] Thus Faustus is "glutted with the conceit" of making spirits "fetch [him] what [he] please[s]," "resolve [him] of all ambiguities," and "perform what desperate enterprise [he] will[s]" (i. 78–80). Similarly, at his first meeting with Mephostophilis Faustus states his desire clearly: "I charge thee to *wait upon me* whilst I live, / *To do whatever Faustus shall command*, / Be it to make the moon drop from her sphere / Or the ocean to overwhelm the world" (iii. 38–41; my emphasis). The extravagance of what he might desire highlights the importance of the sheer command over what it effectively demands.

[3] Here I am about to make a very unhistorical move: I will read into Faustus's speech my analysis of the texts he refers to, with the awareness that Marlowe, however well read he may have been, would not have had such a reading in mind. For my purposes this is not at all problematic, because I am interested in what the intertextual play says about the shifts in models of action I am discussing, of which Marlowe was most certainly not conscious. The move, however, is not ahistorical, as it takes into account the horizon of intertextuality of *Doctor Faustus*.

of the medical art is health, that of shipbuilding a vessel, that of strategy victory, that of economics wealth" (1094a8–9). Faustus in turn wonders and states in disappointment: "Is to dispute well logic's chiefest end?" (i. 8); "The end of physic is our body's health" (i. 17); while the law, he declares, "fits a mercenary drudge / Who aims at nothing but external trash" (i. 34–35). As for the New Testament, it glaringly inspires the terms of Faustus's conditions in the deed of gift: Thus Faustus's desire to be a "spirit," without carnal attachments, takes up a major biblical topos, while that of being a "supermaster" follows (albeit reversing) the Christian precept to serve God. Viewed as a whole, in fact, Faustus's pact with Lucifer is a "faithful" mirror of the New Testament covenant, and the man he wants to become is less alien to Christian doctrine than it is to Aristotle's philosophy.[4] Accordingly it is with New Testament criteria that Faustus dismisses Aristotle's model of action—it "affords no . . . miracle" (i. 9)—to then turn to Divinity ("When all is done, divinity is best," i. 37) and turn it against itself. For, if Faustus evaluates Aristotle's model with Christian criteria, he still finds it necessary to address it, and to do so before "rearranging" the Christian covenant. We must thus look in the New Testament for Faustus's motivations to discard Aristotle's works, and in the latter for the model of action from which Faustus is more fundamentally shifting.

"After the inward man"[5]

Working backward through Faustus's opening speech, let us consider first how his desires espouse the basic precepts of the New Testament through a brief reading of St. Paul's *Epistle to the Romans*, which is not only quoted by Faustus himself but also addresses his central concern with regard to being "but" a man (and

---

[4]This is not only because it stipulates damnation instead of salvation, but, more significantly, because it replaces a policy of "gratuity" (Jesus' death *frees* men from the bondage of sin; salvation is a free gift from God) for one of negotiation and exchange (Faustus *sells* his body and soul for twenty-four years of absolute mastery on earth).

[5]Rom. vii. 22: "For I delight in the law of God after the inward man. "

to actions in general).[6] Schematically, Paul argues that Jesus' cruci-
fixion marks the death of the "old man" (6:6) as characterized by
his likeness to Adam, and the rise of a new, Christian man, defined
in terms of the possibility of salvation by grace.[7] The "old man" is
characterized by his double bondage to sin and to the law: to the
former because he has inherited universal sin, which is part and
parcel of his nature regardless of whether he has "sinned after the
similitude of Adam's transgression" (5:14); and to the latter because he must follow Moses' laws, which reveal sin to the sinner
without, however, being capable of delivering him from its dominion. In contrast, the new Christian man should consider himself "dead indeed unto sin, but alive unto God" (6:11), for Jesus
has delivered him from universal sin, and likewise "dead unto the
law by the body of Christ" (7:4), and hence free from the obligation
to follow the ordinances. With respect to the "old man," then, the
Christian convert is presented as a liberated man—something
Faustus must have liked, as his desire to be master of himself suggests.

The new man, however, has bondages of his own, imposed precisely by the possibility of being saved from eternal death. Indeed, if
the "old man" could do nothing that could redeem him from the
universal sin he inherited, the Christian convert can do nothing to
ensure his own salvation, for his actions cannot determine his access
to the eternal life after death, nor define him as either holy or sinful.
This does not mean that the Christian is not subject to the law of God,
or that he is totally free from sin. On the contrary, he is all the more

[6]I should stress that my reading of Paul's *Epistle* is very partial and lay: It is
concerned with the reconfiguration of actions with respect to agents, and as such
it does not aspire to be theologically competent. In short, it is anything but a
faithful reading.

[7]The new Christian man, subject to salvation, is of course contrasted to the
Jew, defined by his belonging to the chosen people. The whole *Epistle* is in fact
targeted to the Israelites, exhorting them to effect the Christian "inward turn,"
for "he is not a Jew who is one outwardly; neither *is that* circumcision which is
outward in the flesh; / But he *is* a Jew who is one inwardly, and circumcision *is
that* of the heart, in the spirit *and* not in the letter; whose praise *is* not of men, but
of God" (2:28–29). I will not, however, address Paul's polemic with the Israelites.

subject to both in that he is now held personally responsible for what he does.[8] Indeed, insofar as he has been redeemed from Adam's sin, he is now free either to sin or to follow the law, and he is consequently accountable for his actions toward God. The Christian, however, will never be able to follow the law to the letter, for all men "come short of the glory of God" (3:23) except Jesus, who was His Son. Accordingly Paul concludes that "a man is justified by faith, apart from the deeds of the law" (3: 28), faith being a divine gift that can be neither accomplished nor performed, neither deserved nor sought.[9] The convert is thus called upon to yield himself *inwardly* to God and his Son and to "serve in the newness of spirit and not in the oldness of the letter" (6:6).

Faustus, of course, reverses Paul's exhortation, for he wants to be a master in the newness of spirit, but he does this in keeping with Paul's analysis of the double bind in which the renewed man finds himself with respect to his actions—that he is subject to God's law but cannot expect to fulfill it: "for we know that the law is spiritual; but I am carnal" (7:14), and that "the carnal mind *is* enmity against God; for it is not subject to the law of God; *neither, indeed, can it be*" (8:7, second emphasis mine). That it cannot be

[8]It is worth recalling at this point what Nietzsche says about individual responsibility for one's actions in the second essay of *On the Genealogy of Morality*: "Throughout most of human history, punishment has *not* been meted out *because* the miscreant was held responsible for his act, therefore it was *not* assumed that the guilty party alone should be punished" (§4, p. 43); and "for millennia, wrongdoers felt . . . with regard to their offense: 'something has gone unexpectedly wrong here', *not* 'I ought not to have done that'—they submitted to punishment as you submit to illness or misfortune or death" (§15, p. 60). Regardless of their historical accuracy, Nietzsche's remarks are interesting because they postulate a time in which agents could consider their actions, including their wrongdoings, more as something that happened to them, that befell them, than as something they did.

[9]For those readers unfamiliar with the New Testament and with the doctrine of redemption, justification is the act whereby man is declared (by God) to have no charges laid against him, and hence is considered as righteous and worthy of salvation (see *Webster's New Collegiate Dictionary*, or the *Oxford English Dictionary*). Paul's point is that man is not justified—absolved—by virtue of his acts, but only by virtue of the divine gift of grace.

subject to God's law suggests that "the carnal mind" does not refer here to the driving impulses of the flesh or to desires in general, for these, irresistible as they may seem, can, in principle, be mastered—they are in fact precisely what there is to master. What is definitely beyond legislation is the mind of the flesh, understood as a figure for the body's independent functioning and imperviousness to the will, to intentions and to commandments in general. Bodily functions do follow "rules and laws," but these are not commands; they are "given," but not by any willing entity. Similarly, feelings and sensations, experienced on the body, follow their proper rules beyond the will's control, while bodily movements are fundamentally "unruly" in that, although it can sometimes be said that we control them, it is clear that we do not cause them and that we do not dominate their actual moving. In fact, bodily movements may very well fail to occur.[10] It is by virtue of being beyond command, then, that the body is "enmity against God" and can be considered as the site of sin, for by failing to heed God's law, it is guilty of transgressing its precepts by omission.[11]

But Paul goes on to interpret the body's disobedience by omission as an active attempt to take over the entire man: "I see another law in my members, warring against the law of my mind, and bringing me into captivity to the law of sin which is in my members" (7:23). Here "the law of the members" is in fact a conflation of the two possible readings of "the carnal mind": It implies the "intentionality"—the drive—proper to desires, as well as the ab-

[10]Recall that agents cannot be said to cause their bodily movements because, as Davidson points out, "doing something that causes my finger to move does not cause me to move my finger; it *is* moving my finger" (see Introduction, pp. 9–11 and note 13). It is interesting to note here that Davidson's argument is, in a sense, the opposite of St. Paul's: For the former, bodily movements are the only actions that can be said to "belong" to the agent; for the latter, not only bodily movements but all actions are extraneous to the authentic, willing "I" and mark the agent's lack of control over his body and his "outward" self in general.

[11]The body can in fact follow no law at all; it is, as it were, "deaf" to commandments. But this is not the only reason why the Christian fails to follow God's law, for no law can be followed to the letter. And, as we will see in chapter 6, neither should it be.

solute unruliness of bodily functions. This conflation sustains the image of a "warfare" between mind and body, which is in turn necessary, in Paul's argument, to the construction of the inward man who "delights" in the laws of God (7:22).[12] Indeed, to show that he is carnal and "sold under sin" (7:14), Paul explains that "that which I do I understand not; for what I would, that I do not; but what I hate, that I do" (7:15) and concludes that "if, then, I do that which I would not, I consent unto the law that *it is* good" (7:16). What begins as a lack of understanding of his actions thus becomes, first, the inability to do what he wills—a lack of control over his body—and then an actual acting against his will, as if he were under the power of a superior force. But it is because he does what he would not do that he can say of himself that he "consents unto the law," while "it is no more I that do [that which I would not], but sin dwelleth in me" (7:17).[13]

If doing what he does not will to do demonstrates that he follows God's ways inwardly, and hence that he is an inward man,

[12]There are, indeed, many other possible responses to the body's natural "wantonness": It could, for example, be considered as a "gift" from God, exempting us from the arduous task of having to control it constantly. Such a response would hardly have been imaginable given Paul's cultural and historical context, but it is still important to keep in mind that the "war" he stages between body and mind is not natural, and that it is only "logical" according to specific imperatives.

[13]It is worth considering Paul's lack of understanding of himself from the perspective of his being God's creature, for as such he certainly lacks the inside knowledge that God has by virtue of His having made him. In other words, Paul does not know how he is made. In this sense it is not surprising that there should be regions of his person that escape his understanding, and that one of them should be the body, that intimate foreigner. What is more surprising is that Paul should extend his lack of inside knowledge to his actions, for these are what grant human creatures the status of creators, and what also grant them the inside knowledge of their creations. And, as we will see in the next chapter, Locke seizes precisely on the double status of men as creatures and creators to postulate the latter's knowledge of his actions and consequent ownership of himself, while the inner man remains, for him, safely enclosed but ignored. St. Paul does the exact reverse: It is the inner man who is known to the Christian, and his inside that is of his own making, while all that exceeds this metaphor of interiority is foreign, even if, like the law of sin, it invades the Christian man's within.

all that Paul does effectively accomplish "outwardly" is attributed to the ruling of sin through the mediation of body. Consequently, at this moment of Paul's argument what is evil covers all actions that can be performed: "for to will is present with me, but *how* to perform that which is good I find not" (7:18), and "the good that I would, I do not; but the evil which I would not, that I do" (7:19). That he does not know how to perform the good is of course in keeping with the divine nature of the laws that determine it—for, recall, all "come short of the glory of God" (3:23)—and with the precept that God's laws are spiritual, while man is carnal. It does not follow, however, that because he cannot do the good he would, he must do the evil he would not, unless what is evil is understood as what is beyond the commandment of the will. In this case all actions are indeed evil insofar as they involve the body, which in spite of its apparent obedience remains beyond full command. In other words, it is in the light of the mind's aspiration to have total mastery over body and actions that Paul must inevitably do what he would not, for he will inevitably fail to do what he wills, and, more specifically, to will it exhaustively and completely. Hence Paul concludes: "I find then a law, that when I would do good, evil is present with me" (7:21).[14]

The new Christian man is thus a divided man: He wills one thing and does another. This disconformity between will and action follows, as we saw, from the double bind with respect to God's law in which the convert finds himself by virtue of having been redeemed from universal sin. He is now at the origin of his sins and hence held personally responsible for them. He should therefore abide by God's exacting law, but this requires a total mastery over himself that his corporeality renders impossible. The construction of an inner man responds to this predicament: The Christian persists in willing to abide by God's laws, and hence continues to aspire to have total command over himself; but his actions obey the "law of the mem-

[14]Compare this understanding of the good and of how to achieve it with Aristotle's, discussed below. The question of *how* to perform the good is also linked to that of how to follow models and rules, discussed in chapter 6.

bers" and escape his control. Faustus overcomes this situation by effectively dissociating himself from his ungovernable body: He becomes a spirit, pure inwardness and will, but the actions he commands are enacted by Mephostophilis, his powerful servant. In this manner he fulfills the Christian man's aspirations to have total mastery over himself and his actions; he overpowers the "law of the members" and wins the warfare between mind and body. In so doing, however, he dissolves the predicament that was the enabling condition for spirituality, for the inward man exists insofar as he is in conflict with the law of sin, against which he can measure his consent unto the law of God (7:16). In fact, because he can master "his" actions, Faustus now walks fully "after the flesh" (8:1): The selfsame concern to control his actions makes him carnally instead of spiritually minded (8:6). He does not overmaster sin; he becomes the master of sin.

In a sense Faustus espouses too faithfully the Christian aspiration to achieve mastery over body and actions, thus failing to meet the fundamental requisite of servitude to both God and sin: "So, then, with the mind I myself serve the law of God," Paul tells us, "but with the flesh, the law of sin" (7:16). This certainly does not imply that the Christian should actually follow the impulses of the flesh. Against these he must exert his will, although he cannot hope to conquer them on his own—and in this sense he remains a servant of sin, struggling for freedom from it. Only faith can rescue him from the conflict between body and mind, and only faith is a necessary, albeit not necessarily sufficient, condition for salvation. But faith is a free gift from God, implying the Christian convert's acknowledgment of his powerlessness with respect to his own salvation, which acknowledgment in turn implies that he not exert his will with regard to it. He must not, therefore, attempt to act in view of saving himself, for this would reveal an inordinate confidence in himself and his own actions. Instead, he must put his will at the service of God and Christ, and leave his salvation up to them. He must not, however, hope for it, for this would again be an expression of his will. He must hope in the sense of having trust in God's will—"For we are saved by hope. But hope that is seen is not hope" (8:24). Thus the Christian submits to God's will and puts his faith in Him rather than on what he, as a man, is capable of doing. Faustus, of course, does the precise opposite: He puts his faith, his confidence, in his will and in the actions it commands, and he retrieves, as a consequence, his faith in God and in His infinite mercy.

This is apparent in Faustus's failure to repent, which he rationalizes with the argument that his "offense can ne'er be pardoned" (xix. 41).[15] In open contradiction to the New Testament doctrine, Faustus's despair implies that damnation, and by extension, salvation, depend on what a man does rather than on his inward submission to God's will. In this sense it testifies to Faustus's faith in the determining power of his will and of "his" actions, and in particular, in the binding power of his initial "deed of gift." Indeed, to acknowledge the possibility of salvation must entail the recognition that the compact has no binding force, while it presupposes, as a corollary, the Christian resignation to live at once aspiring for the will's mastery over body and actions and renouncing it in servitude to God. And Faustus discards this option from the outset, when, reading, presumably, from Jerome's bible, he quotes St. Paul incompletely: "The reward of sin is death: that's hard" (i. 39–40), reads Faustus; "but," Paul goes on, "the gift of God *is* eternal life through Jesus Christ, our Lord" (6:23). Here Faustus retains that actions—sins—have consequences but chooses to ignore that he could receive the gift of God, a choice that would be incomprehensible if the gift were really free but that makes sense in the light of the conditions the potential beneficiary must fulfill in order to qualify for it. These conditions are obviously unacceptable to Faus-

---

[15]As is well known, Faustus is instigated to repent several times throughout the play, the last occasion being just before Lucifer appears to claim his due, which suggests that his repentance could have canceled the content of the "deed of gift." But Faustus's "heart is harden'd" (vi. 18), and he cannot repent. Instead he *regrets* his past deeds, further asserting the import of their irreversibility as well as the irrevocability of the initial "deed of gift"—for to say that it is too late to invalidate the compact is to say that its terms must, ineluctably, be fulfilled.

tus: He wants "his" actions to obey his will; he wants mountains to be removed by them, and not by faith.[16]

Given the powerful servant he has at his command, Faustus has good reason to have faith in his willpower, for what he wills is bound to be "faithfully" accomplished: Actions are entirely reliable within the terms of the "deed of gift." Taking up the terms of the Introduction, we could say that the compact establishes a formal bond between the ontological and ontic dimensions of action—action as *agere* and as *gerere*, or as *arkhein* and *prattein*—that Davidson's model failed to conciliate and ultimately collapsed into bodily movements. The division of labor between Faustus and Mephostophilis corresponds indeed to the distinction Arendt establishes between action as a beginning of something new—the commandment of Faustus's will—and action as the carrying through of a process—Mephostophilis's task. But Faustus interprets "the beginning" more as Davidson than as Arendt would, for he places himself at the beginning of his actions, the point from which they issue. Because he is not in charge of performing them, moreover, his actions are not limited to bodily movements. Quite on the contrary, they are boundless: Unlike Davidson, Faustus can move the earth, for he can command it be moved. Consequently, and most important, Faustus is not himself "the end" of his actions, as he would be were they mere bodily movements, or simply performed by himself. Faustus's actions, instead, are immediately performed (magically), but he is not immediate to them and remains unmarked by them.

Faustus's physical disengagement from action may well account, in fact, for his nonchalance with respect to the prospect of damnation, for he could, were the terms of the compact eternal,

---

[16]As Hannah Arendt points out, in the New Testament it is not the will but faith that is capable of removing mountains, and this in spite of the Christian emphasis on the former (WIF, p. 168). This is in keeping with the impotence the Christian must feel with regard to God and to himself: He cannot believe that he can actually *achieve* what he wills; he must instead believe in the possibility of its happening through divine intervention.

hope to be exempted forever from the consequences of his deeds. Indeed, to the extent that he does not participate in the action he directs, nothing seems to happen *to* Faustus throughout the play; he is untouched, as it were, by the events he commands to be from his ontological shelter and removed from the passing of time.[17] This suspension of Faustus's being *in time* comes to an end, as is well known, with the end of the play, when the compact comes to term and Lucifer arrives to claim his due. In the meantime, however, Faustus is removed from the effects of the actions he originates as super master and can thus realize, albeit for a short lifetime of twenty-four years, the Christian man's aspiration to control his outward acts and shed his temporal embodiment. Faustus's initial enthusiasm for Aristotle's works, as well as his subsequent dismissal of them, can be understood in the light of this aspiration, because the model of action implicit in Aristotle's philosophy neither posits men at the origin of their acts (or sins) nor emphasizes the government they may have over them.[18] It is, instead, as we will now see, a model that involves men fully into their actions, integrating with them the ontological into the ontic dimension of action. Let us then turn to Aristotle's "Greek" model of action, which, as was anticipated in the Introduction, deserves special attention in view of the part it plays in the various texts discussed throughout this book.

[17]Faustus is occasionally an actor in the game of plotting (cf. scene viii, for example), but he does not perform what he plots. His lack of involvement in the action of the play is further emphasized by the fact that what he commands Mephostophilis to bring about occurs offstage, and appears on the stage only in its finished form—hence the chorus's warning that the play about to be performed will not stage "proud audacious deeds."

[18]Faustus's ambivalence toward Aristotle's philosophy of ends is intimated in his very first words, with which—as if anticipating the difficulty of the *passage à l'acte* that has troubled so many other protagonists—he first exhorts himself to act, to immediately evoke the inward man at the origin of his actions he will become: "Settle thy studies, Faustus, *and begin* / To sound *the depth* of that *thou wilt profess* " (i. 1–2; my emphasis). The term "profess" has religious undertones that announce Faustus's conversion to his "new faith."

Aristotle's philosophy of ends

It is in *The Nicomachean Ethics* that Aristotle develops a model of
what could be called, by contrast to Davidson's, a model of indirect action. He does this through the categories of means and ends,
which are, in his terms and respectively, what is done for something else and what is done for its own sake, and were in Davidson's what we do by doing something else and what we do not do
by doing something else. But Aristotle's and Davidson's understanding of ends do not quite coincide: For the former, what is
done by its own sake and as an end in itself need not be done
without doing something else. Neither *can* it be, for the end of actions, as Aristotle states from the very beginning of the treatise, is
not the end of particular actions: "Every art and every inquiry, and
similarly every action and pursuit, is thought to *aim at* some good;
and for this reason the good has rightly been declared to be that at
which all things *aim*" (1094a1–3; my emphasis).[19] That all actions
are aimed at some good remains a presupposition throughout the
treatise, eventually confirmed only by what it defines—that is, the
good at which all actions aim. This logical twist allows Aristotle to
maximize "some good" into "the good," the ultimate end of action.
The good, however, does not function here as an absolute to be
attained, nor could it be, for the good is not a thing in itself and
cannot be directly achieved, realized, projected, or even wanted;
only particulars can be the end of actions from the agent's perspective. That is, the agent can, for instance, procure food for himself that will do him good, but he will not thereby do the good itself—that will be an effect (or not) of the particular end he has attained. It is thus that, although the good is beyond the bounds of
the agent's specific actions, the good is not beyond the field of actions themselves. The good is still that at which actions aim.

But if agents are at the background of actions in Aristotle's

[19] Arts, inquiries, and pursuits can be considered, for the purposes of our own
inquiry, as forms of action, insofar as there is a practical dimension involved in
all three activities.

opening considerations, they are still the implicit aimers in the metaphor of archery for agency. Their discreet presence is made apparent in the Greek text, where, in keeping with Aristotle's teleological understanding of action, the verb "to aim" is in its passive form (*ephiesthai*).[20] That actions are so aimed at the good obviously implies the aiming agency of the archer, but this aiming must be distinguished from that which concerns the agent's particular aims. For what the agent aims at is not equivalent to the aim of his actions as a whole: Whereas the former can be said to depend on the agent's agency, the latter is conditional on the agent's actions. Taking up Aristotle's image, the agent shoots, as it were, the arrow of his actions to attain a specific end; but he does this with another end in view, at which his actions aim in being aimed at the specific end. In this sense, although it evokes the model of direct action of which archery is the modern paradigm, Aristotle's model is one of indirect action: The ultimate end of actions is only indirectly attained by actions, and only indirectly aimed at by the agent—out of the corner of his eye.[21] Jean Voilquin's French translation conveys a better sense of the indirection of actions toward their ultimate end by rendering the passive aiming of actions with the verb *tendre*, "to tend." Actions thus tend toward the good, while agents intend specific ends.

Aristotle's model of indirect action is bound to be more concerned with what actions do than with what men do, because it

[20]In the second occurrence of "aim at" in the Greek text, the passive form is reinforced by a genitive (*ou ephietai*) that further suggests that actions are effects of—that is, under the influence of, attracted by—ends, rather than the reverse.

All my comments on the Greek text are derived from discussions with George Varsos, who kindly helped me compare the "original" with the French and English translations. He himself used a Greek and English 1934 bilingual edition of *The Nicomachean Ethics* translated by H. Rackham.

[21]Archery is not, therefore, the paradigm of specific actions with punctual ends. These Aristotle discusses in terms of the agent's intentions and continence (or incontinence). But they are englobed in Aristotle's wider understanding of actions as that which we do when we do something, or *in* doing something. What could be called the action of actions thus enframes Aristotle's discussion of specific actions with punctual ends.

ultimately stages what is done in the doing of something instead of what the agent does. In other words, it is a model that gives priority, taking up Hannah Arendt's terms, to what actions begin as opposed to who begins them. But from the perspective of this priority, the issue of the agent's relation to what his actions do is a crucial one, and all the more so given the indirect nature of his agency, which makes it more difficult to grasp the agent's place in action.[22] Aristotle addresses this issue, arguing that, if the agent is to have any influence at all on the tending of his actions, he should have a "mark to aim at," liable to relate to the good and consequently implying the agent's knowledge of it: "Will not the knowledge of [the good], then, have a great influence on life? Shall we not, like archers who have a mark to aim at, be more likely to hit upon what is right?" (1094a22–4).

Here the agent's knowledge of the good is compared to the mark that archers aim at, without, however, the two being equated: What the agent needs is a formulation of the good that can function with respect to the particular ends of actions as marks function with respect to the archer—a mark to keep in view so as to guide actions in their tending. The agent, then, must be aware of what the good might be lest his actions tend nowhere at all: Without the knowledge that, for instance, a specific kind of climate is good for him, the agent is not likely to do what is necessary to expose himself to it. Hence, although the agent cannot attain the good directly, it is up to him to create or find the conditions for the good to occur. The good thus functions like an objective without being one in itself: It is, rather, the temporal end that is attained through achieving specific objectives. To take up the previous example, the agent who seeks a climate that is good for him will not consider that his objective has been attained by simply going to the appropriate place; he will not consider himself satisfied until he feels the good effects of the climate on his health, or mood, or gen-

---

[22]The whole of *The Nicomachean Ethics* can in fact be read as an attempt to elucidate the terms of this relationship, which is, ultimately, the real challenge for all models of actions.

eral condition. The good is thus associated with a fulfillment that does not necessarily coincide with that of particular actions: It occurs in its own time, and it is to that time that actions consequently tend. We could say, then: The good is the fulfillment in time toward which all actions tend.[23] This formulation implies the realization of punctual ends, for there would otherwise be neither fulfillment nor completion. It does not, however, posit the good as an objective to be attained—for only the fulfillment or completion *of something* can be an objective.

Aristotle concludes that happiness is the appropriate formulation of the good as the ultimate end of actions, because it is "final and self-sufficient" (1097b20). It is final because, although it is a condition that can be attained only in attaining other ends, it is not derivable from them: "It is always desirable in itself and never for the sake of something else" (1097a32–34). But it is by virtue of its self-sufficiency that Aristotle considers it to be the "chief good":

> The self-sufficient we define as that which when isolated makes life desirable and *lacking in nothing*; and such we think happiness to be; and further we think it most desirable of all things, not a thing counted as one good thing among others—if it were so counted it would clearly be made more desirable by the addition of even the least of goods; for that which is added becomes an excess of goods, and of goods the greater is always more desirable. (1097b14–20; my emphasis)

In simple terms, Aristotle is pointing out that when we are happy we are content with what there is and desire to go on living. But he stresses this state of contentment by qualifying it in objective terms: It is not that we are happy and consequently in need of

[23] At this point Paul's inability to do the good may have come to the reader's mind. But Paul's definition of the good is quite different from Aristotle's: The good is that which is in accordance with God's law, and, hence, to do it is to follow His law—which nobody can do, because nobody is God. The New Testament metaphor for doing the good is thus a disabling metaphor, for it rules out its possibility altogether. Aristotle's metaphor of "attaining the mark," instead, posits the possibility of its being "done" in spite of the impossibility of doing it directly. See chapter 6 for a discussion of the metaphors of "following" and "obeying" for acting.

nothing else, but it is happiness that makes what there is "desirable and lacking in nothing." This is an important shade of meaning, because it foregrounds happiness, the end toward which all actions tend, as a state of structural plenitude or completion: Nothing can be added to it; it is at once all-inclusive and nonexhaustive, for "of goods the greater is always more desirable."

The structural completion of happiness, moreover, does not pertain to goods that can be possessed but to whatever can be desired. Thus Aristotle clarifies that

> by self-sufficiency we do not mean that which is sufficient *for a man by himself*, for one who lives a solitary life, but also for parents, children, wife, and in general for his friends and fellow citizens, since man is born for citizenship. But some limit must be set to this; for if we extend our requirement to ancestors and descendants and friends' friends we are in for an infinite series. Let us examine this question however, on another occasion. (1097b7–13; my emphasis)

That self-sufficiency, and by extension happiness, should involve the whole polis makes sense given man's inescapable insertion in the interactive network of citizenship. If a man's friends are unhappy, or something happens to his children, he will inevitably desire things be different and hence cease to be happy. In accordance with his conception of men as imbedded not only in action but also in interaction, Aristotle (unlike Davidson) is not interested in discerning actions from each other in terms of the agent's identity, and he does not need to assert agents' exteriority to those events that are not their doing: All men are related by their actions by virtue of their participation in the polis. Even so, the wholeness of happiness is structural, and not exhaustive, for otherwise, as with the goods that can always be added and increase desire, there would be no end to the number of people and of events that a man's happiness would involve. Thus limits must be set to what happiness comprehends to avoid falling into an "infinite series"; and, more specifically, as Aristotle's reference to descendants and ancestors suggests, there must be a temporal end to what it comprehends. If happiness is structurally complete, then it is so by virtue of its temporality.

This is apparent in Aristotle's insistence that, if happiness is to be final and self-sufficient, there can be no "else's" to it: Indeed, any addition or desirable option implies the subordination of present to future or past (the case, for instance, of a situation of regret, which implies that there was a more desirable option that did *not* take place), a subordination that breaks open, so to speak, the plenitude of contentment with what there is. Likewise, happiness is that which is sought for its own sake, and those actions that are done for the sake of something *else* disrupt its temporality: Instead of being attained *in* what one does, they posit an end that will be attained *by* what one does, later on.[24] Those actions, then, cannot tend toward happiness, that state where nothing is lacking, because they produce a temporal lack: Be it in the form of a "will be," a "not yet," or a "could have been," these "elses" parcel the temporal wholeness of happiness. Thus the only kind of action that can indeed tend toward temporal completion, a point we will return to, is the activity of contemplation, of which Aristotle says that it makes the philosopher the happiest of men: "This activity alone would seem to be loved for its own sake; for nothing arises from it apart from the contemplating, while from practical activities we gain more or less apart from the action" (1177b1–4). Gain, here, appears as a factor of incompletion rather than of completion, and consequently those activities that follow this principle will not tend optimally toward happiness. Such is the case with "practical activities," for their end is material and hence temporally separated from the action: Here, again, because the end to be "gained" introduces a lack to be fulfilled in the future, the action itself cannot acquire the quality of being temporally complete that would allow it to tend toward happiness. It is, therefore, the temporal containment of actions that must be preserved or attained for happiness to occur, for that is the only kind of finality that actions can

[24]Here it is worth comparing Aristotle's objections to the "else" of actions with Davidson's, for whom the problem about those actions one does not do for their own sake was that they are not done by oneself, because causality intervenes between the agent and the act.

achieve: They end, are defined and determined in and through time—"afterwards" they are no more; before they are not yet.

At this point it may seem as if Aristotle were arguing that all actions implying a projection in time are marked by incompletion. But that is not the case: When pleasure characterizes the realization of the end, its prospective completion through time does not impinge on the temporal wholeness of actions, because pleasure is the sign that the action (the doing of it) is an end in itself regardless of the eventual result of the action engaged in. Pleasure thus inscribes the overall process of action in the moment of its taking place, as is apparent in Aristotle's comparison between its temporal structure and that of movement:[25]

> For every movement (e.g. that of building) takes time and is for the sake of an end, and is complete when it has made what it aims at. It is complete, therefore, only in the whole time or at that final moment. In their parts and during the time they occupy, all movements are incomplete, and are different in kind from the whole movement and from each other. . . . But of pleasure the form is complete at any and every time. Plainly, then, pleasure and movement must be different from each other, and pleasure must be one of the things that are whole and complete. This would seem to be the case, too, from the fact that it is not possible to move otherwise than in time, but it *is* possible to be pleased; *for that which takes place in a moment is a whole.* (1174a19-b9; my emphasis)

Insofar as the "form" of pleasure is "complete" at every moment, and that moments are themselves temporally whole, pleasure could be said to "fix" actions in time, turning all the stages of their realization into ends in themselves. This does not mean that the objective of actions changes at every moment, nor, indeed, that they must actively aim at each one of them. Rather, the point is that, under the mark of pleasure, actions have an end in time and are thereby as complete in the moment as they are complete in their tending through time toward happiness. In this sense pleasure can be said to preserve the temporal wholeness of the ontic dimension of action by virtue of its temporal wholeness in the mo-

---

[25]By contrast to pleasure, movement has the temporal structure of action through time but without the experience of its happening in time.

ment, and it could thus be said to represent, considered as a purely temporal experience, the ontological in the ontic.

Pleasure also inscribes the agent into the time of his actions as it is structured by their tending toward their double completion in the moment and through time:

We must take as the sign of states of character the pleasure and the pain that supervenes upon acts; for the man who abstains from bodily pleasures and delights in this very fact is temperate, while the man who is annoyed at it is self-indulgent, and he who stands his ground against things that are terrible and delights in this or at least is not pained is brave, while the man who is pained is a coward. (1104b3–8)

Here pain and pleasure measure the degree of acceptance of the activity one is engaged in: Pain is a sign that one would rather do something else (or be elsewhere or in another time); pleasure the sign that one is doing what one is doing for its own sake. And, when one does something for its own sake, one coincides, as it were, with one's actions, regardless of the time of their completion—the man who acts temperately is temperate if he enjoys temperate actions as he engages in them. Pleasure thus establishes a relationship between a man and his actions that reverses the basic postulate of Davidson's model of direct action, for pleasure is the mark of the man's actions on the man. It is, moreover, the mark that the man is in tune, as it were, with his actions, and that he is acting in "accordance" with his character: "for each man," Aristotle explains, "speaks and acts and lives in accordance with his character, if he is *not* acting for some ulterior object" (1127a27–28). To act in "accordance" with one's character, it should be stressed, is neither to "follow" it nor to "obey" it, for character does not precede action. It is, rather, to act in harmony with one's character, where character is already the resulting "sound" of orchestrated actions.[26] Character should thus be considered as the stable trait of

[26]"In rhythm" might in fact best express the relationship between character and action. As Roselyne Dupont-Roc and Jean Lallot point out in their notes to their recent French translation of *The Poetics*, there is an affinity, for the Greeks, between character as the stable disposition of individuals and the rhythm of

actions—that is, what persists of them in time, through time, and on the man.

Action and spectacle

What we have, then, is that the man is most fully inscribed within his actions when pleasure marks his realization of them, for he is then himself contained within the complete whole of the moment—we could say that he takes place in the moment of his actions, or that he *is* his actions, to the extent that they characterize him. If his actions further tend toward happiness, the chief good, he will also be contained within the temporal whole of their completion. But not all men can achieve such states of happiness and pleasure, for these depend on the nature of the activities they are engaged in; practical activities, which, we saw, have particular ends and are future-directed, are unlikely to make men happy because their temporal structure undermines the completeness of the moment and, consequently, of pleasure. Those kinds of activities do not fully inscribe the man in his actions, for they lack the temporal structure that could contain them. Aristotle contrasts such activities, as has been mentioned, with the activity of contemplation, "for nothing arises from it apart from the contemplating, while from practical activities we gain more or less apart from the action." This activity, then, preserves the temporal wholeness required for happiness and pleasure, because nothing is gained "apart from the action"; there is no "else" to turn to, nothing is

---

dance and music that cannot be dismissed as a mere metaphor. Rhythms, for example, can have characters—which would mean, for us, that there is indeed a certain regularity in rhythm (repetition, recurrence) that suggests the persistence of the dance or music in time in spite of (in fact, because of) its progression through time. Thus character could be considered as something like the rhythm of actions: The latter are, as Dupont-Roc and Lallot put it, passing processes with respect to which a man's character qualifies and determines itself. That character *determines* itself in action and emotions means that it takes shape in or with respect to the process of action, which in turn finds a "fixed" or permanent expression in character. For a discussion of action in terms of rhythm in Bakhtin's philosophy, see chapter 5.

missing, and nothing is in excess. Accordingly at the end of his treatise Aristotle concludes that philosophers are the happiest men because they engage in contemplation, and that the "activity of philosophic wisdom" is "the pleasantest of virtuous activities" (1177a23–25). Contemplation thus becomes the optimal activity, for it is that which most tends toward happiness, is most experienced with pleasure, and most fully marks the man.

The self-containment of the activity of the philosopher naturally qualifies it as the most self-sufficient of activities. But slipping from the activity to the man, Aristotle further concludes that the philosopher is, by virtue of his activity, the most self-sufficient man:

> For while a philosopher, as well as the just man or one possessing any other virtue, needs the necessaries of life, when they are sufficiently equipped with things of that sort the just man needs people towards whom and with whom he shall act justly, and the temperate man, the brave man, and each of the others is in the same case, but the philosopher, even when by himself, can contemplate truth, and the better the wiser he is; he can *perhaps* do it better if he has fellow workers, but still he is the most self-sufficient. (1177a28-b1; my emphasis)

The philosopher's activity shelters him most from accident, chance, and even movement, as it depends neither on others nor on actual objects besides the basic necessaries of life. It is transitive action at its most intransitive, and in this sense recalls, strangely enough, Davidson's "mere movements of the body." Like our bodily movements, the philosopher's activity cannot be blunted from the "outside," and it cannot fail, as it has no end beyond itself. Furthermore, the philosopher's activity is self-sufficient, because "it lacks nothing and makes life desirable." We were told before, however, that man was born for citizenship: It is consequently difficult to imagine how, retired from the common space and time of the polis, he could effectively find life lacking in nothing. We were also told that self-sufficiency is not a question of solitary survival, and that it involved so many people that "limits must be set" to avoid falling into an infinite series. Accordingly Aristotle adds that the philosopher's activity *could* be improved, or maximized, by the participation of others. Notwithstanding the desirability of such participation, however, a "perhaps" (*isos*) introduces a doubt as to its possibility, so that the activity of contemplation seems difficult to reconcile with an enterprise of association.[27]

Aristotle does not dwell any longer on this difficulty, maybe because the valorization of the philosopher's self-sufficiency is still only potentially incompatible with the principle of interaction and participation underlying his understanding of man. The notion of a communal self-sufficiency seems indeed to be strong enough to withstand a contradiction noticed in passing; a question is obviously not enough to endanger Aristotle's belief in the intricate common fate of individual citizens and their city. But more important, in Aristotle's works the philosopher, although disengaged, within the limits of the possible, from practical action, is still engaged in action, and, more precisely, in the best sort of action. He is thus still engaged in interaction, although it is in almost exclusively temporal terms that contemplation can be understood to be interactive. To the extent that it is the most temporally complete and stable of activities, in the course of which time passes without the dispersing succession of movement, contemplation is also the activity that most partakes of the temporal whole of the polis, toward which all actions tend.[28] In the light of this, the phi-

---

[27]The French translation emphasizes this doubt: "Sans doute le ferait-il d'une façon supérieure encore, s'il associait d'autres à sa contemplation." The conditional clearly suggests that the association in question is rather improbable.

[28]Aristotle adds in the same section that "happiness is thought to depend on leisure . . . among virtuous actions political and military actions are distinguished by nobility and greatness, and these are unleisurable and aim at an end and are not desirable for their own sake, but the activity of reason, which is contemplative, seems both to be superior in serious worth and to aim at no end beyond itself, and to have its pleasure proper to itself (and this augments the activity), and the self-sufficiency, leisureliness, unweariedness (so far as this is possible for man), and all the other attributes ascribed to the supremely happy man are evidently those connected with this activity" (1177b4–24). In contrast to this ideal of frictionless activity, Locke, whose understanding of action will be discussed in chapter 3, will rely on effort and end-directed action (work) for the constitution of his political subject.

losopher can indeed be said to be the happiest man, for he has access to the experience of the common happiness of the whole polis. It suffices, however, to displace the state of completion from the activity of contemplation to a contemplated object to spatialize the initial temporal whole and place the philosopher in a position of exteriority, on which knowledge (though not happiness!) will depend.[29] Once this is done action can be assessed only in aesthetic terms and as if it were "finished," extended through space instead of through time. Aristotle, I should stress, does not take this step, but he does lay the grounds for the reversal of temporal into spatial wholes by modeling the activity of contemplation on another activity, that of seeing.

Two factors might have determined the subsequent status of sight as the privileged sense of the philosopher. First of all, sight is a sense, but the only one that can be likened to an action, because it can cease its activity. We cannot stop ourselves from smelling; we can stop ourselves from seeing. Then, as an action, it has no physical consequences beyond itself. It therefore presents a self-contained structure. Aristotle compares it to pleasure:

Seeing seems to be at any moment complete, for it does not lack anything whose coming into being later will complete its form; and pleasure also seems to be of this nature. For it is a whole, and at no time can one find a pleasure whose form will be completed if the pleasure lasts longer. (1174a14–19)

Once again, the privileged status of seeing as a "complete" activity resides in its temporal structure—it is directed at the present, contained within the "form" of the moment—and not in the completeness of the contemplated object or process. The point seems to be that whatever we see, we see at once, so that seeing is not achieved through time but in time. Seeing is not movement; in fact sight apprehends the form in the movement and the moment in the sequence. Consequently, from Aristotle's perspective, the activity of seeing disengages the possible from the already-happened—that is,

---

[29]As we will see in later chapters, some of Aristotle's inheritors have interpreted the philosopher's self-sufficiency much more literally.

from the necessity of accident. By anchoring the would-be's and the could-be's in the particular moment, the act of seeing structures contemplation, the activity of the philosopher, who is concerned with the universal and the possible. Now, to the extent that contemplation is the activity excelling all other activities, and the measure of completion of all other actions, seeing becomes the activity that for Aristotle best stages the comprehension of action.

But Aristotle's understanding—and use—of the activity of seeing is far from literal. This is apparent in the *Poetics*, where Aristotle discusses artistic productions that are ultimately destined to be "witnessed" in one way or another by a public, but not necessarily through sight.[30] In fact Aristotle specifies that, in the case of tragedies—the poetic form I am mainly concerned with—the show, "the Spectacle,"

> though an attraction, is the least artistic of all the parts, and has least to do with the art of poetry. The tragic effect is quite possible without a public performance and actors; and besides, the getting-up of the Spectacle is more a matter for the costumier than the poet. (1450b16–20)

We should keep this in mind, because it means that in Aristotle action has not yet been immobilized as if it were a picture, and that his emphasis on the act of sight does not objectify action as what is

---

[30]It could be objected here that the treatment of action in the *Poetics* is not comparable with that of *The Nicomachean Ethics*, which is greatly concerned with the classification of types of characters. But then it should be noted that in the *Poetics*, which one could expect to be concerned specifically with characters, in the modern sense of the term, Aristotle discusses action at great length. This is because both the ethical and the dramatic dimensions of character are intimately linked to Aristotle's model of indirect action, which is eminently poetic. Indeed, the ultimate end toward which all actions tend, and which in the context of ethics is the good or happiness, becomes in poetics the fable or plot—the *muthos*, the "what happens" that gathers temporally the events of the play. It is important to note in this respect that the *muthos* is not equivalent to the actual realization of the play or to the concrete form of the narrative, which according to Dupont-Roc and Lallot, is the *mutheuma* (chap. 24, note 12). Thus the *muthos* is not directly realized, told, or enacted. Taking up the terminology of the previous sections of this chapter, we could say that the *muthos* is the story toward which the *mutheuma* tends.

seen. Instead, understood through the activity of seeing, action emerges as that which happens in the manner of the whole of which seeing is the temporal structure.

Hence Aristotle's characterization of tragedy as "an imitation of an action that is complete in itself, as a whole of some magnitude" (1450b24–26), a definition that basically prescribes a certain relationship—of correspondence maybe—between the unity of action and the unity of perception of the action. The former has been much discussed, and I will come back to it later. The unity of perception is posited by the qualification of the complete action "*as* a whole of some magnitude." Aristotle explains this parallelism as follows:

> Beauty is a matter of size and order, and therefore impossible either (1) in a very minute creature, since our perception becomes indistinct as it approaches instantaneity; or (2) in a creature of vast size—one, say, 1,000 miles long—as in that case, instead of the object being seen all at once, the unity and the wholeness of it is lost to the beholder. Just in the same way, then, as a beautiful whole made up of parts, or a beautiful living creature, must be of some size, but a size to be taken in by the eye, so a story or Plot must be of some length, but of a length to be taken in by the memory. (1450b20–34)

If the criteria of the "size" of the plot, on which depends its intelligibility, and that of the order of the action, which guarantees its unity, are fulfilled, the tragedy conforms to beauty. Here again the metaphor of sight and its concurrent objectivation of action ("size") are a means of preserving the temporal wholeness of action. Memory must be able to take in the whole plot, as sight is able to take in an object of adequate size. The completeness of seeing, which grasps "all at once," is thus transferred to memory, which should conceive of the sequence of events as one, at once. Instead of a long object that the eye must follow to the end, we have a moment, an elastic "once," in which the passing of time and the sequence of events are contained.

Whatever is asked of memory should be simultaneously demanded of what it must remember, the plot, so that it can effectively be remembered "all at once." Hence Aristotle's insistence on the unity of action, which, given Aristotle's own association of the "whole made up of parts" with "a living creature," has often been thought to constitute an organic model of action. Aristotle's organicism, however, is not necessarily grounded on the metaphor of the body. Rather, we should probably hear in the term organic, if we want to use it, the marking of the passing of time in time, the changes (movement, design, the "ontic" dimension) registered in the moment and in substance. Indeed, Aristotle's comparison of the whole to a living creature suggests that what is to be captured in the unity of action is the "being there" of the living in the movement and narrative of action. Thus his insistence on order—"Now a whole is that which has a beginning, middle and end" (1450b26–27)—can be understood as a substantiation of time: "A beginning is that which is not itself necessarily *after* anything else, and which has *naturally* something else *after* it; an end is that which is *naturally* something itself; and a middle, that which is *by nature after* one thing and has also another *after* it" (1450b27–31; my emphasis).

The conjunction of "after" and "naturally" point to an order based on the contiguity of substance rather than on sequences, much in the same way as Heidegger's ontological and ontic dimensions do not take place one after the other temporally but one after the other in a contiguous "taking place." This contiguity is of course rendered by the plot, the *muthos*, which, according to Aristotle, represents the action and is "simply this, the combination of the incidents, or things done in the story" (1450a3–5). Needless to say, this "combination" is not random; as we know, the plot orders time by creating a link of necessity between the different events that constitute the action. This necessity should give the impression that time does not only pass, but it remains as well in the next moment or episode, as what happens leads to what will happen.[31]

---

[31]For Aristotle causality is the best formulation of necessity with respect to the unity of action. It is thus interesting to recall that for Davidson causality is what *separates* events from each other, instead of joining them through time. In Davidson's argument causality lacks the cohesive possibilities it has in Aristotle's because the former is bent on establishing the agent's mark of agency on his actions, whereas Aristotle takes the opposite approach.

This is obvious in the insistence, in the *Poetics*, on the characters' subordina-

The fact that order is imposed from past to future, however, may be misleading, for it may suggest that the unity of the action is based on progression rather than on the kind of temporal wholeness to which the act of sight lends its structure. Hence the importance of the organic metaphor, which articulates the unity of action through time as a figure for the unity of action in time.

The point of Aristotle's insistence on the unity of action, then, is to contain the time of the realization of the action into a temporal whole structured like a moment. In this sense the action of tragedies conforms to the model of the activity of contemplation. But whereas the activity of contemplation is structurally different from practical action, the unity of action in tragedy shares some of its qualities. Action in tragedy, though gathered in the temporal whole of what can be "taken in," still overreaches itself; it has "effects." Thus Aristotle specifies that tragedy does not only imitate complete action but also imitates "incidents arousing pity and fear" (1452a1–3). He is here referring to the much discussed tragic effect (catharsis) that operates on the audience.[32] The action of the

---

tion to the plot in order to enable the unity of the action. When they are not subordinated, causality fails to be cohesive, and the play becomes a succession of events. Thus Dupont-Roc and Lallot explain, paraphrasing chapter 9: "If there are, nevertheless, 'serialized stories' (*des histoires à épisodes*), it is the bad poets' fault, or the bad actors', who seem to put pressure on the poets so as to shine (*briller*) on the stage in the *agônismata*" (chap. 9, note 5, p. 228). The *agônismata* they define as "la *joute oratoire*," verbal confrontation between characters in which one or the other fights to "shine." These jousts disrupt the unity of the action—that is, the *muthos*—as will become apparent in the next chapter throughout my discussion of *Hamlet*: The two kings' agonistic confrontation is eventually "sealed" and silenced by the plot, instead of by the triumph of one over the other.

[32] I should mention at this point that many scholars believe that Aristotle's extant writings "are either notes from which he lectured to his students at the Lyceum, or private records of his observations and investigations, or even simply notes taken by his students from his lectures" (Kenneth A. Telford, *Aristotle's Poetics: Translation and Analysis*, p. xi). Although the issue of Aristotle's authorship does not affect any of the points I make throughout my discussion of the *Poetics*, it spares me a lengthy discussion of *catharsis*, of which much has been made on the basis of very little. What is important for the purposes of my argument is not the nature of the tragic effect but the fact that there is such an effect.

tragedy is of course not directed, or addressed, to the audience. It can be said to function as practical action only within its own unity. But we could say that the action of the tragedy *tends* toward the audience (its effects are not its objective), thus associating it in its temporal wholeness. Aristotle himself does not clarify the relationship between this tragic effect, the audience, and the play. It seems that feeling "pity and fear" is simply what happens when certain actions are imitated, as water boils if left long enough on the fire. Much, however, has been made of very few comments on the tragic effect, which raises the question of what Aristotle's successors see that he did not see in his consideration of the audience.

Aristotle's lack of interest in the audience seems to be related to his lack of concern over the self-confinement of the philosopher. As was suggested earlier, the philosopher's isolation ensuing from his self-sufficiency is a possibility that Aristotle discovers in the course of his argument, and, as such, is far from being an actual and preoccupying state of things. It is only retrospectively that Aristotle's insistence on the "completeness" of the activity of contemplation seems to pave the way for the displacement from a temporal to a spatial understanding of the whole, which definitely retrieves the philosopher from interaction. Davidson's concern with the relationship between an agent and his actions testifies to the setting and persistence of the scene of the agent's exclusion from the time of his actions. And, as will be argued in subsequent chapters, the question of the relationship between spectators and the play is one instance of this setting, in which the philosopher's confinement in his act of sight is figured by the distance between the spectator and the stage. From the perspective of such distance, Aristotle's tragic effect promises to fulfill the function of bridge between agent and action, individual and community.[33]

[33]This is the case for Hans-Georg Gadamer, for whom the tragic effect includes the audience in the definition of tragedy itself. From Aristotle's notion of tragic effect, Gadamer develops the notion of tragic affirmation, which is the act of acceptance of what is—fate—*in* and *on* the audience. Gadamer speaks of the "character of genuine communion" of this tragic affirmation, but eventually concludes that "the spectator recognises himself and his own finiteness in the

From Aristotle's perspective, however, there is no distance to bridge, although there is, as we have seen, an effect of the action of the play on something other than itself. That something is the audience, but Aristotle's indifference to it suggests that what counts is the fact that the action of the play shares the property of actions in general, regardless of its confinement on the stage.[34] In other words, the action of the play takes place, it happens, it is consistent (organic), and this in spite of the fact that what takes place onstage does not have the same status as events that occur offstage. Onstage action has the status of *possibility*, which it retains as it takes place and after it has taken place. Thus Aristotle says of the poet that his "function is to describe, not the thing that has happened, but a kind of thing that might happen—that is, what is possible as being probable or necessary" (1451a36–38). To characterize the action of tragedies as possible is not to say that it has not yet occurred, or that it does not "exist"—indeed the enactment of it on the stage is the enactment of such possibility. What *can* happen is instantiated onstage as what happens, which functions as the "proof" of its possibility: What is possible can only be understood as what is possible, otherwise it is not even impossible, for there is no *it*.

The *what* of action is not constructed as an object but as a temporal whole to which agents participate, without, however, pro-

----

face of the power of fate. . . . To see that 'this is how it is' is a kind of self-knowledge for the spectator, who emerges with new insight from the illusions in which he lives" ("The Example of the Tragic," in *Truth and Method*, p. 115).

The term "insight" certainly suggests participation: The spectator sees "inside"; he is part of what he sees. But the term also leads Gadamer back to the individual subject, for whom the acceptance of "what is" is a form of "self-knowledge." The shift from the acknowledgment of "what is" to "self-knowledge" reestablishes the emergence of the subject from the knowledge of the object that his communal contemplation attempted to prevent.

[34]We will see in the next chapter that the perspective of having the action overflow the stage may be quite alarming. This attitude toward the phenomenality of action is radically different from Aristotle's, and is again a function of the latter's temporal containment of action (in the here and now, as well as through time) as opposed to the attempt to contain it spatially, on the stage.

ducing it as a whole. In Aristotle's view this does not imply the
agent's impotence with respect to fate, which is the "lesson" that
tragedies are thought to teach. On the contrary, Aristotle con-
demns those tragedies such as *Antigone* in which "the personage is
with full knowledge on the point of doing the deed, and leaves it
undone. It is odious" (1453b37–39). Here the character's knowledge renders the deed possible, as the knowledge of the good increased the chances of doing right, and Aristotle's emphatic disap-
proval of the character's failure to act is directed at his not rendering what is possible necessary—that is, at his not doing the possible deed; for only what is done and has occurred is necessary, although it could have been otherwise. The fact that it could have
been otherwise, that what is possible may or may not take place
and acquire the status of necessity, is what opens the space for
characters to act. Of course they can act only in accordance with
fate, because fate is what happens, necessary in that it is the course
events take. To refrain from acting out the possible is thus an attempt to withdraw actions from fate, and consequently from the
way things are, *as they can be known.*[35] Aristotle, then, reprehends
the characters' refusal to participate in that which they are bound
to participate—call it what happens, fate, or destiny—which participation takes the form of actions.

Performing the form

Clearly, then, Faustus's behavior, to which we now return, could
not have met with Aristotle's approval, and this not only because
Faustus attempts to escape from the necessity of the plot. More
important, following his "Christian" aspiration to be master of
himself and of his actions, and the concurrent requisite that he be
at the origin of his actions, Faustus does not act in accordance with
his character. For it is clear that Aristotle's model of indirect action

[35]For Aristotle, knowledge "comes" before action, although the kind of
knowledge he has in mind cannot be staged following the subject-object split.
This split is contested by Wittgenstein and others, as I will show in chapter 6.

does not meet with Faustus's approval either, and that, as he cannot accept the lack of control over action that it implies, he cannot afford to be a *character* in the Aristotelian sense. Indeed, this would imply that Faustus be characterized by his actions, and hence that he be at their end and within their temporal bounds, rather than at their origin and outside time. And this is precisely what Faustus's "deed of gift" would have ruled out, for the formal arrangement between agent and action that it establishes should, in principle, remove Faustus "the man" from the stage of action.[36] In this sense Faustus's compact with Lucifer would achieve the total retrieval of the philosopher from action that Aristotle's model did not quite effect. Faustus thus appears as the spectator of the fate he commands for himself, outside the confines of action and time, himself the whole containing all. At the end of the play, however, Faustus's private fate is shown to have been fully inscribed within and throughout the plot by his repeated failure, or refusal, to repent. Indeed, Faustus's lack of repentance functions as the deed/act that repeatedly confirms the validity of the deed/compact, which, as the Good Angel reminds him, is anything but irrevocable in itself. And it is, ironically, the selfsame permanent status of the deed/compact that demands iterated validation: To the extent that the deed/compact persists through time it becomes accessible, at all moments, to its revocation by a further deed/act, partaking of the time of the plot and hence of what is irreversible (time passes) and necessary.[37]

[36]What remains, as will be fully discussed in the next chapter, is an unqualified Faustus who can, by virtue of his disengagement from action, be called a subject.

[37]In an article entitled "Damnation, Protestant Style: Macbeth, Faustus, and Christian Tragedy," Richard Waswo discusses Faustus's willed participation in his own damnation, pointing out that it is required by the Protestant doctrine within which the play is inscribed: "Even the much-maligned doctrine of 'predestined' reprobation leaves man free to damn himself; for if reprobation is his destiny, he cannot know it and must create it as he lives. It is in this sense that the doctrine . . . is conducive to tragedy, because it postulates an awesome and external fatality with which, *somehow*, man chooses to cooperate. No matter whether his fate has been decided in eternity; he lives in time, and in time he

Faustus's reinscription within action, time, and the plot was, of course, to be expected. But the play problematizes this expectation by staging an oscillation between deed as act and deed as compact. These two deeds confront each other as competing and incompatible models of action, articulating agents to what happens—to what there is, to what is being enacted, and, generally, to the present—according to two different inflections of what could be called the "passive" of action. In the *Nicomachean Ethics* the passive expressed the indirection of actions toward their end, and the agent's equally indirect influence on them. In the *Poetics* the passive of actions is more explicitly related to agents, for the action of the play is, in Aristotle's terms, enacted by agents.[38] Within Aristotle's model, the "passivity" of action is the mark of its being the actualization of possibility as necessity, so that the past tense expresses necessity as *what is done*—which can, however, be effectively done in the present. In this sense, actions must still be enacted—they may be beyond the agent's mastery, but they are not beyond his actual agency. In the model staged in *Doctor Faustus*, instead, the figure of delegation renders the passive of action as the dissociation of action from its "proper" actors. This dissociation in turn posits action as necessary only insofar as it is already done, lost to the present

---

must will it, must *make it happen*" (p. 81; my emphasis). In the case of Faustus, the *somehow* is enabled in his farewell to divinity in spite of the fact that he recognizes that he is "still but Faustus, and a man" and that "the reward of sin is death." As Waswo points out, Faustus's recognition "dissolve[s] into megalomania, thus expressing in microcosm the whole pattern of the tragic action: Faustus renouncing the knowledge of what he is, and so dissolving the possibility of what he could be" (p. 83). In my reading of the play I suggest that such a renouncement and self-blinding is in turn enabled by the model of action as compact that Faustus adopts, the logic of which withdraws Faustus from the man, and from time.

[38]Aristotle says of tragedies that "the subject represented also is an action; and the action involves agents" (1449b36–37). In their French translation, Dupont-Roc and Lallot render this as "la tragédie est représentation d'action et . . . les agents en sont des personnages en action" (p. 53). In a note, however, they argue that the Greek is "even more tautological," for a literal translation would be: "action is enacted by agents"—"l'action (*praxis*) est agie (*prattetai*) par des agissants (*prattontes*)" (chap. 6, note 7, p. 195).

moment even before it takes place: By virtue of being enacted by command and by someone else, action is always already accomplished. Action thus appears as foreclosed to performance, albeit predetermined by command.

The chorus draws the audience's attention to the tension between the two "deeds" from the outset, formulating it precisely in terms of the ambiguous necessity ruling the performance of the play:

> . . . we *must* now perform
> The form of Faustus' fortunes, good or bad . . .
> (Prol., 7–8; my emphasis)

Here the necessity in question may be imposed either by the "form" of the play or by the immediacy ("now") of its performance—without which, there is, of course, no play. An emphasis on performance thus situates necessity in what is enacted and in its enactment, grounding the logic of the play in the deed as act. An emphasis on form situates it, on the contrary, in the deed as compact, which presents what happens as what must be done, because it is predetermined, or already done (by somebody else). Ultimately, the play does not resolve the ambiguity entirely: "Proud audacious deeds" are not quite replaced by "the form of Faustus' fortunes." Neither will they be in *Hamlet*.

2   ☞ From Act to Compact

Bodies placèd to the view, purposes mistook

The new model of action announced in *Doctor Faustus* takes on a new "form" in *Hamlet*.[1] Whereas Faustus could negotiate his disengagement from action—albeit at the cost of both body and soul—and delegate his acts to Mephostophilis, Hamlet can avail himself of neither magic nor powerful servant to accomplish his revenge. His position is in fact the exact opposite of Faustus's, for this time it is *he* who has been delegated to perform someone else's project, and we expect to see him perform this "proud audacious deed" throughout the play. The shift from deed as compact to deed as act, however, proves to be more difficult than the reverse: As is well known, Hamlet spends most of the play pondering his vow and struggling with himself to keep the promise his father's ghost extricates from him. And, when he finally kills his father's murderer, it is not by magic but by accident that he manages it.[2] Thus Hamlet's hesitancy is not just temporary, but,

[1]An early version of what follows on *Hamlet*, focusing more specifically on the tensions between plot and plotting and the concurrent loss "of the name of action" was published in 1994 under the title "Losing the Name of Action" in *New Essays on Hamlet*.

All references to *Hamlet* will be to J. B. Spencer's 1980 edition of the text, which is based on the second quarto (1604), with additions or corrections derived mainly from the first folio (1632), but also, occasionally, from the first quarto (1602).

[2]See. V.ii, where Hamlet is challenged to a combat by Laertes, who, wishing

as I will argue, structural, and directly linked to the introduction of a contractual—or rather, compactual—model of action.

The play in fact begins with a reference to a compact that accounts for its beginning. The ghost has made its appearance wearing King Hamlet's armor, and Horatio, the student in philosophy, concludes that "this bodes some strange eruption to our state" (I.i. 69). At the instigation of Marcellus, who reminds him of other signs of turmoil—"this same strict and most observant guard / . . . nightly toils the subject of the land," while there are "daily cast[s] of brazen cannon / And foreign mart for implements of war" (I.i. 72–74)—Horatio traces the different disturbances to the same origin, a compact between Kings Hamlet and Fortinbras:

> Our last King,
> Whose image even but now appeared to us,
> Was, as you know, by Fortinbras of Norway,
> Thereto pricked on by a most emulate pride,
> Dared to the combat; in which our valiant Hamlet—
> For so this side of our known world esteemed him—
> Did slay this Fortinbras; who, by a sealed compact
> Well ratified by law and heraldry,
> Did forfeit, with his life, all these his lands
> Which he stood seised of, to the conqueror;
> Against the which a moiety competent
> Was gagèd by our King, which had returned
> To the inheritance of Fortinbras,
> Had he been vanquisher, as, by the same covenant
> And carriage of the article designed,
> His fell to Hamlet.
>   (I.i. 80–96)

We are then told that young Fortinbras is making preparations to recover by force "and terms compulsory" the lands lost by his father. This would account for the ghost's nightly apparitions, as well as for the alert reigning in the land. The two "eruptions"

---

to take revenge for his father's death, accepts a role in King Claudius's plot to murder Hamlet. The plot then "falls on th'inventors heads," and Hamlet kills his father's murderer. But he does not himself *plot* it.

eventually part origins, as Hamlet finds out from the ghost himself the reasons for his rambles, and young Fortinbras gives up his claims on his lost inheritance at his uncle's entreaties. But the connection between the ghost and the military threat is not disproved until II.ii and seems reestablished at the end of the play, when young Fortinbras literally takes the place of Hamlet, recovering and even increasing the inheritance he had renounced. Thus the initial—and inaugural—compact erupts to conclude the play.

Paradoxically, the compact inaugurates the play with another act of closure, for it is meant to seal the combat between King Fortinbras and King Hamlet for good. Indeed theirs is not a war but a contest—one king dares the other to combat—and in this sense conforms to the model of the Greek *agon*, or joust. But while there are no absolute winners in the Greek model, this compact does not only ensure the definitive victory of one king over the other; it also guarantees the retrieval of the winner from any further daring or invitation to combat, because it declares him to be the permanent winner.[3] To this end the death of either king is not enough, for their respective sons could take it upon themselves to continue the contest and take revenge. In prevision of this eventuality, the compact stipulates that at the death of one king the other acquires the right of property to his lands, thereby

---

[3] As Nietzsche points out, such an attempt to conclude the joust for good, to stop further jousting, is "anti-Hellenic." He further argues that contest was "necessary to preserve the health of the state, and explains the Ephesians' banishment of Hermodorus because "he is the best" as follows:

> Why should no one be the best? Because then the contest would come to an end and the eternal source of life for the Hellenic state would be endangered.... Originally this curious institution is not a safety valve but a means of stimulation: the individual who towers above the rest is eliminated so that the contest of forces may reawaken—an idea that ... presupposes that in the natural order of things there are always *several* geniuses who spur each other to action. ("Homer's Contest," pp. 36–37)

Leaving aside the issues of the health of the Hellenic state and of genius, let us retain from Nietzsche's text that the function of the exclusion of "the best" is to allow the action to continue.

disinheriting the loser's son and divesting him at the same time of the right to react to his father's death. The compact thus functions like a joint testament that crosses the two kings' lines of descent: Hamlet, to the extent that he is bound to inherit the property his father acquired at King Fortinbras's death, becomes the latter's "compactual son."[4] And so does young Fortinbras become King Hamlet's: hence his claims on Elsinore at King Hamlet's death, and hence the eventual outcome of the play. Young Fortinbras's projected attack can be understood, then, as either a gesture of denial of the transition from act to compact or as the effort to reverse it by bringing the terms of the compact to their proper conclusion. In either case the final "poetic justice" of *Hamlet* depends on the silencing—definitive sealing—of its inaugural compact, which ultimately opens rather than closes a new time for action as deeds.

From the perspective of this framing compact, what appears to be the central plot—that of Hamlet's difficult revenge—functions as the means to the end. In other words, the story of prince Hamlet implements the terms of the compact instead of being an end in itself. The characters are thus formally dissociated from the plot and from the action of the play because the framing plot appropriates both their plotting and actions to the extent that they seem to be "dispensable" once they have performed their part. This is certainly suggested in the fact of their deaths—that is, in their "physical" disappearance from the stage. Indeed, the only surviving character from Hamlet's story is Horatio, who has a task to accomplish, as he has been charged by the dying prince to "report [him] and [his] cause aright" (V.ii. 333). He attempts to do this as young Fortinbras arrives at the end of the play and wonders at the heap of dead bodies:

[4]By stipulating the disinheritance of young Fortinbras, the compact attempts to stop the chain of action launched by revenge. In revenge, courses of action are "inherited" and are thus enacted, albeit not quite in the Aristotelian sense, for they are passed on with an imperative—revenge must be taken. This imperative confers on them the quality of being in the past tense, already done.

> let me speak to th'yet unknowing world
> How these things came about. So shall you hear
> Of carnal, bloody, and unnatural acts,
> Of accidental judgements, of casual slaughters,
> Of deaths put on by cunning and forced cause,
> And, in this upshot, purposes mistook
> Fallen on th'inventors' heads.
>
>   (V.ii. 373–78)

Horatio's language, however, undermines his effort to reinscribe Hamlet in *Hamlet*, for what it reports is ultimately the protagonists' lack of control over their actions—their purposes are "mistook," their acts and judgments governed by chance. The characters' contingent relation to the plot is further highlighted by the generality of Horatio's account, in which they become the "things" resulting from disembodied and "unnatural acts." Thus, as the plotting is integrated in the plot, characters are definitively excluded from it, an exclusion figured by Horatio's demand to have the dead bodies "High on a stage [. . .] placèd to the view" (V.ii. 372). Horatio presumably wants to restore the protagonists on the stage of action with this move, but his attempt "falls on th'inventor's head," not only because dead bodies are by definition beyond action (and they are to be placed *high* on the stage) but also because Horatio needs to create a stage within the stage to point to their centrality. This subjects Hamlet's story to Fortinbras's gaze, enframing it within the logic of the inaugurating compacts and exposing the distance they impose between the bodies and the plot they have served to enact.

Let us linger on these bodies "placèd to the view" for a moment. Their staging constitutes an extreme version of the different scenes of spying or gazing that are the cornerstones of the "action" of the play, articulating reversals in the characters' fortunes and, more generally, change and progression in the plot. It is well known, indeed, that the characters in *Hamlet* (and this is a characteristic of the genre of revenge plays, as well as of comedies of the time) are generally concerned with the elusive nature of action. They take pains to understand each other's acts, the motivations and scope of which seem to be beyond their grasp. As a rule, they assume, and not without reason, that the others' behavior in public is "playing," while only that resumed in "private" is "acting" properly speaking. In other words, the action of the play is hidden and has to be discovered (hence the hiding behind arras, the speculation on "acting" and "playing," "seeming" and "being," and so on); there is a sense that it is taking place in secret and not in interaction. This sense is symptomatic of the aforementioned scission between plot and plotting effected (or confirmed, as we will see) by the framing compact, against which the characters react by trying to ground action in sight, as if what dissociated them from their acts were a lack of *evidence*.[5]

The attempt to ground action in sight should remind us of Aristotle's philosopher, whose activity of contemplation was the most self-sufficient of activities by virtue of its being modeled on the act of sight, the structure of which reproduced the temporal whole toward which all actions tend. But if Aristotle's philosopher was in danger of being enclosed within the temporality of his activity and to be thus incapable of interacting with the polis, *Hamlet*'s characters incur the danger of running out of time—of remaining outside the temporal whole of the plot, which they attempt to reconstitute by *withdrawing* from interaction. For, whereas the activity of contemplation, recall, has no object in Aristotle's model, sight has an object in *Hamlet*: the act. This alters the setup of Aristotle's scene. From the moment the act of sight is given an "object" on which to endow its temporal structure, the viewing philosopher is no longer involved in this structure. Indeed, in order for sight to confer on the act a finitude evoking the temporal whole of the polis, the viewer must be metaphorically situated after the act, at its end and, conse-

---

[5]Accordingly Hamlet's procrastination has often been read as a form of skepticism (see note 7).

quently, disengaged from it. The transition from act to sight thus ensures a certain wholeness of action, but as a counterpart it implies the withdrawal of the agent from interaction and, concurrently, his withdrawal from the time of interaction ("common" time).[6] The bodies "placèd to the view" can be read, then, as the staging of the transition from act to sight meant to reinscribe characters in action but having the reverse effect of exposing their exclusion from it—which exposure can be framed by a plot, although it will necessarily appear as a "foreign" plot.

What Horatio's staging of the dead bodies suggests, more generally, is that the play problematizes the terms of the relationship between the categories of character and plot. More radically, and in Aristotelian terms, the play can be read as the dramatization of the impossible task of foregrounding the character from the unity of the action, and the man from the character. For Aristotle, recall, the former was clearly subordinated to the latter: Not only is the unity of the plot not articulated by the central protagonist, but, in addition, the protagonist must remain subdued to the whole of the action lest he impinge on its coherence. This is in keeping with Aristotle's understanding of the category of character as the persistent mark a man's actions leave on himself. Thus when the man acts according to his character he is harmoniously involved in his actions, he "fits," as it were, the marks it leaves on him, and hence "fits" in the plot. But when the characters of a play are overemphasized, the correspondence between action and character is lost, because whereas action can account for character, character cannot account for action. And this is what happens throughout *Hamlet*: Hamlet, the prominent character, is "out of joint" with the play that bears his name, as well as with his own role as character. Indeed he is incapable of

[6]These two moves are the fundaments of the concept of the subject, which will be discussed in chapter 3—the disengagement of agent from action (who can then no longer be considered an agent), as well as that from the temporal whole of the communal (which, as we will see, deprives the former agent of time). Another formulation of the new concept of the subject could be that the subject is the agent who has no character, who has not been marked by action.

doing what he has been charged to do; he is not in tune with action.[7] This, moreover, is as much an effect of the reformulation of

[7]This is apparent in the history of *Hamlet* criticism, which has focused, whether from the perspective of the plot or from that of its central character, on the inconsistencies between both. T. S. Eliot's famous diagnosis of the play has the merit of expressing the traditional problem succinctly: Hamlet's emotions, he argues, are in excess of the play, which does not provide the "objective correlative" necessary to particularize them. Eliot's conclusion is thus that "*Hamlet* the play is the primary problem, and Hamlet the character only secondary" ("Hamlet," p. 141). Although Eliot's further conclusion that *Hamlet* is a bad play has not elicited much sympathy, the view that there is in it something "out of joint" is now widely accepted. In traditional character-centered approaches, Hamlet's procrastination of his revenge, which remains unexplained, is read as a symptom of his human "depth," which cannot find expression in the mere role he has to play. Hamlet thus appears as grander than *Hamlet*, as if the play were not to his measure (see Martin Wiggins, "*Hamlet* within the Prince"). Plot-centered analysis tends to understand Hamlet's often unintelligible behavior as the expression of his lack of grounding in the play, and even as the play's own groundlessness. This is notably the case with Graham Bradshaw's and Stanley Cavell's readings of *Hamlet* as the staging of the problem of skepticism, dramatizing how the world itself dissolves under the subject's skeptical gaze (see Graham Bradshaw, *Shakespeare's Skepticism*; and Stanley Cavell, "Hamlet's Burden of Proof").

Eliot in fact provides an "empirical" explanation for the play's failure to provide objective correlatives to the central character's behavior, locating it in the superposition of Shakespeare's sophisticated motives on "much cruder material which persists even in the final form" (p. 142). Scholars seem to agree that this material would have been what is known as the *Ur-Hamlet*, a very successful play that may have been written by Thomas Kyd. Bradshaw also seizes on this probable superposition of *Hamlet* the earlier play, suggesting that Shakespeare "grafted" his prince onto the latter: "Even though the phrase 'Hamlet without the prince' is now a synonym for something absurd and unimaginable (like omelettes without eggs), this is precisely what the old play must have offered" ("*Hamlet* and the Art of Grafting," in *Shakespeare's Skepticism*, p. 103). Bradshaw further argues that as a result of such a grafting, "what seems obscure is the *connection* between the [inherited] 'action' . . . and the new play's prince and central nervous system" (pp. 104–5). This would account for Hamlet's overwhelming presence throughout the play (whether he is actually on stage or not) and for the audience's sense that Hamlet is "a 'real' man who finds himself trapped in a play and forced to perform"—what Bradshaw calls the "Pirandellian effect" of the play. It would also account for Hamlet's ungrounded behavior in the play.

The relation of the "new" to the "old" play provides a satisfactory historical

the terms of action imposed by the inaugural framing compact as of Hamlet's wish to be more—or less—than a character, the man *in* the character.

Denote me truly

Immediately after Horatio's articulation of the ghost's midnight rambles to the compact and to young Fortinbras's threat of invasion, but before Hamlet meets the ghost, we learn about the latter's refusal to conclude his mourning. Hamlet's attitude toward the death of his father thus seems to be the factor articulating—or disarticulating—him to the picture Horatio gives of the play, and determining in turn his subsequent fate as a character. The scene introduces from the outset the context for Hamlet's revenge. We learn that the queen has married King Hamlet's brother, Claudius, shortly after her widowhood. Two characters refuse to acknowledge the symbolic order that the marriage should have restored to the state: young Fortinbras and Hamlet. Fortinbras, according to King Claudius, either fails to recognize the new king as being the equal of King Hamlet (and hence denies his full substitution for him) or persists in thinking the "state to be disjoint and out of frame" (I.ii. 20). As we have seen, for young Fortinbras the state is

---

explanation to what Bradshaw calls the "flaw" in *Hamlet*, which he and Cavell then read philosophically. Bradshaw's intuition about "*Hamlet* without the prince" can be further exploited, for the grafting of Hamlet onto *Hamlet* can be understood, in purely dramatic terms, as the grafting of a new notion of character onto a preexistent one of action—which of course entails the readjustment of both. As will become apparent throughout this chapter, the novelty of the "new" character is that it is not a character—it would be undetermined by action. A chorus's warning to the audience of *Hamlet* would thus have to announce, as in the prologue of *Doctor Faustus*, that not only "deeds" but also "characters" will be unexpected in the play. It would also have to emphasize the ensuing difficulties to performing "the form of Hamlet's fortune."

Anticipating the discussion of subsequent chapters, Hamlet's "grafting" onto the old play can also be considered as the grafting or construction of the category of the subject, defined in terms of its dissociation from action, onto a preexisting model of action in which character is "at the service of" action.

indeed "disjoint," but from his person, and in need not so much of enframement but of the implementation of its frame. As for Hamlet, he does not yet have a frame with which to measure the state of things, but he has also been "disjoint" from his state by his mother's wedding and is consequently himself "out of frame." King Claudius is quick to dismiss young Fortinbras's threat—he appeals to the latter's uncle for help—but has more trouble convincing Hamlet to accept the new order of things, attempting—to no avail—to impose it on him: "But now, my cousin Hamlet, *and my son*" (I.ii. 64; my emphasis).

The queen, more subtle, is careful to avoid references to the change imposed on Hamlet and presents novelty as already "old," as just another manifestation of the natural (as opposed to political) order of things:

> *Queen*   Good Hamlet,
>   cast thy nighted coulour off
>   . . .
>   Do not for ever with vailèd lids
>   Seek for thy noble father in the dust.
>   Thou knowest 'tis common. All that lives must die,
>   Passing through nature to eternity.
> *Hamlet*   Ay, madam, it is common.
> *Queen*   If it be,
>   Why seems it so particular with thee?
>
>   (I.ii. 68–76)

The queen is here objecting to Hamlet's overparticularization, and even privatization, of the king's death with a multilayered argument: Death is a common event, because it happens to all, and not to singled-out individuals; but death is also a "common" event in that the individual can experience the death only of others, and only with others, never himself (he is already dead) nor by himself (individuals die for all, not just for any one person).[8] In this sense death is a fundamentally communal event, and experience, be-

---

[8] As it turns out, the king, judging from the ghost's testimony, did, in a sense, experience his own death—but Hamlet does not know this yet. We will return to this point.

cause it is fully exhausted in its public advent, and can be said to *be* (to have taken place) only to the extent that it *seems* (appears) in the realm of the common. Thus the queen's rhetoric collapses the category of the particular into that of the common by presenting the categories of seeming and being as continuous (in the realm of the communal).

Her argument strikes a chord in Hamlet, but he is able to counter it by reversing the relationship between the categories the queen herself introduces:

> 'Seems', madam? Nay, it is, I know not 'seems'.
> 'Tis not alone my inky cloak, good mother,
> Nor customary suits of solemn black,
> Nor windy suspiration of forced breath,
> No, nor the fruitful river in the eye,
> Nor the dejected 'haviour of the visage,
> Together with all forms, moods, shapes of grief,
> That can denote me truly. These indeed 'seem';
> For they are actions that a man might play.
> But I have that within which passes show—
> These but the trappings and the suits of woe.
> (I.ii. 76–86)

It should be kept in mind that Hamlet is here responding to the queen's "demonstration" that his persistent mourning is based on a "logical" mistake, that of considering his father's death as too particular an event. Hamlet does not deny this point, but shifting the subject of the discussion from death to mourning, he contests the corollary that because death is a communal event it should be experienced communally. The death certainly affects all, but not all at the same time—thus it cannot be overcome collectively or inter-actively. Indeed the gist of his argument is that he has "that within which *passes* show," a statement that sounds strange if we read it as the assertion of the sincerity of his mourning, which no one doubts. Hamlet, then, is not denying that he is playing at being sad over his father's death but arguing that his grief occurs in its proper time, and that this time does not coincide with that of "all"; instead it constitutes a "within" distinct from the communal stance. This perspective is based on the understanding of death as a temporal limit (a conclusion) that completes and thereby fully exposes the individual, in opposition to which the living are in the process of completion and, accordingly, not exhausted in seeming.[9] Hamlet thus introduces a discontinuity between seeming and being, corresponding in his argument to that between the categories of the common and the particular: "Nay, it is, I know not 'seems.'"

That he does not know "seems" means, ultimately, that Hamlet does not have access to the communal stance with respect to himself without giving up his particularity. This ignorance, based on the knowledge of his "within," justifies Hamlet's refusal of the common as the grounds for the particular, and the concurrent grounding of being in seeming. His refusal, however, depends on the transformation of the category of the common into that of "the other," enabled by his retreat into the "within" of his private time of mourning. Thus he argues that all the outward signs of mourning fail to "denote [him] truly" because these "are actions that *a man* might play." Here the queen's "all" is reduced to a representative "one" that disrupts the interactive cohesion of the communal. It is when "all" become "others" that the inside / outside distinction can operate to dissociate the show from the act of showing, and seeming from being. The "advantage" of this arrangement, in Hamlet's view, is the acquisition of a *private time*—expressed in fact as a demand for more time, as if his own had to be in excess of that of the others—and concurrently of a *within* of which he can have exclusive knowledge. Its disadvantages are obvious: As he acquires interiority and proper time, he loses his exteriority, which now occurs in the time of the others. By the same token, his appearance—read his being subject to the gaze of the others—"traps" him: Having withdrawn from interaction, he also withdraws from action.

---

[9]This conception of death can be contrasted to that of Aristotle, for whom death is not an end—to the point that he wonders whether a dead man can be considered to be happy regardless of the disgraces that may befall his descendants (*The Nicomachean Ethics*, I.10). The issue makes sense from Aristotle's stance, for he places himself fully within the common time of the polis.

Hamlet certainly has reasons to reject the realm of the common and take refuge in his private time of mourning. He has, as we saw, been displaced from his state (and estate) by his uncle—he has not been able to take his father's place as king. In other words, he has been excluded from his place in the "communal" and reacts against this by rejecting the communal stance in turn. This is not, however, the reason Hamlet himself alleges for his prolonged mourning. In fact, from his perspective he is accomplishing the mourning ritual properly; it is the others who have not taken the proper, or sufficient, time to forget the dead King.[10] More specifically, he objects to his mother's prompt remarriage after his father's death: "a beast that wants discourse of reason / Would have mourned longer" (I.ii. 150–52). But even more specifically, what worries him is that she has married her dead husband's brother, in spite of their lack of resemblance: "My father's brother, but no more like my father / Than I to Hercules" (I.ii. 152–53).

Later on in the play Hamlet repeats this objection to the queen herself, developing the contrasts he sees between the two kings:

> Look here upon this picture, and on this,
> The counterfeit presentment of two brothers.
>   · · ·
> This was your husband. Look you now what follows.
> Here is your husband; like a mildewed ear,
> Blasting his wholesome brother. Have you eyes?
>   (III.iv. 55–66)

Hamlet's suspicion is obviously that she does not have eyes: She does not seem to have noticed the difference between the two brothers, for her one husband is worth another; the queen, after all, defends the category of the common over that of the particular.[11]

---

[10]They have not, as a consequence, taken *their proper time* to do it. In other words, they may not have developed, in Hamlet's eyes, the interiority that he feels he has. In support of readings that concentrate on Hamlet's skepticism, his assertion of that "within which passes show" can be read as an expression of doubt that *others* have it—that is, the suspicion that they only *seem* to be (there) but are not truly—as if they were automatons.

[11]The suspicion that women do not see the difference between one man and

We have reason to suspect, however, that Hamlet might suffer from selective blindness himself. Indeed, although he is trying to convince his mother that she should not have remarried, the comparison between the two kings suggests that the problem is that no difference could make enough of a difference between them, and hence that one brother is effectively worth the other. This belief emerges as an implication of the statement of the worthlessness of King Claudius with respect to King Hamlet, the insistence on which suggests that their lack of resemblance is in fact anomalous and that they *should* have been the same. In other words, the queen's remarriage triggers, or enhances, her son's anxiety over particularity—what *can* "truly denote" being? For if appearance can be played, how can the difference be made between one king and the other? And if one's semblance is under another's gaze, how does one know what it is one is playing at?

Hamlet's overparticularized mourning, his claim to a proper time and to interiority, can thus be read as an effort to ensure particularity for himself. But his concern is, ironically, anything but "particular with [him]"; in fact, it is shared by most of the other characters of the play. The latter actually opens at the moment a change of guards takes place, an operation of substitution that already dramatizes the discontinuity between seeming and being, playing and acting that triggered Hamlet's anxiety over particularity:

> *Barnardo* Who's there?
> *Francisco* Nay, answer *me*. Stand and *unfold yourself*.
> *Barnardo* Long live the King!
> *Francisco* Barnardo?
> *Barnardo* He.
> *Francisco* You come most carefully upon your hour.
>
> (I.i. 1–6; my emphasis)

---

another is common among Shakespeare's male characters whose identities are unfortunately organized around the capacity of their lovers to identify them. I will not expand this aspect of the question, but it is worth noting that the anxiety over fatherhood can be understood not just as the fear of the women's "frailty" and lust but also as the male characters' overidentification among themselves.

We gather that the reason for this "identity quiz" is that Barnardo, although he appears right on time, assumes his office before Francisco bequeaths it to him. In this sense he either plays his part too soon—he acts as if he were already the guard, and questions Francisco, who is still on guard—or too late—he "forgets" he is to play a part (or which part to play), and comes to his senses when Francisco literally tells him what to say (answer with the appropriate greeting to the king) and what name to answer to ("Barnardo?"). Either way, Barnardo's confusion problematizes the relationship between actor and character by exposing to the public the transition from one to the other. This transition corresponds to that from "being" to "seeming," if we follow Hamlet's assimilation of appearances to "actions a man might play" and of being to that "which passes show." Hamlet's distinction sets a distance between the man/actor and the character, formulating the character's actions as *the play* of the man/actor, and consequently presenting them as dissociated from the "within" constituting the being of the man. Thus the character's display depends on the suppression of the actor's being, to the extent that the man appears only as the embodiment of the character. Concurrently, any embodiment may in turn appear, because it necessarily appears as that of a character, and all actions can but seem to be dissociated from the inner man. Hamlet's claim to a proper time further articulates this dissociation as a temporal one, as Barnardo's failure to assume his role on time illustrates—he is out of time with his character. Barnardo, however, does assume his role, in time, and by performing precisely "actions that a man might play." In other words, his playing is the demonstration that a man might not just *play*, but *act*, that the time between "seeming" and "being" is passed in action. This is what Hamlet will strive to do—albeit mostly in vain—throughout the play, asked by the ghost to perform the deed of revenge and thus "set right" its "disjointed time."[12]

---

[12]"The time is out of joint. O, cursèd spite, / That ever I was born to set it right!" (I.v. 188–89).

The questionable shape of deeds

To complement Hamlet's wonder at the queen's behavior, Horatio arrives with the news of the appearance of "a figure *like* [Hamlet's] father" (I.ii. 299; my emphasis), the sight of which he reports right after Hamlet himself tells his friend that he *thinks* he sees his father "in [his] mind's eye" (I.ii. 186). This sudden exteriorization of what is the object of his private mourning and the source of his inner time does not simplify Hamlet's complicated relationship to being and seeming. Even Horatio, the student of philosophy, is puzzled by it, as testifies his incapacity to formulate the figure's *likeness* to the king in unequivocal terms: "I knew your father. / These hands are not more like" (I.ii. 211–12). A person's hands, of course, are only alike viewed as the mirror image of each other—their likeness emerges in juxtaposition and not in superposition. The figure like the king is thus the king-less image of the king. It is pure likeness, pure surface, devoid of an interior but offering the appearance of one. And indeed, the figure appears dressed with an armor, manifesting a "within" sealed in "complete steel" (I.iv. 52). The figure, in short, figures a "within that passes show," but this "within" need not be the king's, for the figure like the king is not necessarily that *of* the king. It is, rather, Hamlet's within it seems to figure, turning him inside out: His inwardness is displayed in the rambling image of his father, the latter's appearance now subsuming all there is to Hamlet.[13] But in accordance with its figurality, the

---

[13]In "Hamlet's Burden of Proof," Cavell actually argues that the ghost's tale is a figment of Hamlet's imagination. Without going into Cavell's argument, it is clear that the privacy that the ghost imposes on Hamlet could support his argument. Taking this privacy literally, however, neglects the fact that other characters see the ghost, and introduces a serious dramatic inconsistency within the play. Indeed, the audience could well witness Hamlet's meeting with the ghost, were it only a product of his imagination, but to have Horatio himself see it is more difficult to account for. To say that the ghost is a figure of Hamlet's privatized mourning does not, instead, imply that Hamlet the character imagines it, because the ghost, as a figure, can be said to serve the plot, which is ultimately what proves his story to be true. As a figure, moreover, the ghost can have the unascertainable existence proper to ghosts with respect to Hamlet, say some-

figure of the ghost at once demonstrates to Hamlet that nothing in him "passes show," and promises to show him what is past showing—with respect to himself, that Hamlet's mourning is justified; that his timing is really private; that he does have something in him that cannot be seen but *is*; and, with respect to the king's death, that it sealed a "deed" that it can, however, no longer occult. "Foul deeds will rise, / though all the earth o'erwhelm them, *to men's eyes*" (I.ii. 259; my emphasis). Thus Hamlet, thinking he will catch a glimpse of his wandering "within," falls prey to the ghost's figurality and is drawn into assuming his "noble father's person" in its stead (I.ii. 244).

At first Hamlet seems to acknowledge the ghost's figural status and engages what could resemble a reading process—"Thou comest in such *a questionable shape* / That I will speak to thee" (I.iv. 43–44; my emphasis). But he immediately lets himself be taken in by the ghost's figurality—"I'll call thee Hamlet, / King, father, royal Dane. O, answer me!" (ibid. 44–45). In the expectation that the figure will reveal its secret to him, he collapses the figure with the king, thus submitting to it: "It will not speak. *Then I will follow it*" (ibid. 63; my emphasis). As he follows the figure of the "foul deed," Hamlet is forced to follow the terms of another deed:

> Ghost   Pity me not, but lend thy serious hearing
>   To what I shall unfold.
> Hamlet Speak, I am bound to hear.
> Ghost   So art thou to revenge, when thou shalt hear.
>   (I.v. 5–7)

Caught by the ghost's figurality, Hamlet becomes bound to revenge, the deed of which he "signs" with his hearing. The logic underlying the ghost's assumption that by "lending his ear" Hamlet is bound to "give his word" hinges on the assimilation of the account of the "foul deed" to a formal "deed" (a compact). This assimilation is enabled by the ghost's figural status, which does not

———

thing about Hamlet to the audience, and be one more character with respect to the play.

recognize the distinction between form and content. Thus as Hamlet is informed of the latter, the ghost argues, he endorses the former—and unwittingly becomes bound to the terms of yet another compact, that between the two kings, which itself concluded a combat, stipulated the crossing of their lines of descent, and will ultimately be concluded with Hamlet's revenge. Hamlet is thus drawn into a complicated pattern of transition from act to compact and compact to act that the ghost delegates him to perform and that constitutes *Hamlet*, the play. The transition from compact to act, however, is obstructed by the same figure of interiority that made possible the ghost's "trapping" of Hamlet.

Indeed, after his encounter with the figure like his father, Hamlet finds himself dispossessed of the inward time he had acquired with his privatization of mourning. On the one hand, the ghost's account of "his" assassination displaces the experience of death from Hamlet to the king, so that he can no longer overparticularize it; on the other, he has, with his vow of revenge, subjected himself to another's time.[14] Hamlet must now remember the ghost, not the king (I.v. 91: "Adieu, adieu, adieu, remember me"), and this in order to "set right" the figure's time instead of his own (I.v. 188–89). And, if his inward time had established the temporal "distance" between the man and the character that Hamlet required for the constitution of his "self-conceit," after his encounter with the ghost Hamlet is doubly distanced, as a character, from the man. First of all, he must plot his revenge secretly: His acts should not be exposed to view. Second, his plot is not his, insofar as he must per-

[14]Interestingly enough, although the ghost's account of his death gives Hamlet reasons for his excessive mourning, it also re-places death in the realm of the communal, as the queen had done before. Indeed, the ghost's detailed account demonstrates to Hamlet that death happens to others, and not to oneself; while the fact that he learns about these details demonstrates, in turn, that death cannot be experienced individually, but only in common—in this instance, between Hamlet and the ghost. In this sense the ghost, while proving Hamlet right to continue his mourning, despoils him of the exclusivity he had over it—in this sense Hamlet "loses" the private ghost of mourning, and with it the time-in-excess of others in which "that within" could "pass show."

form the ghost's demand—as it were, perform its script. He thus finds himself playing, and consequently being, a character, both in private (as he is in charge of the performance of someone else's actions) and in public (as he must pretend he is not engaged in the project of revenge). It is not surprising, then, that after he has seen the ghost he acts "mad" toward others, a behavior that should certainly be read as strategic but also as the logical consequence of the distance he is forced to take, *as a character*, from the man. It also indicates the struggle Hamlet must engage in against his own figurality, which has taken over the "inward man."[15] This is apparent in Hamlet's next "apparition," which, in accordance with Hamlet's new figural status, is as ghostly as the ghost's: It takes place offstage and frightens Ophelia, who then, as Horatio did to Hamlet, reports it to Polonius (and consequently to us, audience and public).

Ophelia, then, has been intruded upon by a transfigured Hamlet as she was "sewing in her closet"—the prince's doublet is unbraced, "his stockings fouled," he has no hat, he is ungartered, and so on. Although he looks "as if he had been loosèd out of hell / To speak of horrors" (II.i. 83–84), he says nothing. Instead he performs a little dumbshow for Ophelia, which she has trouble translating into language:

> *Polonius*   What said he?
> *Ophelia*   He took me by the wrist and held me hard.
> Then goes he to the length of all his arm,
> And with his other hand thus o'er his brow
> He falls to such perusal of my face
> As 'a would draw it. Long stayed he so.

[15]Here Hamlet finds himself in the following predicament: For his actions to remain "hidden," they must not leave their "mark" on him; but how can he then enact them? Locke develops, as we will see in chapter 3, a model to construct the subject from action while exempting him from the marks of his action—as if it were possible not to be "touched" (affected, qualified) by what we do. This model, anticipated in Hamlet's procrastination, ultimately grounds the subject in inaction, suffering from permanent *akrasia* (see the Afterword for a discussion of incontinence as an inability to act rather than as compulsive acting).

> At last, a little shaking of mine arm
> And thrice his head thus waving up and down,
> He raised a sigh so piteous and profound
> As it did seem to shatter all his bulk
> And end his being. That done, he lets me go;
> And, with his head over his shoulder turned,
> He seemed to find his way without his eyes;
> For out o'doors he went without their helps
> And to the last bended their light on me.
>
> (II.i. 86–100)

Ophelia's account fails to determine "literally" what Hamlet's actions say to her, but in her uncertainty over what it is he is performing she succeeds in conveying his absorption into the realm of the figural. Indeed, what starts out as a "sober" description of Hamlet's gestures—the first two lines of Ophelia's account are as "literal" as they can be—soon lapses into imagery, be it in the form of mimicry—Hamlet's hand is *thus* over his brow; he shakes his head *thus*— or similes—his perusal of Ophelia's face is likened to his drawing of it. His sigh *seems* to shatter his bulk; he *seems* to find his way without his eyes. These two types of figuration of Hamlet's behavior in fact collapse as Hamlet's sigh *ends his being*, and his body leaves the room without the guidance of his eyes, leaving Hamlet the subject (that "within which passes show") behind. Whereas Hamlet appears as the subject of his acts in the "literal" part of the account, he disappears into their semblance in their figural counterpart—Ophelia reproduces his gestures, while his sigh operates on his body, ending his being. Ultimately, Hamlet's dumbshow can be read as the performance of the clause that qualifies his love for Ophelia: "Thine evermore, most dear lady, *whilst this machine is to him*" (II.ii. 122–23).[16] The machine in question is the body, the exteriority of which is inaccessible to the "within" of his being, and which he has pledged to the service of the ghost's revenge; but it is also the machine of language, which he loses as he gives his word, a loss that points out his inability to control his own figurality.

[16]This is one of the letters that Polonius shows to King Claudius to account for Hamlet's distraught behavior.

Hamlet's dumbshow can also be read as a plea to Ophelia—
hence his taking of her wrist—to give him an image of himself. In
other words, as the demand to be looked at (with his perusal of
Ophelia's face he could be asking her to draw *his*), and to have access to that view. From this perspective his eyes would "bend their
light" on Ophelia in order to see what she sees. Such a move
would be in accordance with the other instance of Hamlet's recourse to a dumbshow, that which he sets up to "catch the conscience of the King" (II.ii. 603). This time Hamlet is not directly involved in the performance, but his eyes are also bent on seeing
what someone else is seeing:

> I'll have these players
> Play something like the murder of my father
> Before mine uncle. I'll observe his looks.
> . . . The play's the thing
> Wherein I'll catch the conscience of the King.[17]
>   (II.ii. 592–603)

Here again acts take on a figural turn as the players will be asked to
play something *like* the murder of the king. Hamlet hopes to be able
to read in his uncle's "looks"—both his appearance and his gaze—
the latter's recognition of the "foul deed" he has perpetrated. In
other words, he hopes to see his uncle seeing himself in the figure
displayed before his eyes, a discovery of his "within" (his "conscience") that he would then necessarily show in his behavior, as he
would then have no interiority in which to hide from exposure.

Hamlet's reasons to believe in the play's capacity to turn his
uncle "inside out," as it were, finds an explanation at the beginning of the speech, in which Hamlet wonders at the First Player's
ability to play his part so convincingly:

> Is it not monstrous that this player here,
> But in a fiction, in a dream of passion,

---

[17]Note here that Hamlet is out to catch not only King Claudius's conscience
but also that of the other king, or of the figure of the king, as he now suspects the
ghost may be a devil "abusing" him to damn him.

> Could force his soul so to his own conceit
> That from her working all his visage wanned,
> Tears in his eyes, distraction in his aspect,
> A broken voice, and his whole function suiting
> With forms to his conceit? And all for nothing.
>
> (II.ii. 548–54)

Whereas at the beginning of the play Hamlet took it for granted that woe was one of those "actions that a man might play," the fact that a man does play it now seems "monstrous" to him. What provokes his ambivalent admiration is the player's control over his appearance, which Hamlet himself has given up, first in favor of his "within" and then at the service of the ghost. Hence the actor's capacity to figure his own "conceit"—to give it "form"—highlights Hamlet's own inability to shape a "conceit" of himself.[18] Indeed, had the actor the "motive and cue for passion" that Hamlet has, he argues, "he would drown the stage with tears," whereas Hamlet "can say nothing, no, not for a King." Thus Hamlet seems stuck "within that which passes show," whereas the actor, who has nothing to pass it, can perform the show. But this selfsame disparity between the latter's capacity to perform the feelings of the former induces in Hamlet a fit of self-deprecation, that proves to him that he can at least *say* a lot. In other words, the player's successful figuration of his conceit draws Hamlet's own, "catching his conscience": The actor's play forces Hamlet's "within" into display. It is not surprising, then, that after this demonstration of the demonstrative power of figures Hamlet should trust them to disclose his uncle's participation in the "foul deed."

It is worth insisting on the change of status that "play," display, seeming, showing, and the like undergo for Hamlet: Appearances can be feigned, he argues at the beginning, and consequently do not "denote truly." By the time of the play-in-the-play, however, appearances have become reliable means of revealing truth. Thus

[18]Recall Doctor Faustus, who, "swollen with cunning of a self-conceit / His waxen wings did mount above his reach, / And, melting, heavens conspir'd his overthrow" (Prologue).

Hamlet comes to accept that the "trappings and the suits of woe" can precede and even create the woe "within," to the extent that he believes they are able to "trap" in their embodiment—and do justice to—the guilty conscience of the king.[19] The fact that the king's conscience finds expression in the performance of the "foul deed" that he silences suggests that "that which passes show" is not hidden or by nature invisible, but simply not shown. For what is not shown—"being," for Hamlet—need not be understood as that which is *within* and which it is impossible or not desirable to display *without*; showing does not necessarily imply a transition from an inside to an outside.[20] The act of showing, like other acts, can be done or not done, and the "actions that a man *might* play" are likewise actions that he may or may not play, rather than the cover for what the man is "acting" within. Accordingly the distinction within / without that Hamlet strives to keep disappears under that of showing / not showing, or doing / not doing.

But Hamlet makes yet another distinction in the course of this speech, which he first formulates as that between "fiction" and its counterpart—let's call it reality, even though he does not use that term himself. The player could give form to fictitious feelings, whereas Hamlet failed to express his "real"—well-grounded— passion. He eventually does manage to be drawn by the example of the actor and to vent his desire for revenge. At the end of this display of feeling, however, in which he successfully "forces his soul . . . to his own conceit," Hamlet realizes that revenge demands another kind of unfolding:

> Why, what an ass am I! This is most brave,
> That I, the son of a dear father murdered,

[19]It is interesting to note that the creation of an internal space seems to be linked to sorrow or guilt—Hamlet's mourning, his uncle's "foul deed"—and not to happiness (which Aristotle set as the end of all actions) or pleasure.

[20]Things can be perfectly visible and yet not be actively shown, either because they are not relevant (it would not cross my mind to show my new pair of shoes to the first passerby) or because showing them is not called for or is even superfluous (I show the room to my guest, but not each of its items).

> Prompted to my revenge by heaven and hell,
> Must like a whore unpack my heart with words
> . . .
> About, my brains.
>
> (II.ii. 580-86)

Words—figures of speech—are not enough for the kind of "play" Hamlet feels bound to perform. His revenge cannot take place on a stage; the figure of the deed needs to be unfolded in action, and not just to sight. Hence Hamlet's decision to set his brains working on the *conceit of the act*, instead of on the conceit of himself. For, if he is to effect the transition from the vow of revenge to revenge, Hamlet must effect yet another transition, that from the conceit of the deed to its unfolding in action.[21] But that he manages to do only when challenged to a combat by Laertes, who ultimately precipitates his revenge by drawing him into action.

To the mute audience of the act

Before the final combat between Hamlet and Laertes seals the inaugural contract, another combat takes place by Ophelia's grave, in which Hamlet challenges Laertes to outdo him in emphasizing his sorrow:

> What is he whose grief
> Bears such an emphasis, whose phrase of sorrow
> Conjures the wandering stars, and makes them stand
> Like wonder-wounded hearers? This is I,
> Hamlet the Dane.
>
> (V.i. 250-54)

[21]I discuss the relationship between contracts and conceits—basically, contracts as conceits of action that enable the conceit of the subject—in the next chapter. In chapter 6, I turn to *Hamlet* again, discussing Hamlet's problems with the transition from the conceit of action to action more fully. For the time being it suffices to anticipate that, while Hamlet plans his revenge, he "loses the name of action," a name that he will not utter himself but that will be left to the spectators to pronounce.

> I loved Ophelia. Forty thousand brothers
> Could not with all their quantity of love
> Make up my sum. What wilt thou do for her?
>   (V.i. 265–67)[22]

Hamlet has obviously not managed to leave the stage yet, as this combat of words demonstrates. On the contrary, he relapses into the attempt to control the figural while preserving his interiority. Hence he warns Laertes, who has grabbed him by the throat: "Though I am not splenitive and rash / Yet *have I in me* something dangerous" (V.i. 250–57; my emphasis). What it is that threatens from within is never named, which suggests that its menacing nature resides in its interiority. This is supported by Hamlet's self-qualification: that he is not "splenitive and rash," that he does not act on the spur of the moment but takes his time to consider a course of action. And indeed, Hamlet takes plenty of time to think about the best way to revenge his father (as he does before to mourn him), to the extent that by the end of the play he gives the impression of being a rather harmless character.[23] But we can consider the danger in question to be linked, not so much to his private preparations for revenge as to the time he has accumulated during its postponement. Indeed, recall that Hamlet understands his "mission" as one of "joining" the "time" that is "out of

[22]Hamlet is here taking the place of the player in II.ii, of whom he says:

> What would he do
> Had he the motive and the cue for passion
> That I have? He would drown the stage with tears
> And cleave the general ear with horrid speech,
>   . . .
> Confound the ignorant, and amaze indeed
> The very faculties of eyes and ears.
>   (II.ii. 557–63)

He is also engaging in the kind of *joute oratoire* that Aristotle reprehended because it put the characters to the fore, thus impinging on the unity of the action.

[23]He does, of course, kill Polonius and arrange Rosencrantz's and Guildenstern's deaths; but the former he does by mistake, and the latter by delegation. Otherwise, he is not much of a hero, and is not presented as a physically dangerous character: As his mother points out, "He's fat and scant of breath" (V.ii. 282).

joint"—the "time" between the inaugural contract and its fulfillment, between King Hamlet's death and its compensation in revenge, between, in short, the past and the future.[24] We could say that
Hamlet is a time bomb contained by figures of speech until he is
thrown into interaction (which could be qualified as the actual unfolding of action, in contrast to its conceit), at which point the bomb
explodes and events break loose.[25]

The explosion of Hamlet's time bomb is announced by Hamlet
himself when he confides to Horatio his apprehension over fighting
Laertes at King Claudius's request. Hamlet's presentiment is of
course grounded in the plot, for King Claudius has arranged for him
to be killed during the combat. But Hamlet is not informed of his uncle's plotting, and, although he feels "ill" about his heart, he is convinced he will "win a the odds" (V.ii. 205–8)—about which he is,
again, at least partly right. Nonetheless it is not to the prospect of
winning to which Hamlet alludes when he answers Horatio's plea to

[24] A word on the structure of revenge: It suspends time at the moment the
wrong was perpetrated, thus presupposing that it can be "undone" and that
time can flow again at the moment of its doing. Until that moment, the present is
destructured in function of the past.

[25] In a recently published article, the dramatist Alexander Weigel, discussing
Heiner Müller's "translation" of *Hamlet*, as he calls it (*Hamlet/Maschine*), makes a
similar point. He states that "at the heart of Shakespeare's *Hamlet* there is the
question of time in general." He argues that there are different and mutually exclusive times in the play, and that the only "real" time, which intrudes upon the
action, is that of the "undeniable immediacy of war and global destruction." His
essay is mainly concerned with Müller's parallelism between the walls of Elsinor
and those of Berlin, figuring the "conversion of historical time into dramatic
time." It concludes with an appeal to resist "the machine of time," reflected in his
argument by the events leading to the Gulf War, and to "recapture time and return it to its original state: slower, more adjusted to human beings and nature."
He thus echoes Hamlet's claim for more time, reformulating this claim as the resistance against historical time as figured in the dramatic time of the play (that of
the plot). In terms of my reading of *Hamlet*, Weigel is here pointing out the "intrusion" (his essay is entitled "Hamlet, or the Intrusion of Time in the Action"—
"*Hamlet o La Intrusió del Temps en l'Acció*") of the course of events imposed by the
inaugural compacts, which impose in turn a time of their own through the "gap"
of the disjunction claimed by Hamlet between "private" time and public or
common time.

"obey" his mind's dislikes (ibid. 211):

We defy augury. There is a special providence in the fall of a sparrow.
If it be now, 'tis not to come. If it be not to come, it will be now. If it be
not now, yet it will come. *The readiness is all.* Since no man knows of
aught he leaves, what is't to leave betimes? Let be. (Ibid. 213–18; my
emphasis)

It is significant here that while Hamlet defies augury, he surren-
ders to providence. He thus challenges what he can know of the
future, by foretelling or foreboding, and places his trust, instead, in
what he cannot know: the time of his death, the moment of its occurrence.[26] The gist of Hamlet's argument is that, to the extent that
one's own death is beyond the power of one's decision, there is
nothing one can do about it except be "ready" for it. In this sense,
although the reference to Matthew introduces a religious dimension in Hamlet's reflections, divine predestination seems to take
significance for Hamlet with respect to the "faculty" of readiness,
which he may or may not have, rather than with respect to God's
will, which will necessarily be accomplished. Earlier in the play
Hamlet had already reflected on providence and readiness in
similar but more explicit terms, when he told Horatio how he had
escaped from certain death by following his impulse to read the
letter Rosencrantz and Guildenstern were carrying to England:

> Sir, in my heart there was a kind of fighting
> That would not let me sleep . . .
> Rashly,
> And praised be rashness for it—let us know
> Our indiscretion sometimes serves us well
> When our deep plots do pall, and that should learn us
> There's a divinity that shapes our ends,
> Rough-hew them how we will . . .
>   (V.ii. 4–11)

Here "rashness" takes over when plots "pall," and its success dis-

---

[26]It is interesting in this respect that, etymologically, defiance is related to the
loss of faith and trust: Hamlet's challenging of the future thus reflects his mis-
trust of his own projections. See chapter 6 for a discussion of Hamlet's problems
with projects.

closes the existence of an end-shaping divinity. The ends so shaped can be known only retrospectively, and, accordingly, it is with "indiscretion"—with a certain lack of discernment or foresight—that they are most adequately implemented. This is not to say that plots are not subject to divine ends—to this the entire play testifies—for, whether they succeed or fall on the inventors' heads, they will ultimately accord with this higher purpose. But when there is no plot, and agents act without the guidance of their own projections, yielding to impulse and seizing opportunities, then it is clear that they can but be accomplishing what *should* happen—which means, ultimately, that they are actualizing possibilities and making them necessary, for whatever happens becomes necessary by virtue of its having happened.

Hamlet's "surrender" to providence is thus less a form of resignation to predestination than the acknowledgment that what will make things happen is not foreknowledge but a certain disposition to act. Indeed, readiness does not evoke only preparation and prevision, with the relation to time that both imply, but also availability and the capacity to respond to the "now" of events. And it is to this "now," to the present tense of action, to which Hamlet is ultimately yielding with his reflections on the unpredictable inevitability of death—for, by virtue of these two "qualities," death comes to epitomize one's relation to the future in general.[27] Thus, whereas at the beginning of the play Hamlet interpreted it in terms of mourning, death now opens the future to action for him. Taking up the pun with which the ghost drew Hamlet into "signing" the deed of revenge and assuming the two kings' inaugural compact, Hamlet is now *bound to act*, rather than to *revenge*: He sheds, as it were, the imperative of the act-to-be-accomplished in favor of the readiness to accomplish it. He is accordingly willing to effect the transition from the figural combat with Laertes to a combat with foils.[28]

---

[27]There is in fact an interesting reversal: From the perspective of one's own projects, only suicide has a foreseeable end. And Hamlet, as is well known, contemplates its possibility.

[28]I return to the issue of Hamlet's readiness—and courage—in chapter 6.

But if words are daggers—Hamlet knows this—daggers are not words: this demonstrated by his and Laertes' deaths, as by those of part of the public of their performance. The fight takes place within proper bounds until Hamlet and Laertes "change rapiers in scuffling" (these are the stage directions), a moment of literal inter-action that "seals" their deaths, as the foil that passes from one to the other is poisoned. The king wants to *part* them ("They are incensed"), but it is too late: Their acts are unleashed off the stage of the combat, involving the spectators one after the other (the queen falls, Laertes reveals the truth, the king dies) until they all die. Before he dies, however, Hamlet quickly recontains the spreading interaction by addressing a "new" audience—either the public of the play or that within the play:

> You that look pale and tremble at this chance,
> That are but the mutes or audience to this act,
> Had I but time—as this fell sergeant, Death,
> Is strict in his arrest—O, I could tell you—
> (V.ii. 328–31)

With this gesture he reconstitutes a stage and reestablishes a distance between act and sight that can then be mediated (figured) by words. Hence his plea to Horatio to reconstitute the figure of this "foul deed" ("report his cause aright"), and Horatio's subsequent insistence on the *staging* of the dead bodies "lest more mischance / On plots and errors happen" (V.ii. 387–89). In the meantime, however, Hamlet has lost his time, and his "within" is denied by the prospect of death—which was, recall, the event that first made possible its construction.

Although we can read death as the cause of Hamlet's loss of private time and space, the fact that it is itself caused at the moment of interaction with Laertes suggests that the "fell sergeant," as Hamlet calls it, functions as the figure of what happens then. And what happens can be formulated as follows: Hamlet engages in interaction with "readiness" (he does not have the time to prepare a "conceit" for what will happen), which implies that he "joins" a common time that comprises his. He concurrently loses his "within," for the within / without distinction is not operative from the stance of the communal. Indeed, the overflow of deaths offstage demonstrates that interaction does not respect the categories of within / without, and further suggests that it does not allow their imposition, insofar as it does not allow viewers to circumscribe the time and space of the stage. According to this formulation, the conceit of Hamlet's being as "that within which passes show" is not compatible with the communal realm (time and space) of interaction. Hence the introduction of such a category upsets the possibility of action—to which Hamlet's postponement testifies—and conversely the engagement in action overturns Hamlet's conceit of himself.

We thus find in *Hamlet* a tension between the deed as contract and the deed as act that is manifest in the different transitions from combats to compacts, and in the difficulty surrounding the enactment of the latter. The tension arises from the (temporal) dissociation of the agent from his actions, which introduces, as I will further argue in the next chapter, the category of the subject as conceptually independent from action. This dissociation renders the form—whether through sight or compact—of Hamlet's inscription in *Hamlet* questionable. Hence Hamlet's appeal to the mutes or audience, who could stop, with their silence, the continuous transformations of the plot. Reproducing the ghost's gesture toward himself, Hamlet here assumes that, as the audience is bound to hear, so should it be bound to set his story right. This, however, can be done only in silence, and more specifically, in the "silence" of the performance itself, where words do not exhaust deeds, be they acts or compacts.

3 ⌒ Locke and the Performative Subject

Authorizing the individual

The oscillation between deed as act and deed as compact staged in *Doctor Faustus* and *Hamlet* was accompanied, as we have seen, by the protagonists' efforts to formalize a "conceit" for themselves, enabling them to act and yet remain unmarked by their actions. Faustus, recall, situates himself at the origin of his actions and acquires command over his actions by delegating their performance to his powerful servant; while Hamlet, who has "that within that passes show" struggles to keep his own time and interiority and engage in action all the same. In both instances, however, compacts eventually give way to performance, and the protagonists become full characters, if not once and for all, at least once again. The conceit of the "new" agent thus follows the to's and fro's from act to compact: It is fixed when the law of compacts takes over, but only until it is disproved by the necessity of acts. Giving this conceit a name—the legitimacy of which this chapter will confirm—it can be said that the category of the subject does not have a proper figuration in either of the two plays. It surges with the disruption of the Aristotelian model of action as the abstraction of the man from the character, the displacement of the temporal whole from actions to agents, and the withdrawal of individual from communal time—but it lacks modeling: It is unconfined by action and cannot contain it in turn.

To say that the category of the subject surges with the disruption of the Aristotelian model of action is not, to be sure, unequivocal, and can lead down the slippery slope of causality and determinism. In some narrative circumstances it might appear that it is the introduction of the category of the subject that causes the disruption of the Aristotelian model and the shift from act to compact; in others, that the category of the subject coins its own compactual model and then displaces the Aristotelian one; and yet in other circumstances that it is because compacts become the new paradigms of action that the category of the subject "must" surge to replace that of character. As long as these circumstances are circumscribed as narrative, however, the temptation to recount the story of the configuration of the categories of subject and action need not be resisted, for what is at stake is less how such a configuration took place historically than how it could be possible, and what its implications are. Succumbing to temptation, then, this chapter recounts how John Locke elaborates a conceit for the subject in his *Two Treatises of Government*. Needless to say, Locke does not set out to coin such a figure, but the latter emerges in the course of his account of the origins of civil society as he theorizes the relationship between individuals and their society on the basis of the concept of property.[1] Locke's figuration of the subject thus begins, as we will see, with the individuation of the agent from the communal by means of action and through the category of labor; it continues with the derivation of action, in the form of compact, from the individual agent, owner of himself and of his acts; and it ends with his reintegration into an interpactual (rather than interactive) social network (rather than whole).

---

[1]Readers with a strict philosophical background might find that this account does not render Locke's argument with rigor—that it dwells too much on linguistic "details" and too little on the substance of his argument. But philosophers, as much as poets or novelists, must avail themselves of metaphors, images and, in general, figures of speech to develop their arguments, and this all the more so when they are being innovative, for they then need new terms with which to overcome the limits of the philosophical tradition they have inherited. In this sense, to consider the terms of Locke's account is to take his argument all the more seriously.

The terms of Locke's argument, are, of course, more specific and recall in fact the political context of Hamlet's inaction. Indeed, Locke presents his *Treatises* as the refutation of the political stance represented by Sir Robert Filmer in his *Patriarcha*, where he argues for the absolute power of monarchs over their subjects and for the perpetuation of this power through inheritance.[2] Locke opposes the social compact to inheritance as the legitimating source of power, in much the same manner that the system of inheritance is contested in *Hamlet* by different compacts—the compact between the two kings, on the one hand, the legitimacy of which young Fortinbras questions and validates simultaneously, and the queen's remarriage, which disinherits Hamlet. But whereas in *Hamlet* the interruption of the cycle of inheritance by the "new beginnings" imposed by compacts is the source of temporal and political disorders—the time, recall, is "out of joint"—for Locke it is clear that only compacts can bind "the times." According to him, it is self-perpetuating sovereign powers that threaten the continuity of political societies, laying "the Foundation for perpetual Disorder and Mischief, Tumult, Sedition, and Rebellion" (II.§1).

Interestingly enough, these are the same effects that Hobbes, whose political theory coincides with Locke's in most other respects, attributes to governments elected according to the social compact.[3] Hobbes's argument is that in the interval between the

[2]According to Locke, Filmer would argue that "Men are not born free, [and] therefore could never have the liberty to choose either Governors, or Forms of Government. Princes have their Power Absolute, and by Divine Right, for Slaves could never have a Right to compact or Consent. Adam was an absolute Monarch, and so are all Princes ever since" (I.§5).

[3]I am here following C. B. Macpherson's comparison between Hobbes and Locke in *The Political Theory of Possessive Individualism: Hobbes to Locke*. According to Macpherson, Hobbes's and Locke's political theories share the same basic assumptions, converging in all respects except the issue of the manner of continuation of political governments. They would both uphold that governments are meant to implement the protection and order for which political societies are created. And they both conclude that, if governments are to guarantee such order, governments must have sovereign power. For Locke, political government must indeed be perpetual, in the sense that there should always be one, but the

end of one government and the election of the next chaos is bound to erupt, rendering election itself impossible. Thus for Hobbes political government must be absolutely continuous, a seamlessness that is not possible when the physical succession of government depends on the people's repeated consent. While this argument is not historically grounded, as, indeed, Locke's is not,[4] Hobbes's objection to elected governments does have some logical ground once it is granted that men are naturally bent on fighting each other—this is a point that Locke himself grants. Indeed, the gap of time between one government and another, the period of "disjointed" time, can at least give the occasion for the ghost of oppression to rise and unchain revenge, revolt, and chaos. The reasons for the "perpetual Disorder and Mischief" that Locke ascribes to self-perpetuating governments, instead, are less obvious. They are, in fact, more formal than logical, as is apparent in the terms with which Locke refutes Sir Filmer's defense of inherited governments.

Locke's main objection to self-perpetuating governments is that they lack authority, simply because neither it nor power can be passed on or inherited:

It is impossible that the Rulers now on Earth should make any benefit, or derive any the least shadow of Authority from that, which is held to

---

individual person or persons assuming its functions must be sanctioned by the majority of the members of society (for a summary of Locke's and Hobbes's "political theory of possessive individualism," see Macpherson, pp. 263–64).

[4]There are clearly sufficient examples of long-lasting and relatively orderly self-perpetuating sovereign powers to contradict Locke's argument against them, as there are also reasons to consider Hobbes's fears about the total breakdown of society historically unjustified. Thus Macpherson argues that the cohesion of the ruling classes in Hobbes's time does not justify his fear of the upsurge of chaos. According to Macpherson, Hobbes's erroneous judgment would be due to his unawareness of—or failure to theorize—the existing social classes of his society. Locke would have "seen" through this mistake and perfected the model of possessive individualism that Hobbes had begun (Macpherson, pp. 93–95). And in his introduction to the two *Treatises*, Peter Laslett is in turn amazed at Locke's capacities of historical abstraction: "Neither Machiavelli, nor Hobbes, nor Rousseau succeeded in making the discussion of politics so completely independent of historical example, so entirely autonomous an area of discourse" (p. 78).

be the Fountain of all Power, *Adam's Private Dominion and Paternal Juris-diction.* (II.§1)

The problem, moreover, is not that a government lacking authority cannot subsist, or that it can do so only by sheer force and hence in "tumult and mischief." The "disorder" that the self-perpetuation of governments entails must thus be understood with respect to the order proper to its palliative, authority, which Locke presents as the criterion for legitimacy that should replace hereditary right. Authority, Locke argues, is also a right, but it issues from an author's act and hence entitles only (design as the "right" person, and also as the owner, as we will see) the author of that act. Thus the most apparent order that authority presupposes is that between author and act: The author has rights because he is at the origin of the empowering act, and he is its ordering principle.

The possibility of attribution of act to author is in turn allowed for by the temporal order implied by the postulate that the right-giving acts issue from the author, which basically reverses the temporality of inheritance. Indeed, whereas in the latter the past determines the present, in the former it is the present that determines the future. The present, moreover, is the agent, the origin of the act, whose presence marks the beginning of new acts turned toward the future and determining it. In this sense, if authors inherit anything, it is the future of their own making. Opposed to this future-oriented order, which is of a prescriptive nature, the subjection of the present to the governing drive of the past imposes a system of necessity that removes actions from the command of agents. Accordingly in a regime of inheritance authority is ultimately irrelevant because there are no beginnings, only the continuation of what came to pass before—to the extent that actions themselves seem to be transmissible, as if they were passed from agent to agent, carrying them in their flow. Inheritance thus precludes a strict correspondence of acts to agents, introducing indeed a form of disorder, linked, however, less to social upheaval than to the "world order" Locke is keen to ensure.

Before he can "set down what [he] take[s] to be Political

Power" (II.§2), then, Locke must dispel the possibility that acts are transmitted. Accordingly, his first *Treatise* is dedicated to a thorough refutation of Filmer's biblical version of the origins of political society, according to which (1) God gave the earth to Adam to the exclusion of all other men, and appointed him to have dominion over it and its creatures; (2) all other men were consequently not born free because they were at birth subject to Adam, Father and Monarch of all; and (3) political power is hence transmitted from Adam to all successive Princes.[5] In other words, in Filmer's account the transmission of power is a consequence of an inaugural transmission of property from God to Adam and of the former's appointment of power to the latter. Locke's first objection to Filmer's argument, as summarized at the beginning of his second *Treatise*, is accordingly "that *Adam* had not, either by natural Right of Fatherhood, or by positive Donation from God, any such Authority over his Children, or Dominion over the World, as is pretended" (II.§1). Locke can dismiss with ease Adam's Paternal Right, from which his absolute power should have derived, on the grounds that it is not in fact an exclusive right, because according to the Scriptures children should honor both mother and father.[6] The proper term of this authority, Locke argues, would in fact be parental authority (I.§15), but that is a shared source of power and does not correspond to the kind of power that was supposed to be transmitted. Indeed, Locke argues that parental authority is not to be con-

[5]Locke himself will argue exactly the contrary: The earth was given to all men in common and no one was appointed to dominate it over other men; men are consequently born free, even from their parents and monarchs; political power cannot be transmitted but is created through consensus. Hence Locke replaces Filmer's myth of the (causal) origins of political society with his own foundational myth (he will talk of the commonwealth as a "house").

[6]It is worth noting that although Locke appeals to the equal status of mother and father to make his point against Filmer, women lose their equality with men when Locke discusses the marriage contract: "But the Husband and Wife . . . will unavoidably sometimes have different wills too; it therefore being necessary, that the last Determination, i.e. the Rule, should be placed somewhere, it naturally falls to the Man's share, as the abler and the stronger" (II.§82).

fused with regal authority, which could be what Filmer is thinking about: They are two distinct types of power and nowhere in
the Scriptures are they equated (II.§52–76, §169–74).

But dismissing the rights Adam would have acquired with
God's Positive Donation is a more complicated—and fundamental—matter. Locke's basic argument is that possession of the world
cannot be a source of Adam's power for the very simple reason
that he did not, in the first place, possess it. God gave no exclusive
dominion of the Earth to Adam, Locke declares, but on the contrary, "God in this donation, gave the World to Mankind in common, and not to *Adam* in particular" (I.§30). If anything, then,
Adam is a metonymic representative of mankind, a "particular"
standing for the "common" of which he is a part. Filmer is obviously a literal reader, unskilled at recognizing figures. Locke, instead, manipulates figures with ease. He is aware, for example,
that metonymy is both a figure of substitution and of identity, as
the part that stands for the whole is itself, by definition, part of the
whole. Filmer errs because he privileges the function of substitution over that of identity—that is, he takes Adam for the whole of
mankind. Locke himself privileges, in this case, the function of
identity, maintaining the connection between Adam and the whole
from which he steps forward. In this manner, Adam's individuated status is "temporarily" suspended; he is not "Adam" for all
practical purposes, particularly for those of inheritance.[7]

Having dismissed Adam's qualifications as a legatee, Locke
addresses the modalities of the transmission of rights and property. Thus the second point of his summary argues that, even if
Adam had the authority over his children and the dominion over
the world that Filmer pretends, "his heirs yet had no right to it."
This time Locke's objection pertains to the definition of what can
be effectively inherited, rendering it dependent on the manner of

[7]By converting Adam into a metonymic representative of mankind Locke
denies him not only the possession of the world but also his existence as Adam.
Having established, through metonymy, the commonality of all, Locke will then
proceed, through metonymy, to individuate each.

its original acquisition. Hence: "In all Inheritance, if the Heir succeed not to the reason, upon which his Father's Right was founded, he cannot succeed to the Right which followeth from it" (I.§85). If Adam acquired his rights from God's donation, and this was a personal donation, then no one but Adam has a right to them unless God himself repeat his donation:

for positive Grants give no Title farther than the express words convey it, and by which only it is held. And thus, if as our A—— contends, that *Donation*, Gen. I.28. were made only to *Adam* personally his Heir could not succeed to his property in the Creatures. (I.§85)

God's donation is performed verbally; like all of God's acts, it is a speech act. Accordingly the physical operation of passing the Earth from God's hands to Adam's need not be accomplished, and should not, in fact, be accomplished, for the sake of Locke's argument. Indeed, if the full import of the donation had to be conveyed in a single gesture, how could it be known whether Adam received the Earth as Adam or as the metonymic representative of mankind? Once the distinction is available, as Locke renders it, the decision as to whether "one" is a part of a whole or a whole part (an individual, in this case) comes into force with the declaration of intent of the donation—hence the importance of the donation being a speech act. Having granted, then, that God's donation was personal—that is, addressed specifically to Adam—it follows that no one else can take Adam's place or represent Adam in an attempt to reconstitute a metonymic flexibility. A personal donation is an individuating act inclusive of one and therefore exclusive of all (the rest).

Not only is the recipient of a donation irreplaceable, but the donor's agency is not transmissible. Only God can grant what he grants; the act itself is what it is in virtue of the fact that God enacts it, and only he can enact it again. Thus Locke "closes," as it were, the act of donation at both of its poles, which enables him to ground rights on acts: Origin and end are established by the act and retain their positions through time—centuries after God gave the Earth to Adam, God still has a unique right as donor, and

Adam as recipient of the donation. The fact that for Locke the power to alter the structure that is thus set up remains with the agent/author, here speaker, qualifies donation as an act of institution. According to Locke, then, the act of donation is an act of institution of a relation of rights that provides for the relation's persistence through time, until a similar act of institution renews the parameters (the individuals, for example) upholding the relation in question. Because each act of institution must be performed in the present tense, there is no place here for the intervention of the past. By insisting on the performative nature of God's donation, Locke relates the individuation of subjects to their position within a structure enforced by an act that is then contained through time in the structure itself. Thus the act of donation is, as it were, fixed through time, and so are the "rights" it establishes, the subjects it individuates.

There can be, then, no such thing as "transmission" of rights (in the two senses of "right position" and "right individual"); there are only instituted rights. The relations that confer rights are mapped from receiver to giver, originator and end of action, and the act of donation that first set the relation in place persists between these two invariable poles. We cannot imagine in this context the "contagious" proliferation of actions that caused havoc in *Hamlet* and motivated Horatio's attempt to contain them in the stage-within-the-stage. Locke contains all actions in contracts, equating all action to speech acts; the dangerous oscillation from act to compact seems to be precluded. All actions perform appointments that guarantee their field of operativity. Locke further specifies that

any Government begun upon either [*Paternal Right, Consent of the People,* or the *positive Appointment of God himself*], can by Right of Succession come to those only, who have the Title of him, they succeed to. Power founded on *Contract,* can descend only to him, who has Right by that Contract: Power founded on *Begetting,* he only can have that *Begets*: And Power founded on the positive *Grant* or Donation of God, he only can have by Right of Succession, to whom that Grant directs it. (I.§96)

Unsurprisingly, for Locke "positive Appointment" and "positive Grant or Donation" seem to be equivalent to each other. Their equivalence is traced on the common ostensive element through which both acts delimit and enforce their effectiveness. Similarly, all of Locke's three types of empowerment comprise an ostensive dimension of assignment: Contracts designate "the right" successor "by right" (that is, by the terms of the contract), and the right successor binds the terms of the contract through time; grants are directed to someone who is by virtue of that direction the right beneficiary, and delimits the physical and temporal reach of the act of donation; the act of begetting—whatever that is!—operates as the criterion for the relation between father and son that empowers the father and in which the son points to his father as his origin.[8]

The power conferred by paternity is particularly interesting because it functions "backward": whereas both contracts and grants appoint specific individuals to hold specific powers, the father's power is consequent to his own act of begetting. It is therefore the consequence of the act that qualifies the act, which in turn appoints—authorizes—the "right person"—the author—to benefit from the rights of fatherhood.[9] What allows this retrospective empowerment, or what follows from it, is the assurance that not only do individuals act, but actions are individual. They do not merge into the common drift of events but retain their specificity by virtue of their having an origin.[10] Thus actions can be considered as individuating, whatever their stretch through time (nine months after). Accordingly Locke concludes that, as the empowerment derived from paternity follows a strictly personal act, it cannot be inherited or passed on. In fact passing it on would be like inheriting a Relation:

[8]There is no question of daughters here, not even of mothers: "For Paternal Power, being a Natural Right rising only from the relation of Father and son, is as impossible to be Inherited as the Relation itself" (I.§98).

[9]The appointment of the right person—the right father—when fatherhood is concerned is of course not an easy task, even in our times. The uncertainty of fatherhood, well thematized in literature, is probably one of the reasons why Locke will not rely on it for the creation of his political subjects.

[10]In this sense Locke's preoccupations are similar to Davidson's, who, we recall, distinguished actions from events by the "mark" the agent left on them. Locke, however, does not conclude that all actions are bodily movements—on the contrary, his solution is to consider them all as primarily speech acts.

and a Man may pretend as well to Inherit the Conjugal Power of the Husband, whose Heir he is, had over his Wife, as he can to Inherit the Paternal Power of a Father over his Children. (I.§98)[11]

Inheriting a relation, as the above "absurd" example shows, is akin to being entirely replaceable, to being successible oneself, to being passed on by time instead of constituting the order of time—hence the hint of incest, the generational disorder that would allow a son to replace his father in his mother's bed. We are back to God's "positive Donation," also a "personal," specific, and individuating act that cannot be transmitted (inherited) because neither the agent nor the recipient or object of the action can be substituted. If acts are to ground rights and function as a technique of individuation for Locke's subjects, they cannot be themselves transmissible— they must only be repeatable.

Locke addresses the issue of the criteria of the determination of the "right" heir in the remaining points of the summary. First he argues that they are simply not reliable, because they are in fact neither stated nor could cover all possible cases, "there being no Law of Nature nor positive Law of God that determines, which is the Right Heir in all cases that may arise, the Right Succession, and consequently the bearing Rule, could not have been certainly determined." Hence inheritance as the legitimating practice of political power leaves open the possibility of usurpation, even if by "mistake." This, moreover, is necessarily the case even if the criteria of identification of the right heirs existed, because, as Locke states in the last point of his summary, "the Eldest Line of *Adam*'s Posterity being so long since utterly lost . . . there remains not to one above the another, the least pretense to be the Eldest House, and to have the Right of Inheritance." In other words, whatever these criteria are, they do not apply to any existing (present) candidate, because the individual candidate does not exist. Again, Locke melts the individual back into the common, into "the races of mankind." Inheritance fails in the best of cases to be an individuating practice and practi-

---

[11]As an important trend of *Hamlet* criticism argues, it may well be that Hamlet hoped he would inherit his father's title as a husband with that of king.

cally amounts to usurpation in its incapacity to legitimate or authorize the reign of a given—"donated"—and only if given (specified) right, individual.

Strangely enough, Filmer himself would have agreed with the
equation of inheritance and usurpation. As Locke points out, Filmer's insistence on the genealogical descent of monarchy from
Adam is relative if not irrelevant within his own argument. Locke
even quotes Filmer's statements to this effect: "All power on Earth
is either derived or usurped from the Fatherly Power," and "It
skills not which way kings come by their Power, whether by Election, Donation, succession or by any other means, for it is still the
Manner of the Government by Supreme Power, that makes them
properly Kings, and not the Means of obtaining their crowns"
(I.§78). At this point an exasperated Locke suggests that Filmer

> might have spared the trouble of speaking so much, as he does, up and
> down of Heirs and Inheritance, if to make any one *properly a King*,
> needs no more but *Governing by Supreme Power, and it matters not by what
> Means he came by it.* (I.§78)

The reader in turn wonders why Locke did not spare himself the
trouble of refuting Filmer's system of inheritance, given the facility
with which he could have simply dismissed the matter altogether.[12]
Locke's preoccupation with the issue suggests that Filmer's conflation of inheritance, usurpation, succession, and even election makes
dangerous sense unless the notion of "rightful" individuals is firmly
secured through a properly individuating relationship between
subject and action. This relationship, as Locke hints, is that of
authorship, that actions authorize their authors. But such a relationship can be secured only if the metonymy of the part for the whole

[12]My own detailed discussion of Locke's argument against inheritance reflects the fact that he also speaks "up and down" of inheritance: The four longest
sections of his first *Treatise* are on the question of inheritance ("Of the Convey-
ance of *Adam's* Sovereign Monarchical Power," "Of Monarchy, by inheritance,
from *Adam*," "Of the Heir to the Monarchical Power of *Adam*," "Who Heir?").
The last of these sections, "Who Heir?" is not only the longest of all but also
closes down Filmer's doctrine of "inherited" monarchy on the grounds that
there is no determinable candidate for the inheritance of Adam's reign.

that it undoes remains undone—that is, if the part can be literally detached from the whole as a whole part—if the author can be identified. Thus Locke sets out to secure each man's individuation from mankind "once and for all" by definitely closing down the possibility of reversing the status of the individual back in time and into its "pre-individual" origins.

The person in labor

Against the all-confusing practice of inheritance, which fails to distinguish individuals by the mark they leave on their acts and only follows the organizing principle of the passage of time, the second *Treatise* provides the account of "another rise of Government, another Original of Political Power, and another way of designing and knowing the Persons that have it, than what Sir *Robert Filmer* hath taught us" (II.§1). The other "original" will of course be the individual, for whom Locke's founding myth must provide an existence previous to society. Consequently Locke posits, in a conventional contemporary move, an intermediary State of Nature between God's positive donation of the earth to all men in common and the creation of society, in which individuals already have full rights. In this state,

all Men are naturally in . . . a *State of perfect Freedom* to order their Actions, and dispose of their Possessions, and Persons as they think fit, within the bounds of the Law of Nature, without asking leave, or depending upon the Will of any other Man. (II.§4)

Man's "state of perfect freedom" is limited only by natural law, which prescribes, in accordance with God's purposes, the preservation of mankind.[13] Each man must follow this law of preservation by preserving himself and contributing, if possible, to the preservation of other men:

For Men being all the Workmanship of one Omnipotent, and infinitely wise Maker; All the Servants of one Sovereign Master, sent into the

---

[13]For a full discussion of the relationship between God's purposes and the law of nature, see James Tully, "The Law of Nature," in *A Discourse on Property*.

World by his order, and about his business, they are his Property, whose Workmanship they are, made to last during his, not one another's Pleasure. . . . . Everyone, as he is *bound to preserve himself*, and not to quit his Station willfully; so by the like reason, . . . ought he, as much as he can, *to preserve the rest of Mankind*. (II.§6)[14]

All men are equally God's property, but they are not his property "in common." By qualifying the relationship between man and God in terms of property instead of government, Locke can derive individual freedom from equality. Hence, because all men are owned by God, each man must be his own watchdog and govern himself to the end of his self-preservation, leaving other men alone to "order their actions . . . as they think fit." Thus the status of being God's property creates in each man an individuating and self-subjecting bond that distinguishes him, as a unit, from the rest. The only "commonness" left to mankind is their individual link to God, who comes to represent, in Locke's founding myth, the individual imparting individuality.

From this first step of individuation, which subjects man to himself ("bound to preserve himself") instead of to a social group, the relationship between men is defined in terms of each man's freedom from "the will of any other man," and consequently each man's respect of the other's will: "No one ought to harm another in his life, health, liberty or possessions" (II.§6). This prescription creates a negative subjection to the other's will, in that the other's will must be "followed" by not impinging on its willing. The space of the individual is consequently created by God, preserved by the individual subject himself, and acknowledged and permitted by other individuals. But other men's acknowledgment of one's individuality and recognition of one's will is problematic. God has criteria for the individuation of a subject and the subject himself "has" them in turn in the sense that he is their product, but there is nothing in the relationship between different subjects that could force the "rest" of mankind to be anything other than an amor-

[14]For a discussion of what Tully calls the "workmanship model" of the relationship between God and man, see also his chapter on "The Law of Nature."

phous, unified mass. The only criterion available for the recognition of the individuality of others is the assumption that they are like oneself, but this opens the way for exactly those metonymic appropriations—substitutions—that Locke wanted to ward off in his refutation of inheritance.

The fact that God's criteria are inaccessible to man and other men might explain Locke's apprehensions with respect to the relations between individuals. Other individuals represent a threat to any given individual because they may fail to respect the self-binding "fence of freedom":

> For I have reason to conclude, that he who would get me into his Power without my consent, would use me as he pleased when he had got me there, and destroy me too when he had a fancy to it . . . and reason bids me look on him, as an Enemy to my Preservation, who would take away that *Freedom*, which is the Fence to it. (II.§17)

Homo homini lupus est, and freedom is that which fences off the intrusion of other wolfmen (into the boundaries of the individual). Locke's conceit posits men as real estate (land), with defined boundaries that determine them as private property in the eyes of others, inviolable within those boundaries. If the fence of freedom is trespassed without the key of consent, then the boundaries of this property are blurred and there is, properly speaking, intrusion and usurpation. Man, like real estate, is dependent on the recognition of the boundaries that he sets out to enclose himself. God recognizes these boundaries, as he himself created them and "owns" them. But He has "delegated" his ownership to the "owned," by which act he naturalizes—that is, does not change—the boundaries of individuals, legitimating them. Between men themselves, however, man's individuality is as conventional (and for Locke this means "consensual") as private property—witness the purely symbolic nature of fences. As fences can be trespassed, and conventions denied, so can individuals be de-defined.

Locke deals with this problem through a peculiar reversal: He naturalizes the boundaries of property through the category of "labor," which he in turn conventionalizes ("consensualizes"); and he transfers the power of self-preservation to an agreed-upon political government. The argument is spelled out in his chapter on *Property*, where Locke explains how the transition from God's grant of the earth to all in common to the actual partitioning (sharing) of it into private property takes place. The initial postulate is that

> Though the Earth, and all inferior Creatures be common to all Men, yet every Man has a *Property* in his own *Person*. This no Body has any Right to but himself. The *Labour* of his Body, and the *Work* of his Hands, we may say, are properly his. (II.§27)

What we have is that whereas the man is God's property because He created him, the person is the rightful property of the man, and this, presumably, for similar reasons—man must be, in some sense at least, the maker of his person. Now, as Tully points out, God's ownership of man is grounded on His workmanship to the extent that He has an "inside" knowledge of his product.[15] By contrast, fathers, who are the other "creators" of mankind, do not own their children because they have an observer's knowledge of them: They do not know how to make their children; they do not know what it takes for their children to be what they are. Accordingly it must be on his maker's knowledge that man's property in his person must be grounded. In Locke's formulation the person is associated with the labor and work of the man's body and hands, which suggests that the distinction between "man" and "person" corresponds to that between the body and what it does. It is of his actions, then, that the man has an internal, and even prophetic, knowledge, which grants him in turn an internal knowledge of his person and hence an interiority. The person thus designates the internal and "private" space of the man, as defined by his body's labor and the work of his hands. On the basis of the privacy that actions demonstrate, the person acquires in turn a right over himself as a man, for "no body . . . but himself" has the right to occupy the space of the enacting body. "Himself" is here the figure of the

---

[15]See Tully's *Discourse on Property*, pp. 104–10.

person as traced by the actions of the body, which actions, as it were, return to the body enclosing it within the person.

A closer analysis of Locke's use of the terms "work" and "labor" will be enlightening at this point. Tully explains that the term "labor" can cover most sorts of action in seventeenth-century literature but that it is, more strictly, "coterminous with non-recreational actions," and "free, intentional actions."[16] Thus labor and work, the two activities defining the person, are basically productive, end-directed, and transitive actions, from which enjoyment—pleasure—is precluded or at least incidental. In Aristotelian terms, they are not actions done for their own sake, and they are not, consequently, actions that can contain the man by reason of their temporal structure. They do, however, refer back to the man, by virtue of their productivity—work, because it produces goods that are, in Locke's scheme, the rightful property of the maker, bearing his mark of "origin" by their existence. In this sense work could be said to "point back" to the maker. Labor, instead, could be said to "close back" upon the laboring agent. Indeed, as Hannah Arendt points out, the products of labor are goods for consumption that, although they can at times be said to be "made," are destined for the biological maintenance of the body, the needs of which are constantly renewed.[17] Thus labor, unlike work, has no temporal end and is instead endlessly repetitive. But it does have a physical end that coincides, in principle, with its origin. And in this sense

[16]Ibid., p. 109. Tully actually quotes Locke's opposition of recreation and labor in a letter to a friend, where recreation would be "the doing of some easy or at least delightful thing to restore the minde or body tired with labour, to its former strength and vigor and thereby fit it for new labour." Here it is interesting to recall Aristotle's own conception of leisure: "For we are busy that we may have leisure, and make war that we may live in peace" (*The Nicomachean Ethics*, 1177b4–6). If Aristotle wants to "free time" and have leisure, Locke wants to be free from time, through work.

[17]See Arendt's 1957 lecture on "Labor, Work, Action," where she develops the distinction between the concepts of labor and work on the basis of Locke's comment. The lecture can apparently be found among "The Papers of Hannah Arendt" in the Library of Congress. I consulted a recently published Spanish translation of it.

labor is an action that returns to the man: It begins and ends in the man. Accordingly it is with labor, rather than work, that Locke develops the figure of the person, enclosing the man within its temporal and physical circuit.

The figuration of the person through labor is apparent in Locke's derivation of private property from the property in the person. The world, recall, was given to all men, and consequently all have rights on this common property. But a person is entitled to the exclusive use of whatever he labors for, because with this activity he singles out something from the common property and "instills" himself in it or, alternately, integrates it within himself:

Whatsoever . . . he removes out of the State that Nature hath provided, and left it in, he hath mixed his *Labour* with and joined to it something that is his own, and thereby makes it his Property. It being by him removed from the common state Nature placed it in, it hath by this *Labour* something annexed to it, that excludes the common right of other Men. (II.§27)[18]

In other words, labor leaves the person's mark on its product, whereby other men lose their right to use it upon themselves, for they are not the right "destination" of the product of the labor, and they are not legitimately included within the figure of the person. This figure must remain closed to enclose only the "right" man within the person. Accordingly, Locke postulates that appropriation is only legitimated by use, which activity completes the cycle of labor and hence also the figure of the person:

It will perhaps be objected to this [appropriation through work], That if gathering the Acorns or other Fruits of the Earth, etc. makes a right to them, then any one day may *ingross* as much as he will. To which I Answer, Not so. The same Law of Nature, that does by this means give us Property, does also *bound* that *Property* too. . . . As much as any one can make use of to any advantage of life before it spoils; so much he may by his labour fix a Property in. (II.§31)

---

[18]Or yet: "*As much Land* as a Man Tills, Plants, Improves, Cultivates, and can use the Product of, so much is his *Property*. He by his Labour does, as it were, inclose it from the Common" (II.§32).

"Use" thus becomes the last stage of the process of appropriation of the common by the individual, binding the product to the man: "And thus, I think, it is easie to conceive, without any difficulty, *how Labour could at first begin a title of Property* in the common things of Nature, and how the spending of it upon our uses bounded it" (II.§51).[19] Thus labor first "entitles" one to property, designating the "right" man to the right product, and then use secures the figure of the person, completing it and binding the man within the person.[20]

It is worth considering at this point how Locke's configuration of man, action, and person innovates Aristotle's and St. Paul's respective configurations of man, action, and character, and "old man," action, and Christian man. Because he is theorizing the nature of the relationship between members of a political society, Locke, like Aristotle, is particularly interested in the category of action without referring to which he cannot figure political subjects. Thus his person bears a certain resemblance to Aristotle's

[19]Hence slaves cannot own property, because their labor does not "return" to them, and they do not, consequently, own their person.

[20]We could reformulate the circuit that Locke is attempting to define in the following terms: "Appropriation," the entitlement to property, is a function of an act when the act is understood as productive (that is, end-directed and transitive) and its product is put to use by the selfsame agent (enacting body) of the action. Or: "I pick up an acorn" designates a process whereby an individuating (entitling) relationship is set up between the "I/person" and the "acorn" whereby, as the "I," in Locke's formulation, "by his labour does, as it were, inclose [the acorn] from the common" (II.§32), the acorn's return to the "I/body" in turn encloses it from the "all" owning the common. If the move of individuation of the object through the action "begins" the person's title to property, the person and the title are secured only when the "I/body" effectively uses (in this case, eats) the apple, closing upon itself the movement of appropriation, and enclosing the man in the person. Hence the acts that the "I/body" directed toward the "common" objects, singling them out and drawing the figure of the person, must revert toward the "I/body" again, singling it out in turn to the person. Without this return we could say that the "I" is lost to its actions, the person is not "materially" bound by action. "Use" "binds" property—encloses, engrosses, singles it out—and defines its boundaries within the realm of the "I"/"agent," operating the inclusion of the "I" within itself.

character, because he is defined in terms of what he does. But unlike Aristotle, Locke's concern is to legislate action rather than in-
quire into its ultimate ends, and cannot, consequently, admit that
men are marked by their actions and that character is the term for
their full temporal inclusion and display in action. Accordingly, in
Locke's model the man is spatially circumscribed—recall "the
fence of freedom"—by his actions in the person, which is the figure that in turn contains both man and action.[21] In this Locke's person is comparable to St. Paul's Christian man, for his actions define
his inwardness, which inwardness is, in turn, their originating instance. But whereas the Christian gained inwardness by virtue of
what he could not do, and in opposition to what he did following
the law of the members, Locke's man is interiorized by what he
does and in continuity with the person. Indeed, Locke could not
admit the radical division between the inner and the outward man
and the law of the spirit and the law of sin postulated by St. Paul,
for this would concede to Filmer the legitimacy of self-perpetuating governments. Thus whereas in St. Paul's model there is an inner "I" in struggle with a body that acts like a "he," in Locke's the
"he" is the inner man, whose actions demarcate its containment
within an enclosing "I." With this shift from the third to the first
person Locke's agents are able to preserve "that within that passes
show" and, unlike Hamlet, act at the same time.

What makes possible Locke's slide from the third to the first
person, recall, is the concept of property. Man, which would correspond to St. Paul's "he," is God's property; for He has an inside
knowledge of him. The man, in turn, has an inside knowledge of,
and consequently owns, his actions, occupying with respect to
them a first-person position. The person, finally, defined in terms
of the man's actions, occupies with respect to the man the first-
person position that the man occupies with respect to his actions.
In this manner the third and first person are conflated, and the in-

[21]A way of formulating the difference between character and person is that
the former is a temporal category within a philosophy of ends, whereas the latter
would be its spatial correlative in a philosophy of origins.

ner "he" passes show. But the person's knowledge and correlative possession of "his" actions have an uncertain status, corresponding to that of an observer rather than a maker—indeed, to the extent that the person is drawn by actions, he cannot be said to "be" inside them. There is, in short, a first- to third-person fluctuation at the heart of Locke's figuration of the person that emerges, as we will now see, when the circuit of action is broken by the imposition of another's will onto the person. Locke responds to his own fluctuation from first to third person with the notion of consent, which posits the property in one's actions—labor—by conventionalizing the appropriation of one's actions by others. Thus all action is further regulated by the act of consent, which is the condition for the "creation" of the political subject.

The performative subject

We can now better understand Locke's imagery of freedom as a fence that preserves the person, for to the extent that the latter is circumscribed by his end-directed and productive actions, to deflect their course or impede their return to the person in self-use is akin to breaking open the circle of individuality. Indeed, to force someone to do something is to ignore the distinction between one's and another's actions, and consequently between one person and another. Accordingly Locke concludes that to be forced to do something, or simply be under someone else's power, amounts to the destruction of the "I": "He who would get me into his Power *without my consent* would use me as he pleased when he had got me there, and *destroy me too* when he had a fancy to it" (II.§17; my emphasis). Locke is not here referring to the physical destruction of the man but to the reduction of the free person to the state of slavery. The latter, however, should not be understood literally either, for Locke further specifies that "it is Lawful for a Man to *kill a Thief*, who has not in the least hurt him, nor declared any design upon his Life, any farther than by the use of Force, so to get him in his Power" (II.§18). We are thus entitled to understand the above destruction of the "me" that follows from another's "use" as the dissolution of the boundaries of self-property, which implies the restoration of metonymy and its potential for substitution and the return of one's person to the common "all" of mankind, free for anyone's use. The danger disappears, however, when the use of one's person is granted, or consented to, by the selfsame person. Then there is no possibility of treating an "each" for an "all," a given person for a "common" person (common to all). "Consent" here constitutes the criterion of differentiation between "use" and "usurpation."

We encountered this term in Locke's heated refutation of Filmer's defense of inherited monarchies. For Locke, recall, inherited government amounts to usurpation because inheritance does not fulfill what he considers to be criteria for entitlement. In inheritance, indeed, there is no question of consent on either part of the transmission of rights; in fact inheritance would function by transmitting people to rights. As far as Locke is concerned, this is akin to usurpation, which he defines—negatively, how else?—as follows: "It being no *Usurpation* but where one *is* got into *the Possession of what another has Right to. This, so far as it is Usurpation,* is a change only of Persons, but not of the Forms and Rules of the Government" (II.§197). Usurpation then occurs as a system of circulation of persons, in a context where private property or titles to property are already in place. There is usurpation when the rightful owner, proprietor, or ruler is substituted in his relations to others and things by somebody else. In other words, there is usurpation when the specificity of individuals that supports and is granted by right proves to be fictional or at least unessential because it can be equally obtained by force. In other words, "usurpation" reveals the unnecessary and alienable nature of "self-ownership," and consequently, of the agent's centrality to his actions.

The transition from the State of Nature to the political would thus be motivated—theoretically, if not historically—by need to ward off the risk of usurpation. This transition is effected when men agree

to joyn and unite into a Community, for their comfortable, safe, and peaceable living one amongst another, in a secure Enjoyment of their Properties, and a greater Security against any that are not of it. (II.§95)

The interest of such an agreement is obviously the protection of each from all, the preservation of one's properties—in one's properties and of one's person—from others. Consequently as men agree to join in a community, they divest themselves of their natural liberty and "put on the bonds of Civil Society" (II.§95). The bonds of civil society are that each individual delegates his right to protect himself and do justice to himself to the community. Thus each individual subjects himself to a common government. In effect, subjects of a political society delegate their protective "fence of freedom" to an approved government, and consequently delegate the self-binding power of their agency, which had "enclosed" them from the rest of men in the State of Nature. But they have not thereby reimmersed themselves into an unindividuated whole, because the government to which they delegate their self-government functions itself as an individual:

For, when any number of Men have, by the consent of every individual, made a *Community*, they have thereby made that *Community* one Body, with a Power to Act as one Body. (II.§96)

Each individual's relation to the common government is therefore a one-to-one relationship (as opposed to a one-for-one relationship), in which both poles maintain their individuality (they are both known and designated), as established by an act (the "origin" of political power) that ascribes rights and maintains "the right" through time.

The act that empowers political government but yet preserves the individual over whom it has been empowered is the act of consent, a speech act functioning like God's original "positive donation" or grant of the world to all in common. As earlier observed, speech acts require reenactment in the present tense for any change in the relation they prescribe to take place, so that they "act" as if there were neither past nor future and as if the acts themselves were isolated from other historical events. In this sense, the individual's consent to subject himself to government does not affect his individuality (again, he cannot be thrown back into a preindividual state), because he retains in himself the temporal origin of the power to act that he gives away with his "positive donation." The interest of the founding speech act of "consent," then, is that it centers the origins of political power in those who are themselves subject to that power. The power in question is the power to govern one's actions, which constitutes the fence of freedom preserving a subject's individuality. To consent is to preserve the property in one's person as one's actions, or at least as a great field of decisional power over one's actions is given away. It is to assert self-agency—origin, individuation—at the very moment it is abandoned. This is possible because to consent is in fact to enter a symbolic order where actions are structured like grants—who gives what to whom—and where the subject takes his position as he gives his actions away.[22]

Locke's political subjects are thus doubly preserved from the risks of usurpation, by their mutual agreement to respect and protect each other's fence of freedom, on the one hand, and by their new grounding, as subjects, in the act of consent, which is in Locke's argument the sole act that cannot, under any circumstances, be either extirpated from or forced upon the person. For, recall, if labor could ensure the person's individuality over nature, it could not guarantee it over other subjects: Actions can always be forced from an agent, as Locke rightly and repeatedly points out throughout his treatise, which appropriation entails the trespassing of the fence of freedom and the destruction of the person. The best solution to the threat of the appropriation of each other's actions, is, ultimately, not to "have" them—and not to be individuated by them—in the first place. This is what happens when subjects put on the bonds of civil society and delegate the active protection of their fence of freedom to a political government, for they then retain only the power to originate actions as the criteria for their individuation. The sole category of actions that is now neces-

---

[22]In this sense, C. B. Macpherson's argument, in *The Political Theory of Possessive Individualism*, that the alienation of labor is a central aspect of Locke's theory of property seems to me to be correct. It is also central to the notion of the political subject, which takes shape in Locke's writings.

sary for their enclosed individuality is speech acts, and, more specifically, those speech acts that, like donation and consent, "accord" their actions to others. In this manner, reversing the initial
situation in the State of Nature, subjects retain property in themselves while they delegate the government of their actions. At this
point, formally speaking, God is no longer necessary: Through the
category of labor to that of speech acts, Locke definitely "detaches"
the individual subject from his original Creator. Persons are now
able to donate to themselves their individuality and temporal origins.[23]

The paradigmatic status of consent as the self-binding act of the
subject is apparent in the following scenario, where Locke considers

whether *Promises, extorted by Force*, without Right, can be thought Consent, and *how far they bind*. To which I shall say, *they bind not at all*; because whatsoever another gets from me by force, I still retain the Right
of, and he is obliged presently to restore. He that forces my Horse from
me, ought presently to restore him, and I have still a right to retake him.
By the same reason, he that *forced a Promise* from me, ought presently to
restore it, i.e. quit me of the obligation of it; or I may resume it myself,
i.e. chuse whether I will perform it. . . . Nor does it at all alter the case,
to say *I gave my Promise*, no more than it excuses the force, and passes
the Right, when I put my hand in my Pocket, and deliver my Purse my
self to a Thief, who demands it with a Pistol at my Breast. (II.§186)

Here the act of consent is the silent act that regulates the donation—actions are, after all, the person's property—of all other acts,
including speech acts such as promises. Accordingly, although the
thief can force a promise from Locke as easily as he can steal his
purse, Locke retains his property rights (his originating individuality) in both his promise and his purse because the transaction
was not ratified by his own consent. Practically this means that, in
spite of the appearance of what he has done, Locke does not consider he has given either purse or promise—in this case, and paraphrasing Hamlet, his are but actions that "a man might play." To

[23]It might be more precise to say that God's individuation having served the
function of grounding the individual "before" society and "as" property, it can
now fade into the background, as it indeed has faded through time.

the extent, moreover, that he did not designate himself as the origin of these actions (promising and handing over), Locke can even argue that it is not he who acted—that their genuine author is ultimately the thief, via his persuasive pistol; or that Locke inherited them from him. At any rate, Locke's consent has not taken place.

Had he consented, however, he would have uttered the same words, and the difference between consented and forced promise would not have been discernible. Indeed, whereas it is easy to grant the absence of consent in circumstances where the use of force is clearly involved, it is impossible to ascertain when it does take place, because consent is postulated as a private, inward, and silent act. There are thus no criteria for determining whether it has been enacted or not, and hence ultimately no criteria for the others to respect the fence of freedom it defends. For to the same extent that it is necessary for someone's labor to be recognized by others as having been performed for it to be attributed to its rightful agent, so should it be possible for others to acknowledge that consent, the act that regulates the subject's transactions of all his other acts, has effectively occurred.[24] The invisibility—or inwardness—of the act of consent does not, however, worry Locke, because in his relational mapping of subjects and actions, he conflates the "internal" knowledge of the "I" with the observer's knowledge of the "he." Hence the subject's inner ratification of the intent of his actions is already akin to the ratification of the first person's actions by a third person. What we have, then, is a circular relationship between the "I" and the "he," mediated by consent. My consent establishes my right to dispose of my actions over a third, potentially usurping, person, and my consent has already been "consented to" by the position of the third, knowing person, which I take as I consent. In other words, Locke grounds his individuating

[24]J. L. Austin discusses whether performative utterances should be thought to be legitimated by an inward act, and concludes that this would "open a loophole to perjurers and welshers and bigamists and so on. . . . It is better, perhaps, to stick to the old saying that our word is our bond" ("Performative Utterances," p. 236).

techniques on the constant slide between the subject and other subjects that he wants to prevent. Freedom from others seems to be an impossible state.

Locke's performative subject encounters a number of problems in the next chapter, one of which can be formulated precisely in terms of the fluctuation from the third to the first person inherent to his figuration. Indeed, in Locke's account, the performative subject that is the protagonist of civil society is a subject that, ideally, does not act, and hence never incurs the dangers of deindividuation and "doubling" into a "he/I." Confronted, however, with the necessity or impulse to act, the model of a subject preserved from action is problematic: The selfsame act of consent constituting the performative subject's "fence of freedom" may well become an act confining the subject from action. Thus one of the questions the performative subject will ask itself as it is caught in the moment of consent and decision is that of how action can in effect be deployed: How can decision (consent/the will) give way to action? How does the first-person position of action take over? How can its temporality be established?

4   ⌒ The Harness of Necessity

Binding acts

How can courses of action be stopped? This was a central concern in both *Hamlet* and the *Two Treatises of Government*, both of which investigate means to contain action—"lest more mischance / On plots and errors happen," as Horatio puts it; or, in Locke's terms, lest "perpetual Disorder and Mischief, Tumult, Sedition and Rebellion" become the foundations of human intercourse. Horatio, recall, stages the dead bodies at the end of the play, in an attempt to withstand the inhuman flow of action and restore the characters' lost protagonism by placing them at the center of their acts. Locke further protects his subjects from the current of inherited deeds by enclosing them within the act of consent and positing them at the origin of their acts. The postulate that the act of consent regulates all of a subject's actions finally formalizes the shift from act to compact. Consent thus becomes in Locke's argument the paradigm of all actions, at once grounding the subject in action and dissociating him from it. The performative subject can now "administrate" his actions, but at the risk of being confined by the selfsame act of consent that gives him fundament. Indeed, consent is meant to regulate not only those actions the subject delegates—or alienates—but also those actions the subject undertakes. Here the act of consent becomes, more specifically, an act of decision or of willing, anticipating and generally creating or affirming the origin from which a predicted course of action should ideally "flow."

Action then implies a transition from performativity to performance, requiring an impulse or incitement for decision to deploy
into action. As Hamlet's procrastination testifies, however, such a
transition is not easily effected—it is in fact difficult to "perform
the form." Thus the question of how the actual *passage à l'acte* occurs is raised: What makes it happen? How do courses of action
begin? This will be the performative subject's main concern.

It is important to keep in mind that when models of action do
not need to accommodate the category of the subject, the question
of the beginning of actions does not imply that of the *passage à
l'acte*. The difficulty surges when the *passage à l'acte* is isolated, as a
moment, from the duration of action, and posited as the moment
of demarcation of the subject's inwardness from action—then the
incitement to act must surge from within, self-generated, out of
nowhere. When there is no inwardness to safeguard, instead,
agents deliberate and make decisions, but they are not themselves
the source of their impulse to act. In Aristotle's understanding of
action, we saw, the man will act in accordance with his character:
If he is courageous, he will act courageously; he will follow his
character traits, which traits are in turn the marks that his actions
leave on him. In other words, the impulse to act is not figured as a
source but as a manner or a modality of acting that gives shape to
decisions and deliberation. Hannah Arendt calls this impulsing
modality "principles," a term that stresses their role in the initia-
tion of courses of action without, however, positing them as points
in either time or space. In contrast with motives, Arendt argues,
"principles do not operate from within the self . . . but inspire, as it
were, from without"; they are manifest, moreover, "only in the
performing act itself"; and, unlike its goal, "the principle of an action can be repeated over and over again."[1] In pseudo-Aristotelian
terms, principles could be understood as prevailing tendencies in
and of action. Without regard for terminology, however, what

[1] Hannah Arendt, WIF, p. 152. The examples she gives of such principles of
action are "honor or glory, love of equality . . . or distinction or excellence . . . but
also fear or distrust or hatred."

counts is that principles account for the actual undertaking of actions, and that they are operative in decisions rather than issuing from them.

There is a moment in *Agamemnon*, the first play of Aeschylus' *Oresteian Trilogy*, that illustrates with particular aptness how the issue of the beginnings of actions is resolved when agents are not performative subjects.[2] Early on in the play, the chorus recounts how Agamemnon decides to give up his daughter Iphigenia for sacrifice to placate the goddess Artemis, who has sent an ill wind preventing the Hellene troops from sailing for Troy. Holding her husband responsible for the death of her daughter, Clytemnestra kills him and explains to a distraught chorus that *he* had killed *her* "for a charm to stop the Thracian wind!" (1418). From Clytemnestra's perspective, Agamemnon's decision is not only criminal but lacks grounding as well—he had the choice between spilling his own blood and giving up his participation in the attack on Troy, and he settled for the former, as if the two options were commensurable and it were possible to weigh them with the same scale. Agamemnon himself lacks criteria at first to decide for either option, both of which have nefarious consequences, but when he gives further thought to the prospect of leaving the project he has undertaken unaccomplished, he is unable to contemplate the possibility of sparing his daughter:

> Disband the fleet, sail home, and earn
> The deserter's badge—abandon my command,
> Betray the alliance—now? the wind must turn,
> There must be sacrifice, a maid must bleed—
>
> (211–14)

Here the criterion that allows Agamemnon to make up his mind seems to be that of which of the two options has a sequitur. Iphigenia's survival leads nowhere, it is not inscribed within a course of action to be taken, it is an ending. Her sacrifice, instead, is the condition of possibility for the sailing of the troops and for their

[2] I will be referring to Philip Vellacott's translation of *The Oresteia*, which I have checked with that of Robert Fagles.

participation in the Trojan War, and it is consequently necessary for the achievement of that course of action. It is not, it is worth stressing, necessary in itself—Agamemnon can betray the alliance, the fleet can be disbanded—but it will be necessary, in view of what will happen, if it does happen. In other words, Iphigenia's sacrifice is compelling because it is impelling; it can be conjugated in the future anterior as an event that *will have been necessary*.

Hence the chorus's comment on Agamemnon's "decision": "Then he put on / *The harness of necessity*" (217–18; my emphasis). Here decision appears as the device of self-harnessing that binds Agamemnon to action and resembles more an act of submission to a principle of necessity than an exercise of free choice. Indeed, Agamemnon "chooses," ultimately, to submit to the guidance of a defined course of action, to enable and follow its flow: He harnesses himself with necessity to draw action forth. Agamemnon's agency thus appears as an enabling rather than a commanding agency; he leads, but because he is guided; he carries through events to their proper end. By contrast, and as figured in Locke's *Treatises*, the performative subject would have the principles of action within himself and generate the impulse of necessity without harnessing himself to action. If in Aeschylus' image actions guide, necessity harnesses, and agents carry through, the performative subject would like to be the guiding instance and harness action with necessity. To do this it is not sufficient to be at the origin of actions; the subject must yet interiorize their anterior future, the impelling "it will have been" of necessity. And he does this through his proper device: performatives. More specifically, he does this with promises, which imply the agent's capacity to predetermine the future.[3] But promises also imply the agent's capacity

[3]In *On the Genealogy of Morality*, Nietzsche qualifies promises as "a desire to keep on desiring what has been, on some occasion, desired, really it is the *will's memory*: so that a world of strange new things, circumstances and even acts of will may be placed quite safely between the original 'I will', 'I shall do' and the actual discharge of the will, its *act*, without breaking this long chain of the will" (*Second Essay*, §1, p. 39). For man to acquire such a control of the future, however, he must "become *reliable, regular, automatic*, even in his own self-image" (ibid.).

to attune the present to the future—and this, as we will see, is not an easy task. Promises, moreover, like all illocutionary acts, introduce other subjects in relation to whom the speaker's words—whether uttered or not—acquire their performative force, for it is always to an audience—albeit a tacit one—that the "I will" is addressed.[4] The performative subject's "I will" thus binds him to other subjects, reintroducing an extraneous force that "harnesses" him to action when it does not (as we will see) harness him to himself.

The difficulties the performative subject encounters as he attempts to be the source and harness of his actions can be traced through Milton's *Samson Agonistes* and Shelley's *Prometheus Unbound*, both of which feature their heroes reduced to inaction and "freed" into action again after a reshuffling of the conditions of their performativity. Significantly, both texts are conscious rewritings of a third, "model" text, Aeschylus' *Prometheus Bound*, in which the mythical figure of Prometheus is staged bound to a rock, suffering Zeus' punishment for his theft of fire and subsequent gift

---

For this and other reasons, Nietzsche "wonders" whether becoming an "animal able to make promises" is not the "real problem *of* humankind" (ibid. p. 38)—presumably because man will never acquire such a degree of automatism. For our purposes, it is interesting to note that Nietzsche speaks of the "*sovereign individual*" as a "man with his own, independent, durable will, who has *the right to make a promise*" (ibid. §2, p. 40). Not all men have this right, according to Nietzsche, because not all men can keep their word. And this is because not all "are strong enough to remain upright in the face of mishap or even 'in the face of fate'" (ibid.). In other words, promises make sense when one is strong enough to be self-confident enough to know that one can actually do what one has promised. This may sound like a banality, but it is not in view of the performative subject's difficulty to act: He promises *in order to act*, as opposed to promising because he *can* act.

[4]Indeed, as P. F. Strawson points out, an important feature of those acts that we "perform *in* saying something" is that the speaker intends to produce a certain response in the audience by means of "the recognition on the part of the audience of the intention to produce that response, this recognition to serve as part of the reason that the audience has for its response, and the intention that this recognition should occur being itself intended to be recognized" (see "Intention and Convention in Speech Acts," p. 159).

of it to the human race.[5] Prometheus' gift delivers men from the rage of Zeus but also frees them into action, for with fire he offers them the skills that enable them to articulate time, predict the future, and generally shape their purposes and acts. Milton and Shelley seize on the paradox of having the donor of action himself bound to inaction, but they provide a version of their protagonists' "unbinding" rather different from that of Aeschylus, who makes it

[5]Milton and Shelley basically respect the "skeleton" of Aeschylus' play, reproducing it quite literally at times. Aeschylus' play begins at the moment that the punishment of Zeus is being implemented, and Prometheus is nailed to a rock. Prometheus' isolation is broken after a brief period of lamentation with a series of visits: First the chorus, which will stay with him throughout the play, then Oceanus, and then Io arrive. Finally Hermes arrives and threatens Prometheus with heavier punishments unless he reveal to Zeus how to avoid the defeat he predicts. Prometheus refuses, and the play ends as "threat gives way to performance" (1081). Milton's play opens as Samson, who has tried to free the Hebrews from the Philistines and has been imprisoned and blinded by them, is lamenting his situation. He is then visited by the chorus as well as by Manoa and Dalila, and is challenged by Harapha, who allows him to express his defiance of the Philistines. Finally his presence is required at a feast in honor of Dagon, in which he is asked to make a spectacle of his defeat. He first refuses to go, and then, after a moment of introspection, complies. During this feast, "threat gives place to performance" as Samson collapses the roof of the theater on both spectators and himself, thus fulfilling God's promise that he would deliver the Israelites from the Philistine yoke. As for Shelley's Prometheus, he is also bound as the poem begins, by reason of his own foresight, which has given him confidence to curse and defy Jupiter, thus binding his will to the god's. Like Aeschylus' Prometheus and Samson, Shelley's Prometheus laments his lot, is visited by different figures, is threatened by Mercury, whom he defies, and is further punished by the Furies. His own delivery is brought about by an act of introspection similar to Samson's that frees him from his inner bonds to Jupiter. The latter's fall follows, Prometheus is freed, and the poem does not end tragically.

Milton's and Shelley's stress on the unbinding of their Prometheus figure points out their concern with the difficulties the subject encounters when the time comes to perform. In this respect it is worth noting that neither *Samson Agonistes* nor *Prometheus Unbound* is a play; they are, respectively, "dramatic" and "lyrical" poems. The move from play to poem already marks a change of focus away from performance.

For the sake of consistency, I will refer to Philip Vellacott's translation of *Prometheus Bound*, counterchecked, however, with the translation by J. Scully and C. J. Herington.

clear that it is Prometheus' foresight that will eventually free him
from his bonds, as he knows how to prevent the otherwise im-
pending fall of Zeus. By contrast, Milton's and Shelley's promethean figures are delivered by a change in their attitudes toward their adversaries and to their imprisonment, a change effected by an act of insight that contrasts significantly with the foresight of the mythical Prometheus. Thus, as they unbind the "father" of action, *Samson Agonistes* and *Prometheus Unbound* stage the
advent of a second "gift" of action, issuing, this time, from the
subject himself.

Prometheus Bound: the rule of time

While Prometheus is being bound, Strength explains to the sym-
pathizing God of Fire, Hephaestus, that the theft of fire and subsequent gift of it to men is "an offence / Intolerable to the gods, for
which [Prometheus] now must suffer, / Till he be taught to accept
the sovereignty of Zeus / And cease acting as a champion of the
human race" (8–11). Prometheus, however, does not understand
his deed as an act of rebellion against Zeus' rule as such, but as the
refusal to acquiesce to a particular instance of its application—
namely, his projected annihilation of the human race. Hence he
explains to the chorus that Zeus,

> on succeeding to his father's throne
> At once . . . appointed various rights to various gods,
> Giving to each his set place and authority.
> Of wretched humans he took no account, resolved
> To annihilate them and create another race.
> This purpose there was no one to oppose but I:
> I dared. I saved the human race from being ground
> To dust, from total death.
> (228–37)

Prometheus is here directing the chorus's attention to a significant
injustice in Zeus' treatment of the human race. Having himself
come to power through a regime of succession, Zeus refuses to
mankind the benefit of the same—not satisfied with their individ-

ual mortality, he wants their "total" death. He is thereby attempting to submit to his rule the conditions of possibility of his ruling. This, as we will see, is not possible.

We find a hint of the logic behind, if not the reason for, Zeus' denial of continuity (immortality) through succession to the human race in the myth of the advent of the Olympian rule. According to Hesiod's *Theogony*, "at the beginning" there are four primary beings: Chaos, Gaia, Eros, and Tartaros. These four beings are not created, and they are there "first" only in a logical sense, for they exist "before" time, or outside of it. Gaia eventually conceives Uranus and then conceives Kronos with Uranus, allowing for the possibility of time. But Uranus prevents Kronos from being born, until he is overturned by Kronos. Then Kronos, in turn, swallows the children he had had with Rhea, except for the last one, Zeus, who overthrows him. In other words, both Uranus, who creates time, and Kronos, who is in charge of its passing and articulation, attempt to inhibit its succession and stop it at the moment of their own reign.[6] Thus in this "Succession Myth," as M. L. West calls it, the succession of moments and that of rulers coincides: Impeding the passing of the former is tantamount to preserving the power of the latter; ruling over the gods implies ruling over time.

When Zeus eventually vanquishes Kronos, with the help of Prometheus, the Olympian gods become immortal. Under the rule of Zeus all are allowed to be born, as it were, but further succession is arrested by the appointment of each god to "a set place and author-

[6]As George Varsos pointed out to me, Kronos does not mean time, but rather something like "fulfiller," or, less elegantly, "passer of time." The term comes from the verb *kraino*, which means "to accomplish, to fulfill, *to bring to pass*." In Homeric language, *kraino* further means "to finish the story of." Hence Kronos is the principle that enables things to happen or be fulfilled, which necessarily implies the passing of time, and consequently, time itself. It is in this sense that Kronos, not to be confused with Chronos, can still stand for the inauguration of time. In *The Oresteia* it is Zeus who becomes the "fulfiller" (*Zeus kronion*), in accordance with his having succeeded his father and inherited the function of "passing time" and enabling events to take place.

ity." In this manner succession is transformed into multiplicity. The human race, however, obviously exists and persists within the temporal order of succession that Zeus needs to abolish. It is indeed only through succession that it attains continuity as a race; the mortality of its members is both required and overcome by the longevity of the race. Hence Zeus' wish to wipe it out as a race is basically the wish to bar the passage from mortality to immortality that humankind crosses and that gods may "slip" through individually. In other words, the human race, by simultaneously upholding and overcoming the temporal regime of succession, threatens Zeus with its reintroduction into the realm of the gods, following which, as successor to his father and ruler of Olympus, he would be in turn ruled over and replaced. And in fact Zeus' actions as he takes over repeat with regard to the human race what his ancestors had done to their descendants.

The antagonism of Zeus makes sense if the human race is his creation, which it is in the sense that the temporal continuity of the race is accessible only to the gods, in that it is safeguarded by the gods in general and by Prometheus in particular. Inversely, if the human race is considered to have created the gods, in order to keep its time (as it were), then Zeus' attempt to "succeed" it— finish their story once and for all—is only "natural." In both cases, however, Zeus would deprive the human race of the immortality that stabilizes his regime. From a more anthropological position, it is obvious that the human race must survive the unaffectionate concern of Zeus because otherwise men could not account for their still being here, telling the story. In this case, Zeus' failed attempt to destroy them would tell the story of the gods' acknowledgment of men's responsibility for the telling of the story of the gods, and therefore, of men's responsibility for the permanence of the gods. Thus the myth in which the human race attributes its creation to the gods and then features them trying to destroy it, would constitute the myth of the gods' acknowledgment of their creation by the human race. Concurrently, the gods' wish to wipe out the human race would signify their fear of it, and would constitute in turn the acknowledgment by the human race of its creation of the gods.

All of the above perspectives show that gods and men are subject to each other as if they were each other's creatures. In this context Prometheus is a figure of mutuality and mediation, representing both the gods' responsibility for the human race (he saves them) and men's responsibility for the gods (he helps Zeus establish the new order). This is apparent in the fact that he mediates between human and godly time, mortality and immortality, as his gift of fire to man—his "ungodly" act—shows. Thus Prometheus explains to a questioning chorus that yes, he did more than "save the human race":

> *Chorus*   Did your offence perhaps go further than what you said?
> *Prom.*   Yes: I caused men no longer to foresee their death.
> *Chorus*   What cure did you discover for their misery?
> *Prom.*   I planted firmly in their hearts blind hopefulness.
> *Chorus*   Your gift brought them great blessing.
> *Prom.*   I did more than that:
> I gave them fire.
> *Chorus*   What? Men, whose life is but a day,
> Possess already the radiance of fire?
> *Prom.*   They do; and with it they shall master many crafts.
> *Chorus*   This then was the offence for which you suffer here—
> (248–58)

Prometheus grants men the ignorance of the advent of their own death; beyond this "blessed" blindness, and worse, Prometheus gives fire to men. The two gifts are related: The first grants each man the sense of immortality within the cycle of succession, based on mortality, that comprehends him. The second gift, fire, grants men, "whose life is but a day," the capacity to provide for themselves through the mastery of crafts. The mastery of crafts amounts to nothing less than "all human skill and knowledge" (507), including the craft of prophecy. In other words, Prometheus teaches men what I will call a "technology of time," which allows them to produce the future but forces them to submit to it, "read it," as they devise it.[7]

---

[7] I use the term "technology" rather freely, as a "technical method of achieving a practical purpose" (*Webster's New Collegiate Dictionary*), and derive the term

Indeed men learn from Prometheus how to do things, and, more generally, how to act purposively:

> In those days they had eyes, but sight was meaningless;
> Heard sounds, but could not listen; all their length of life
> They passed like shapes in dreams, confused and pur-
> poseless.
>   . . .
> Their every act was without knowledge, till I came.

(447–54)

---

from Wlad Godzich's title to his foreword to Didier Coste's *Narrative as Communication*, "The Time Machine." Here Godzich discusses Aristotle's classification of narrative as part of the genre of deliberative discourse: "The function of this genre is to prove to the assembled citizens the need for, or indeed the necessity of, a particular course of action that one wishes to see them execute, or conversely, to dissuade them from a given course of action. Deliberative discourse, in other words, leads to action or to its abrogation. It is not, itself, a representation of action and is never meant to be a substitute for it. The best way of thinking about it is as enabling (or disabling) action" (p. xv). The object of deliberative discourse, Godzich goes on to explain, is a decision, and more specifically a decision to "escape" from the "inexorable logic" of a process the assembly feels is "inimical" to them. Hence the decision is meant to "escape into a new temporal dimension free from as many of the constraints of the old one as possible" (p. xvi). The creation of this new temporal dimension involves *prohairesis*, "the future projection of a course of action," which projection constitutes the construction of a story that can "arrest" history and "produce more time," opening an alternative that can then be treated as history. Action can then unfold within this "new" historical time.

By technologies of time I do not mean only those techniques of projection but also of retrospection involved in the making of stories. In Godzich's account the technologies of time and the act of decision that triggers their productivity are not effective in the homogeneous time of philosophy (the time of concepts), in which decision is deferred indeterminately. Milton's and Shelley's Prometheuses start out by inhabiting such philosophical time. In the context of Aeschylus' plays, as I discussed earlier, deciding is not only an act of liberation from a given situation; it also involves an act of submission to the new temporality, which act effects the passage from story to history. After all, it is only in historical time that events are necessary, and this, because they happen—it is in this time that they happen. Agamemnon's "harnessing unto necessity" could be said to figure what Godzich calls "double catachresis" from history to story and from story to history.

The knowledge men acquire here is, basically, that of hindsight and foresight, the awareness of time and form that enables eyes to "see" and identify, and ears to "listen" to a song instead of to unstringed sounds. Prometheus' gift thus enables man's entrance into a world where the passing of time is marked, where there are beginnings and endings, and hence where there are purposive artifacts requiring and implementing memory as well as "foresight" or projection into the future. These purposive artifacts enable men to determine the future to some extent, although they will always have to experience its advent as a trick of Fate and remain subject to it as if it were god-given. For the gods, however, the fact remains that Prometheus has in effect given men the power to manipulate time, and hence also the ability to intervene in godly affairs. And indeed, the Olympian gods and men will constantly interfere with each other, pass from mortality to immortality, establishing a firm tradition of intercourse between the two orders of temporality and between what man decides, gods rule, and Fate prescribes.

But if Prometheus has initiated men to action, he lacks "even one trick" (466) to free himself from the punishment of Zeus. The god who taught men different technologies of time cannot himself appoint the time of his deliverance. Prometheus' impotence is almost a joke in the play:

> *Prom.*   So, here's the whole truth in one word:
>   All human skill and science was Prometheus' gift.
> *Chorus*   Then do not, after helping men to your own hurt,
>   Neglect to save yourself from torment.
>   (502–5)

The joke is a tragic one, however, for Prometheus himself:

> Fate fulfils all in time; but it is not ordained
> That these events shall yet reach such an end. My lot
> Is to win freedom only after countless pains.
> Cunning is feebleness beside Necessity.
>   (507–10)

Prometheus knows that he will strike a deal with Zeus and will be freed. But he remains bound to the "when," to the moment destined for his unbinding, in place of which no other moment will do. Hence the punishment fits the crime: Prometheus must endure the passing of time, which no technology can accelerate. In other words, as his bound body testifies, he must endure his subjection to the present. He may foresee the future, as mankind "foresees" it in its attempts to determine it, but this does not exempt him from being subject to its happening.

What could have appeared as an opposition between Prometheus and Zeus is thus further unbalanced by the agency of Fate. As Prometheus cannot anticipate the appointed time, or fly from his present condition, Zeus cannot force from Prometheus the secret of the conditions of his own fall from power before the same appointed time. Hence their fates are related, but concurrently rather than causally, temporally opposed, as it were, as their promised "accord" appears to be an accidental (in the sense of *accidens*, chance, what happens) concordance. The lack of any causal link between the fates of Prometheus and Zeus is confirmed by the former's contradictory prophecies: He first presents his freedom and the continuing reign of Zeus as the result of a pact (189–91) but announces elsewhere that only the deposition of Zeus will save him. He explains to Io that he could save Zeus, "once set free" (782–83). He also predicts the inevitable fall of Zeus: He will be "humbled," and his marriage "shall hurl him out / Of throne and sovereignty into oblivion" (912–14). These inconsistencies can certainly be explained by the fact that Prometheus is a boaster as much as he is a "prophet." But they are consistent with the complex situation that his knowledge of the future creates. On the one hand, he knows that Fate decrees the fall of Zeus; on the other hand, he knows that his knowledge of Fate will produce an alternative Fate—the continuing reign of Zeus—itself decreed by Fate. We can either consider this production of Fate as part of the technology of time that Prometheus masters, and which he would, this time, operate in favor of the gods, or consider the first of the Fates as a trick of Fate, in which case, of course, it is the Fates, instead of Prometheus, who boast. But whether tricked by or producing Fate, Prometheus is ultimately as subject to it as Zeus.

It is therefore not so surprising that Prometheus should at times "forget" his own foreknowledge:

> I groan in anguish
> For pain present and pain to come:
> Where shall I see rise
> The star of my deliverance?
> What am I saying? I know exactly every thing
> That is to be; no torment will come unforeseen.
> My appointed fate I must endure as best I can,
> Knowing the power of Necessity is irresistible.
>
> (79–86)

The only Necessity distinct from Fate is that of the present manifestation of Fate. Its irresistible power can be understood as the simple immersion in actuality, which can be neither fought nor avoided. Prometheus' name already suggests this, for it could be translated literally as "providence": Indeed his foresight does not allow him to prevent future events but rather to prepare for them beforehand, to create, as it were, a perspective or framework to cope with them. His foresight, however, does not apply to what happens now—for this, preparation comes too late, even when it has preceded the immediate "now." Hence, as Prometheus' foresight falls short of the present, he finds himself surprised by his own technology of time: "Yet I did not expect such punishment as this—" (268). Prometheus' talents, like the rule of Zeus, are operative only in the future. In the present he can only remember, occasionally, that he is plunged into oblivion of the future—that is, that no preparation prepares for what comes, when it happens.

As Prometheus cannot "foresee the present," he cannot "will" it either—only the future can be wanted, what happens "now" can neither be wanted as it is nor as it is not, but only as it will not be. This insight can be heard in Prometheus' words to the chorus: "Wrong? I accept the word. I willed, willed to be wrong!" (266).[8] Prometheus' "will to be wrong" is not a willing reconcilable to the notion of

---

[8]In Arnott's translation the terms are: "I know all this. / I sinned *with full intent*" (265–66; my emphasis).

agents as decision-makers. Indeed, by willing to be wrong Prometheus accords his will—that is, his orientation to the future—to the agency of Fate and time, espousing a course of action of which he does not claim to be the source but in which he does claim his necessary—because actual—involvement, albeit "in" the wrong. Prometheus' "willing to be wrong" is consequently an acceptance of his agency in Fate, a form of agency that, without positing him as the producer of what is to happen, posits him as the producer—performer—of what is happening, through his subjection to what will happen. In this sense, the kind of willing Prometheus endorses is anything but "willful" in the modern sense of the term: It does not posit the will as an originating force but as an instance of performance that enables the future by binding agents to the present. Prometheus' foresight thus functions like Agamemnon's "harness of necessity"—it is the principle of necessity of his endurance of the present, which endurance will enable his eventual delivery.

Turning now to Milton's *Samson Agonistes*, we will see how the performative subject attempts to free himself from the harness of the present by grounding the acquisition of foresight on that of introspective powers. Introspection will function in Milton's poem as a device to produce, instead of performing, the present.

Samson's "uncontrollable intent"[9]

In *Samson Agonistes* we can trace the fate of Prometheus' gift of fire among the human race and its concurrent interiorization by the individual subject. Samson, as is well known, has received from God the gift of superlative strength, which comes to represent, given the apparently unlimited capacity for action it grants him, the gift of action itself. Indeed, before his blindness Samson was, in the words of Manoa and the chorus, "irresistible" (126), "strongest of mortal men" (168), "invincible" (341); capable, in short and in

---

[9]See the chorus's closing speech (1749–54): "His uncontrollable intent" is of course God's, whose purpose can be neither predicted nor countered. But Samson's "intent" proves "uncontrollable" too, as we will see.

his own words, of "the mightiest deeds" (638). But his strength is not meant to remain abstractly wondrous; with it he received a purpose from God—to deliver the Hebrews from Philistine rule, and, Prometheuslike, offer them in turn the gift of action in the guise of freedom. As he was himself "promised by Heavenly message twice descending" (635) to his father, so does he become the bearer of God's *promise* to his chosen people: "Promise was that I/Should *Israel* from *Philistian* yoke deliver" (38–39). Samson is thus in charge of the promise that he represents with his mighty strength, but its being a promise he has not himself made, he is not the principle guiding his actions, nor indeed, that containing his strength. He is, instead, "led" (638) and "motioned" by God (222), prompted by "Divine impulsion" (422) and even "divine instinct" (526), when not by the irresistible drive of his own strength, which protagonizes the descriptions of Samson's feats as if it were his body that "insupportably . . . advanced" (136) rather than Samson who guided its steps.[10] In other words, the source of Samson's actions is anything but inner, as is emphasized by the fact that his strength hangs in his hair, fully—although secretly—displayed.

Before his blindness Samson is, in short, a Greek hero ("That heroic, that renowned / . . . Samson," 125–26), "design'd for great exploits" (32), and destined to act by reason of his decisive strength, which is for Samson what foresight was to Prometheus. Accordingly, when Samson loses his strength in a moment of indiscretion, he also loses his sight, his foresight, and the purpose to which he was destined—none of which he recovers as his locks grow forcefully again. Thus the play begins with Samson's demand for guidance: "A little onward lend thy guiding hand / To these dark steps, a little further on" (1–2). His despair at the loss of direction—of destiny, purpose, guidance—recurs throughout the

[10]This a "free" adaptation of the following passage, which features not Samson but his foot: "But safest he who stood aloof / When insupportably his foot advanced, / In scorn of their proud arms and warlike tools, / Spurned them to death by troops" (135–38). In most descriptions of Samson's feats it is apparent that he is possessed, as it were, by his strength, which is a property of all of his body. He is rarely, if ever, described administrating it, or using it strategically.

play, bordering on sin as he wishes for death and finds no hope in life: "as for life, / To what end should I seek it?" (521–22). This, however, is precisely the question that is proper to the process of interiorization that Samson's blindness very obviously figures: What end should I seek? To this process corresponds, in the manner of St. Paul's "inward man" who arises from the death of the "old man," one of mourning for "what once [he] was" (22) and inner contemplation of "what [he is] now" (ibid.).[11] Thus, as he oscillates between the "old" Samson, who had only eyes, and the "new" one, who should have a properly intending "I," Samson lives "a life half dead, a living death, / And buried" (100–101): "Myself, my sepulchre, a moving grave" (102).

This wavering between "what he once was" and "what he is now" is displayed, and put into play, in his evaluation of his lot, for which he blames an incomprehensible divine will when nostalgia wins him over, and himself when he recalls the circumstances of the turning point of his heroic past. Thus he wonders how to fit his present situation in the pattern of his once purposeful life:

> O wherefore was my birth from Heaven foretold
> . . .
> Why was my breeding order'd and prescribed
> As of a person separate to God,
> Design'd for great exploits; if I must die
> Betray'd, Captived, and both my Eyes put out,
> Made of my Enemies the scorn and gaze;
> To grind in Brazen Fetters under task
> With this Heav'n-gifted strength?
> (23–36)

More bitterly, he complains of the treatment he has received from God: "I was his nursling once and choice delight . . . / But now hath cast me off as never known" (633–41).[12] But when the pre-

---

[11] This should also remind us of Hamlet, who carves his interiority with the death of his own "old man."

[12] Resentment and regret are in fact Samson's main torments, as corresponds to his inability to act: "My griefs not only pain me / As a lingering disease, / But finding no redress, ferment and rage, / No less than wounds immedicable / Rankle, and fester, and gangrene, / To black mortification" (617–22).

sumptuousness of his judgment of God's will dawns on him, he presumes, in turn, to be himself entirely responsible for his state:

> Yet stay, let me not rashly call in doubt
> Divine Prediction; what if all foretold
> Had been fulfill'd but through mine own default,
> Whom have I to complain of but myself?
>
> (43–46)
>
> Nothing of all these evils hath befall'n me
> But justly; I myself have brought them on,
> Sole Author I, sole cause . . .
>
> (374–76)

At this stage it is clear for Samson that either God willed his fall, and he did not cause it, or that he caused it, and God did not will it: Agency must be on either side; he cannot reconcile the new status of "author" that he has earned with his indiscretion with the fulfillment of "divine prediction." And yet he must, for, as Manoa, his father, repeats to him, his "miraculous" strength must have grown back to some end: "His might continues in thee not for naught / Nor shall his wondrous gifts be frustrate thus" (588–89). In other words, he has the capacity for wondrous action again, and he must, again, put it at the service of God. He must, moreover, do it on his own.

That Samson should lose his purpose as he gains his authorship makes sense in the light of the event that triggers his coming into subjectivity (into being a subject). For it is clear that it is when he falters and reveals his secret to Dalila that he discovers that he has a will of his own—precisely because, like St. Paul's inward man, he does what he would not. Indeed, as Samson acknowledges, somewhat puzzled by his own unpredictability, he "knew" that his wife would betray him: "This well I knew, nor was at all surprised, / But warn'd by oft experience" (381–82). He acts, therefore, against his best judgment, and more specifically, as he tells Dalila, against himself: "I to myself was false ere thou to me" (824). And it is by so being "false to himself" that Samson's will first reveals itself to him as a source of actions apparently unguided by divine purpose, and even responsible for changing the prescribed course of events. With this negative will, however, Samson can do nothing, nor, indeed, will much, for it is a will that is bound to fail in action. In other words, as long as he remains the "sole author" of his wrongs, Samson must be without a purpose and devoid of foresight, consequently unable to intervene in the course of events to redress his betrayal of God's will.

It is worth noting that Samson's knowledge or intuition of Dalila's betrayal puts him in a situation akin to that of Prometheus, who knows but cannot avoid what will happen. There is, however, no conflict between Prometheus' foresight and his conduct—he does not disclaim his actions nor, indeed, claim authorship for them. Instead he does what he foresees: His "I willed to be wrong" is consequently neither the negative will of regret nor that of denial, but an acquiescent acknowledgment of his necessary participation in time, in his wrongs, and in his being wronged. Prometheus' foresight frees him, in fact, from having to struggle with the adverse circumstances—he knows he must wait, that there will be a time for his deliverance. Samson, by contrast, does indeed what he foresees but must then disclaim his foresight in order to claim his authorship. As a result, Samson is at odds with time: There is no future for his will to will, no time for deliverance to occur. His will can thus exert itself only on the present and in adversity and dissent, instead of on his recovered and promising capacity to act. For Samson to become the deliverer he was to be he must redress not only the course of events but also his will, which he must attune to time.

The selfsame event that reveals his authorship and deprives Samson of God's purpose ultimately prepares the ground for his reconciliation with the present and the eventual emergence of his "positive will" and proper purpose. Dalila, recall, wins over Samson's "fort of silence" "with blandish'd parleys, feminine assaults," and "tongue batteries" (403–4). Whereas the biblical account lingers on Dalila's strategies without problematizing Samson's "weakness," Milton insists on the latter and has Samson, somewhat perplexed, surprised, and full of regret, lament over his ignominious failure to respect his pledge and himself.[13] Doubtless Milton's point is to illustrate that physical strength is weakness without a guiding spiritual strength. Still, the question of why—and how—Samson eventually gives up remains one of the big question marks of the text. What is troubling, as Dalila remarks, is that he seems to have made known his secret "for importunity, that is for naught" (779). "Importunity," however, is not "naught." As Samson himself remarks, with her constant nagging Dalila is ultimately waiting for the right moment for her request to bear fruit: "At times when men seek most repose and rest, / I yielded, and unlocked her all my heart, / Who with a grain of manhood well resolv'd / Might easily have shook off all her snares" (406–9). In other words, her importunities are, more than plain nagging, opportunely inopportune—she creates the occasions to achieve the objective she has in mind and is ready, with Promethean "providence," when the time of its fulfillment arrives.[14]

Seizing the occasion—opportunism, in its Machiavellian sense— is not one of the skills Samson is liable to master. Indeed, he is more likely to have stormed in on occasions whenever he was not acting under divine "motion" and with a prescribed course of action. It is, however, one of the skills that seems to be required for the exercise of free choice, and, judging from the outcome of the play, it seems indispensable that Samson should acquire it in view of the realization of God's project. For according to Manoa, and Samson confirms this, the latter marries Philistine women under "divine impulsion prompting how [he might] / Find some occasion to infest [the] foes" (422–23)—that is, to infiltrate the enemies and seek for appropriate

[13]In the Old Testament, Samson just gives up, vanquished by Dalila's constant nagging: "And it came to pass, when she pressed him daily with her words, and urged him, so that his soul was vexed unto death; That he told her all his heart" (Judges, 16.16–17).

[14]It is worth pointing out how Dalila's agency is presented as entirely different from Samson's: She is weak, yet capable of overpowering him because she does not counteract; rather than attempting to harness events, she knows how to shape occasions to her favor and how to attune the present to her vision of the future.

moments to attack them from within. As it turns out, it is Dalila who infiltrates Samson and "finds the occasion," but in so doing Samson is placed in the most ideal position for assault: He is held captive, considered harmless in spite of his strength, and thus led into the heart of a major Philistine congregation. From a strategic point of view, then, Samson's inward turn could appear as a device to hide God's purpose from the enemies and thus better bring about its achievement.[15] And this seems to be the assumption that finally leads Samson to agree to participate in Dagon's feast, which occasion marks Samson's reconciliation with his destiny, for it reveals to him how the latter can be fulfilled: Thus Samson manages to accomplish with "inward eye" what was foretold, proceeding according to his own "prediction" of events.

The decisive change in Samson takes place between the first and the second visit of the messenger, who comes to summon him to make a show of his strength at the feast the Philistines are giving in honor of Dagon. Samson at first refuses to "abuse this Consecrated gift / Of strength . . . / By prostituting holy things to Idols" (1354–58), and the chorus, accepting Samson's new situation, tries out different arguments to soothe his defiance and convince him to comply:[16]

[15]I am of course talking from the perspective of the plot, and not from a theological standpoint. From the latter, Samson's inward turn must rather be seen, as I suggest, as the conversion of the Old Testament into a New Testament man who can, however, act. His previous exploits, in this sense, are presumptuous, as Samson himself acknowledges: He behaved like a "petty God" until, "swoll'n with pride," he falls into the "snare . . . / Of fair fallacious looks" (532–33). But Samson is humbled and renewed by his defeat.

[16]The chorus's other argument is that Samson is already serving the Philistines with his work, and consequently with the selfsame "consecrated strength" that he refuses to "prostitute to Idols." Samson replies by making a difference between his "labor / Honest and lawful to deserve [his] food / Of those who have [him] in their civil power" (1365–67), and the spectacle he is asked to give. The logic seems to be that his work relates to the Philistines' "civil power," and not their religion, for he is earning his food and thus paying the debt he would otherwise hold toward his own captors. To participate "freely" (for free) in their religious rites, instead, would mean giving up the (economic) freedom his labor grants him.

> *Chorus* Where the heart joins not, outward acts defile not.
> *Samson* Where outward force constrains, the sentence holds;
>   But who constrains me to the Temple of *Dagon*,
>   Not dragging? the *Philistian* Lords command.
>   Commands are not constraints. If I obey them,
>   I do it freely; venturing to displease
>   God for the fear of Man . . .
>
>   Yet that he may dispense with me or thee
>   Present in Temples at Idolatrous Rites
>   For some important cause, thou needst not doubt.
>   (1368–79)

Adhering to the distinction between outer acts and inner consent that allowed Locke to symbolically save his purse, Samson argues that only the physical overpowering of his body—as with the robber's pistol—can effectively "save" his inner freedom. Unwillingness is not sufficient to preserve authority over one's actions and exempt oneself from their defiling "outward" character. But as he argues with the chorus, Samson's purpose surges unawares in his own words, which once again give him away, this time to himself: "If I obey them, / I do it freely." Thus Samson has still the free choice to will to go, but his acts need not correspond to what his enemies think he is doing, precisely because "commands are not constraints." He can change the content of the command, while pretending he is following "their" content. He can exchange, finally, the author of the command, the source of knowledge and the foreknowledge that will eventually rule the outcome of the show. In this manner "the heart joins" and the "outward acts defile not," and, rather than "willing to be wrong" and submitting to the present and to the Philistines' "plot"—recall the theater of the last scene—Samson elaborates a subplot that submits the Philistines' command to his own.

Samson thus generates the impulse to act from within himself: "I begin to feel / *Some rousing motions in me* which dispose / To something extraordinary my thoughts" (1381–83; my emphasis). His internal source of action, however, is enabled on the one hand by the circumstances, which he aptly seizes, and on the other by the postulate of an "important cause" that could become the end of his actions and thus enable him to originate them in himself. In other words, he cannot generate his own purpose entirely—he needs to align it to God's. What we have, then, is Samson's authorship at the service of God's purpose. Samson's authorship thus "produces" his actions only to the extent that their purpose is projected onto a third person, God, who becomes the depository of the "will have been" of Samson's actions. This third person has the peculiarity of being at the same time outside, elsewhere, and "later" in time, and inside Samson himself. Indeed, the fact that Samson postulates a knowledge of God's intentions implies God's knowledge of his. It is thus that, like Locke's performative subject, Samson ratifies his internal knowledge—his insight—by collapsing it with God's knowledge, which is the observer's knowledge par excellence. The third-person position that Samson internalizes can thus fulfill the function of necessity because it is a position external to himself. Being interiorized, however, the "necessity" this position can impose becomes Samson's own production. Samson thus becomes the "harness of necessity" of his actions, which have their origin in him and find their end in God.

Dalila's words to Samson, however, haunt the end of the poem: "Fame if not double-faced is double-mouth'd / And with contrary blasts proclaims most deeds" (971–72). With this image Dalila had explained to Samson that, if she was considered a traitor by the Hebrews, she was a heroine for the Philistines. Nothing in her actions proclaimed her as one or the other; only the different accounts of them did. Similarly, Samson's final performance is subject to the "blasts" of fame, which return him to the public sphere from which he had withdrawn with "inward eye": "*Samson* hath quit himself / Like *Samson*, and heroicly hath finish'd / A life Heroic" (1709–11). With these words Manoa transforms Samson into a Greek hero again, a gesture that points out that Samson's newly acquired authorship is not recognizable in his acts, and suggests that Samson's inward and invisible

change has been erased by the selfsame deeds it "originated."[17]
God, of course, would still "know" about Samson's authorship,
but God does not speak out in Milton's poem. He has already
been interiorized.

Prometheus Unbound: undoing the bonds of the will

Shelley's counterpart to Aeschylus' *Prometheus Bound* seizes on the
announced compromise between Prometheus and Zeus and sets out
to dissociate the destinies of the two gods. The gift of fire, with its
related enabling of action through forethought, has been neutralized
by Jupiter's power over Prometheus and is reflected in mankind's
oppression under various tyrants. Prometheus' deliverance from
Jupiter will consequently reflect mankind's deliverance from tyranny. The two gods thus become "the Champion and the Oppressor
of mankind," related in opposition rather than in apposition, as we
saw they were in Aeschylus' play.[18] Shelley's polarization of the two
gods, however, is not just a "misreading" but constitutes an attempt
to disrupt the oppositional structure upholding the performative
subject, which is assimilated in his play to the structure of political
oppression. Indeed, in *Prometheus Unbound* the internalized other
who ultimately enabled Samson's authorship to generate actions is
presented as the "harness" impeding the flow of events, and, more
specifically, of time—it is the knot tying the will to a permanent
"would not." This internalized other thus becomes the internalized
oppressor, and the subject appears to be disabled by himself. This
connection between subjective and political imprisonment is not in-

[17]Manoa's words also leave the question of Samson's suicide open: that he
has quit himself as Samson suggests that he owes nothing for his death, or life,
not even to God. At the same time, the gesture returning Samson to his former
Greek self may be an attempt to avoid judging him as a New Testament man.

[18]Shelley states his objection to Aeschylus' reconciliation of the gods in the
Preface to the 1820 edition of *Prometheus Unbound*: "I was averse from a catastro-
phe so feeble as that of reconciling the Champion with the Oppressor of mankind" (p. 63).

consistent with Locke's account of the origin of civil society, according to which, recall, man gives up the management of his outward actions in exchange for authorship. But for Shelley this initial social compact, whereby man bows "before tyrants to whom he [has] himself given power," is very clearly a perversion.[19] *Prometheus Unbound* stages the conditions of man's voluntary self-oppression in an effort to elucidate this perversion.

The lyrical drama opens with the statement of the opposition between the two gods, and immediately establishes the conditions of its undoing. Prometheus' first words are addressed to Jupiter: "Monarch of Gods and Daemons, and all Spirits / But One" (I. 1–2); it is a clear statement of his fundamental imperviousness to his enemy's tyranny.[20] But if he would be exempted from Jupiter's rule, Prometheus does not seem to be exempted from his own, for which subjection, moreover, he accuses Jupiter:

> Whilst me, who am thy foe, eyeless in hate,
> Hast thou made reign and triumph, to thy scorn,
> O'er mine own misery and thy vain revenge.
>
>   (I. 9–11)

"Eyeless in hate," Prometheus is yet blind—Samsonlike—to his participation in Jupiter's rule, as he "reigns" over the latter's revenge, allowing the "thou" to command, and take the place of, the "I." Again like Samson, he recovers his insight as he hears himself slide into a moment of identification with the tyrant, which points out to him their mutual exchangeability:

> And yet to me welcome is day and night,
> Whether one breaks the hoar-frost of the morn,
> Or starry, dim, and slow, the other climbs
> The leaden-coloured east; for then they lead
> Their wingless, crawling Hours, one among whom—
> As some dark priest hales the reluctant victim—

[19]These are P. H. Butter's words in the notes to *Prometheus Unbound* (p. 258). Butter points out that this instance of man's perversion was a recurrent theme for Shelley.

[20]The exempted One seems in this context to be Prometheus, though it could also be the appointed Hour of his deliverance.

> Shall drag thee, cruel King, to kiss the blood
> From these pale feet, which then might trample thee
> If they disdained not such a prostrate slave.
> Disdain? Ah no! I pity thee. What Ruin
> Will hunt thee undefended through wide Heaven!
> How will thy soul, cloven to its depth with terror,
> Gape like a hell within!! I speak in grief,
> Not exultation, for I hate no more,
> As then, ere misery made me wise. The curse
> Once breathed on thee I would recall.
>
> (I. 44–59)

As day and night alternate, so will Prometheus' and Jupiter's situation be reversed, Jupiter then a prostrate slave. The formulation of this reversal renders Prometheus aware of the symmetry ruling his opposition to Jupiter; hence his pity, his regret, and his wish to take back the words "breathed" as a spell on his now former enemy.[21]

The successful recalling of the curse, in the form of Jupiter's phantasm uttering it back to him, will turn out to be the necessary condition for Prometheus' self-unbinding. We understand why when we realize that the curse is articulated like a contract establishing the terms of his captivity, and that Prometheus has bound himself with his own words. Here is the curse, as "returned" by Jupiter's phantasm:

> Fiend, *I defy thee!* with a calm, fixed mind,
> *All that thou canst inflict I bid thee do.*
> Foul tyrant both of Gods and Humankind,
> One only being shalt thou not subdue.
> (. . .)
> Ay, do thy worst. Thou art omnipotent.
> *O'er all things but myself I gave thee power,*
> *And my own will.* Be thy swift mischiefs sent
> To blast mankind, from yon aetherial tower.
> Let thy malignant spirit move
> Its darkness over those I love:

---

[21]Hence also the reversal from "exultation" to "grief," which is so symmetrical that it needs to be explicitly announced lest we mistake one for the other. The implication seems to be that "grief" and "exultation" differ only in tone.

> *On me and mine imprecate*
> *The utmost torture of thy hate,*
>   And thus devote to sleepless agony
> This undeclining head while thou must reign on high.
>
> But thou, who art the God and Lord—O thou
>   Who fillest with thy soul this world of woe,
> To whom all things of Earth and Heaven do bow
>   In fear and worship—all-prevailing foe!
> *I curse thee! Let a sufferer's curse*
> *Clasp thee, his torturer, like remorse,*
> Till thine Infinity shall be
> A robe of envenomed agony;
> And thine Omnipotence a crown of pain
> To cling like burning gold round thy dissolving brain.
>   (I. 262–291; my italics)

Prometheus, then, first defies Jupiter to inflict pain on him and then curses him with a "sufferer's curse." In this context his defiance constitutes a double move that reappropriates Jupiter's power and sets the conditions of the curse in Prometheus' own suffering. The underlying logic is that because Prometheus suffers, Jupiter can be cursed, so that the curse binds Prometheus to his suffering as it binds Jupiter to be cursed because he makes Prometheus suffer.

Jupiter's effective power to torture Prometheus is thus presented as an effect of Prometheus' defiance: "All that thou canst inflict I bid thee do." In other words, Prometheus' sufferings seem to be caused by his own will, through the agency of Jupiter. The assimilation of Prometheus' will to Jupiter's "body" is reinforced as Prometheus excepts from Jupiter's omnipotence Jupiter himself: "O'er all things but thyself I gave thee power, / And my own will." "Thyself" and "my own will" are identified insofar as they share the same status of exception and are mutually inclusive as exceptions. In order for Jupiter's self to be excluded from his omnipotence, it must be included in the will that excludes it, and, inversely, Prometheus' will is exempted because Jupiter's self provides the "space" for its exclusion. In other words, as he sets the conditions for the utterance of the curse in his own suffering, Prometheus collapses the opposition between Jupiter and himself into identification. As Jupiter's ghostly body is possessed by the will of Prometheus' lost words—"A spirit seizes me and speaks within" (I. 254)—the crossed assimilation between the two gods is redressed, and Prometheus frees himself from the bonds of opposition. Now Prometheus' "other word," the prophecy of Jupiter's fall, can materialize, and the appointed Hour arrive.

Prometheus' self-cursing curse establishes the participation of the performative subject in his incapacity to act. Here the act of will, the speech act, becomes the act of authorship itself, not only replacing but also impeding the unfolding of action in time. In this sense Shelley's choice of the "curse" to characterize the performative subject is very appropriate, as curses are by definition not performable by the speaker. Unlike promises, of which they are the reverse, and which keep to the form "I will," curses are of the form "you will," or "it will." In the "you will / it will" the *passage à l'acte* is missed out, and the curser is bound to the moment of the utterance of the curse, suspending the time of the event indefinitely. This suspension and containment of action in the past in the anterior future would be the peculiar perverseness from which "man" suffers, subjecting himself to the selfsame forces he authorizes. Shelley's deliverance of Prometheus from his curse should thus mark the possibility of a transformed subject, capable of exteriorizing into action "again," of comprehending himself within the exteriorization of action.[22] The fact that Prometheus is literally unbound with the arrival of the Hour supports this point: The curse undone, the intervention of "Fate, Time, Occasion, Chance, and Change" is allowed for again, time flows, events occur, and the deployment of action is now, in principle, enabled.

But Shelley has Demogorgon specify that to these five temporal characters "all things are subject but eternal Love" (II. 119–20). And "eternal Love" is the motif upon which the "new," nonoppo-

[22]Compare to Nietzsche's "superman," the man who has been delivered from revenge—that is, from "the will's revulsion against time and its 'It was'" (*Thus Spoke Zarathustra*, Part II, "On Deliverance," quoted in Martin Heidegger, *What Is Called Thinking*, p. 93).

sitional relations between men are based in *Prometheus Unbound*. "Love" is the principle of the relations between Asia, Ione, Panthea, and Prometheus, who will live united in a cave,

> A simple dwelling, which shall be our own,
> Where we will sit and talk of time and change,
> As the world ebbs and flows, ourselves unchanged—
> What can hide man from mutability?
>
> (III. 22–25)

This latter question seems to find an answer in the "idle" chat about "time and change," which eventually collapses the distance between subjects. In accordance with the inevitable intersubjectivity of language, which Shelley's lyrical drama exploits thoroughly, subjects are here presented as primarily hearers and speakers whose interiorities mingle with words to the point of constituting a single, unified subject for whom the question of action simply does not arise.[23] Hence Prometheus and his Oceanides will "search, with looks and words of love, / [Their] unexhausted spirits" (III. 34–36), and man, "free from guilt and pain / Which were, for his will made, or suffered them," will rule "chance, and death, and mutability," "like slaves" (III. 198–201). In other words, man will renounce his manmade technologies of time, which enabled the creation of other times (and of more time), and cosmic time will return to its pre-Olympian status, contained by the Gaia and Uranus figures of the Earth and the Moon, who unite in turn in love in Act IV (see lines 356–69). Here "Love" is a motif of timelessness because, if language is the most intersubjective human medium, love is traditionally the most intersubjective of relationships, the figure for the intermingling of subjects at which Prometheus excels with his Oceanides.[24] "Love"

---

[23] It is worth noting the movement from sight to hearing, which also takes place in *Hamlet* and in *Samson Agonistes*—recall that Hamlet would have told his tale before dying, had he had the time, and that Samson's decisive insight was into his own words. There seems to be a "linguistic turn" in reflections on actions, which, as we will see in chapters 5 and 6, is effected by Bakhtin, Beckett, and Wittgenstein.

[24] I say "his" because they seem to be an extension of himself. Shelley's use of female figures for Prometheus' intersubjective experiences is, to say the least, questionable.

would thus be the relation that short-circuits in the present the passing of time, folding together the two poles of the relationship—a "consummation devoutly to be wished" which, however, does not leave any interval for action to unfold. And there is, indeed, not even much place for the body in the "chainéd link of thought" which, "man, oh!, not men" would constitute in his new undivided state of "love and might" (IV. 394–95). In *Prometheus Unbound* performance is still retained in the "might" of performativity.

What emerges from the above account of the adventures of the performative subject is a fundamental discontinuity between himself and his actions: Whenever he ventures to act, he dies as a subject, like Samson, and, if he survives as a subject, it is because, like Prometheus, he does not act. Milton's Samson, recall, "enters" the field of action again (remember that he was heroized "before" his disgrace) once he internalizes the external position of God, which thus functions as the other "end" of his actions enabling Samson to seize the time and "produce" action while aligning his behavior to God's purpose. This move constitutes an acknowledgment of the interactive nature of action and is the enabling condition for Samson to act again. Once he engages in "performance," however, Samson the subject literally disappears from the scene: Not only does his own deed kill him but, in addition, he does not seem to be there as it is performed. Indeed we are told that he has won the contest, a victory that in all appearance returns Samson to his "former" self (Greek hero), before blindness revealed to him his interiority. What we have, then, is Samson as a performative subject, alone and unable to act (to guide his actions), or Samson in performance, "agonistes," heroized, triumphing but without interiority—not, in brief, a subject. We are left with a situation in which no continuity is thinkable between subject and action: Either one acts or one is a subject.

Milton overcomes this discontinuity, without resolving it, through a change of perspective: Samson does not see himself acting (he is blind!), but others see him act. The introduction of the perspective of the others "saves" the narrative but does not do away with the problem: The fact that such a change of perspective

is necessary actually emphasizes, or expresses, the lack of continuity between, in a sense, the subject of action and the subject in
action. Shelley's Prometheus resolves this predicament by positing not so much different positions from which to construct a continuity between subject and action, but rather a temporal discontinuity that makes possible such a construction. Recall that Time
rescues Prometheus once he realizes that he must not turn his will
against the past, that he must not, in short, resist the passing of
time and consequently *what happens*. Once his will becomes at-
tuned to the present, time can "flow" again, and with it change
takes place. But here time functions as the agent: It is the arrival of
the moment that brings significant change with it, mainly Prometheus' liberation—a liberation that does not lead into action, as in
the case of Samson. Prometheus is freed into a purely intersubjective world, abstracted from actions. He contemplates, and comments on, men's doings from above, caught again, or sheltered, in
a temporal discontinuity between his subjectivity (the fact of his
being a subject) and actions: The subject Prometheus exists in eternity, from which he contemplates action, occurring more properly
speaking in time, in mortal time. The discontinuity first "solved" is
thus recreated, as Samson's spatial discontinuity (unseen by himself, seen by others) was at his death.

5 ⌒ Ought and Act

Ought to act

How to act? How can the *passage à l'acte* take place? How is it possible? These questions are bound to rise once the subject is posited as the source of action, and expected to generate himself its impelling principle. The performative subject, we saw, attempted to interiorize the "harness of necessity" of his actions. But the will became itself subject to the necessity it had to generate, and the subject found himself reduced to performativity. Unable to accord the categories of necessity and of the will, the performative subject failed, as a conceit, to ground the springs of action in himself. In his *Fundamental Principles of the Metaphysics of Morals*, Kant develops another model of subject and action that could be read as a response to the performative subject's predicament.[1] Very schematically, Kant's treatise presupposes that all free actions are com-

[1]See in particular the third section, "Transition from the Metaphysics of Morals to the Critique of Pure Practical Reason."

It should be noted that Kant's treatise on ethics follows in many ways Aristotle's *Nicomachean Ethics*, although it displaces significantly its basic postulates. Thus, instead of inquiring into the chiefest good toward which all actions tend, Kant inquires into the nature of the supremely good will from which they all stem, and upon which even the desire of happiness depends. He does this, however, with Aristotelian categories: The good cannot be a means to an end but deserves to "be highly esteemed for itself, and is good without a view to anything further" (p. 21). It is not enough for a man to do a good action for him to be good: He should do it out of duty, and not for pleasure; and so on.

manded by the will and that the will itself is free—which implies, in his argument, that it is also free from any object of volition, that it simply *wills*. Thus the will is the principle of morality, of that which "ought to happen," as opposed to that which does happen. A good action is that which follows the ordinances of a good will, and a good will, because it is also free and cannot be subject to any law, is a will that follows the principle of "universal conformity of its actions to law in general," as expressed by the maxim "I am never to act otherwise than *so that I could also will that my maxim should become a universal law*" (p. 27). This is the well-known categorical imperative, otherwise formulated as "*Act on maxims which can at the same time have for their object themselves as universal laws of nature*" (p. 66).

The question of how to act thus becomes, in Kant's terms, that of *how is a categorical imperative possible?* (p. 85). The problem is the following: The categorical imperative would determine our actions completely were we exclusively rational beings. In this case, the will would function as the efficient cause of our actions; it would be their principle of necessity. But, because we are also "affected . . . by springs of a different kind, namely, sensibility" (p. 81), and do not always do what reason dictates, the necessity of the will is expressed only as an "ought," so that the subjective principles of action—which should, according to the categorical imperative, hold as universal principles—are different from its objective principles. In other words, Kant's question is, How does the will determine our actions, once it is established that it does not, practically speaking, function as the "efficient cause" it should be by virtue of its freedom and autonomy?

According to Kant, this is possible because man partakes of two distinct worlds: "In respect to mere sensations and receptivity of sensations" he belongs to the *world of sense* and is subject to the laws of nature; but as a rational being he belongs to the *intelligible world* or *world of understanding* and is ruled by laws that "have their foundation in reason alone" (pp. 84–85). If he belonged to only one of these two worlds, his actions would conform, respectively, to "the natural law of desires and inclinations" or to "the principle of autonomy of

the pure will" (p. 86). This is not the case, but the world of understanding is more determinant for man as a rational being than the
world of sense is, because reason presupposes man's freedom and
"independence on *determining* the causes of the world of sense" (p.
87).[2] Accordingly, to the extent that he can *transfer* himself (and this
is Kant's term) to the world of understanding, man must consider
himself as free, and subject himself to the autonomy of the will, regarding "the laws of the world of understanding as imperatives" (p.
86). In the world of the senses, then, man subjects himself to the obligation to conform to the categorical imperative, to which he would
necessarily conform were he only a member of the world of understanding. The moral "ought" is thus man's recognition of the will as
a principle of necessity, and this acknowledgment is in turn a form
of implementation of this necessity: "What he morally 'ought' is then
what he necessarily 'would' as a member of the world of understanding" (pp. 87–88).

Through the postulate of the two worlds, Kant avoids, at least
theoretically, the pitfalls of the performative subject, for then man
can be free by virtue of his will, and be subject to it at the same time
without losing his freedom. He is, moreover, free as an intelligence,
and hence as a *being in himself*, and subject as a *phenomenon*, which is
a *thing in appearance* (p. 94). Aware of his existence as a being in himself, man-in-appearance bows to the dictates of his free will, which,
although it has no compelling force in the realm of the senses, is
binding to the extent that man considers himself as free. The question, however, remains of how the "ought" is effectively operative,
or imperative: How does it mediate between the efficient cause that
is the will, and actions, which are to be its effect? For this requires, as
Kant himself points out, that the subject "take interest" in the categorical imperative, which is not, we saw, an efficient cause in the
world of sense. But "nothing *urges* me to do this," Kant "allows,"
"for that would not give a categorical imperative" (p. 81).[3] Conse-

[2]More precisely, "*the world of understanding contains the foundation of the world
of sense, and consequently of its laws also*" (p. 86).

[3]In Kant's terminology "interest" is "that by which reason becomes practical,

quently another "spring of action" is required for the subject to *want*, basically, to submit, in the world of sense, to the will the existence of which he acknowledges in the intelligible world. What is missing, in short, is the mediation between the two worlds, something enabling the transition, in Kant's terms, from pure to practical reason. This transition, however, is "beyond the power of human reason": We cannot explain how the mere principle of the categorical imperative "can of itself supply a spring, without any matter (object) of the will in which one could antecedently take any interest" (p. 95).

What we have, then, is that man's will and his actions are, as it were, split in two worlds again: St. Paul's inward man comes to mind, whose will followed the laws of God but who could not do what he *would*. Kant's subject, to be sure, is not inward: He is transcendental, his will is free because he can transfer himself to the intelligible world, abstract himself from the world of sense, and thus command, from this perspective, his actions-to-be in the realm of appearance. But he can still not do what he *would*, for he lacks the compelling "ought" that would enable him to cross the distance from command to act. This distance is at the heart of what M. M. Bakhtin calls, in *Toward a Philosophy of the Act*, "the contemporary crisis," which, he argues, is "fundamentally, a crisis of *contemporary action*" (p. 54; my emphasis)—of action in the process. Under the influence of Kantian ethics and, in general, of binary models of action, "an abyss has formed between the motive of the actually performed act or deed and its product" (p. 54); there is "a fundamental split between the content or sense of a given act/activity and the historical actuality of its being" (p. 2). There is, in short, a prevailing difficulty to conceptualizing "the actually performed act," as a result of which what should be a single step into action becomes, once again, an inhuman or superhuman leap.[4]

i.e. a cause determining the will. . . . Reason takes a direct interest in action then only when the universal validity of its maxims is alone sufficient to determine the will. Such an interest alone is pure" (p. 93, note 8).

[4]In the preface to his translation of *Toward a Philosophy of the Act*, Vadim Liapunov explains that Bakhtin's term for "act" is not *akt*, which would be the Russian equivalent of the Latin *actus* and *actum*. Bakhtin's term is *postupok*, which

Against the division of the act that skips performance, Bakhtin foregrounds the unity of what he calls "the answerable act or deed," which resides, above all, in the irrevocability of its performance, in the fact that once it is performed it is performed once and for all:

The performed act concentrates, correlates, and resolves within a unitary and unique, this time, *final context* both the sense and the fact, the universal and the individual, the real and the ideal, for everything enters into the composition of its answerable motivation. The performed act constitutes a going out *once and for all* from within possibility as such to *what is once-occurrent.* (p. 29)

What is once-occurrent has the character of necessity by virtue of its irrevocability, which makes the act "answerable" insofar as it necessarily involves the individual agent in its irrevocable process. The notion of "answerable" act thus introduces the individual, not at the origin of action but in the process of action. Only the individual can answer for his actions and reply to a response to his actions; it is only as an individual that he must do this, because his actions are his mode of being in the world. The ought, Bakhtin concludes, is "a category of the individual act" (p. 25).[5]

---

means, etymologically, "a step taken" or "the taking of a step" (p. xix). Bakhtin's choice of words is significant in the light of my argument and seems to be motivated by the same observations as mine: that there has been a (theoretical) separation of the realm of actions (what Bakhtin calls the "world of life") and that of the subject (what Bakhtin calls the "world of culture"), the theoretical nature of which is "forgotten," or treated as a given. Hence acting requires a "crossing" uniting the two realms (we will return to Bakhtin's two worlds), a crossing that is evoked in the image of action as "the taking of a step."

The term *postupok*, which Liapunov translates as an "individually answerable deed or performance" (usually "mine") could also be translated as "procedure," or proceeding—the French *démarche* is even more evocative of the implication of a specific manner *of* doing in Bakhtin's answerable deed. In the next chapter we will see how this is relevant to Wittgenstein's treatment of action.

[5]Here is the full quotation: "The ought is precisely a category of the individual act; and even more than that—it is a category of the individuality, of the uniqueness of a performed act, of its once-occurrent compellentness, of its historicity, of the impossibility to replace it with anything else or to provide a substitute for it."

In other words, Bakhtin's argument is that the imperativeness of the ought is conditional, and that it is only by being conditional that the ought is imperative. In this sense his position is radically different from that of Kant, for whom, we saw, the ought must have universal validity—one must act according to a maxim that can be willed to become a universal law. But then, Bakhtin objects, "the will itself prescribes the law to itself":[6]

The will-as-deed produces the law to which it submits, i.e. it dies as an individual will in its own product. The will describes a circle, shuts itself in, excluding the actual—individual and historical—self-activity of the performed act. (p. 26)[7]

For Bakhtin, instead, "the will is really, creatively active, in the performed act." The ought does not, therefore, have the structure of a command issuing from a third (or abstracted) person. It is grounded in the individuality and actuality of the "I," and more specifically in the acknowledgment that "that which can be done by me can never be done by anyone else"; that "I, too, *exist*": "Here lies the point of origin of the answerable deed and of all the categories of the concrete, once-occurrent, and compellent ought" (p. 40). The ought, then, is the individual's response to and experiencing of the singularity and irrevocability of his present existence (which is, itself, necessarily an actually performed deed). It is, moreover, because one's existence is irreducibly singular, and not simply "an" existence, that it is compellent.[8] The "I" cannot be replaced, cannot abstract itself

---

[6]Bakhtin also objects to the notion of a prescribing law, for the law, he argues, can be justified only theoretically—that is, in terms of a specific theoretical discourse (sociology, aesthetics, and so on) that ignores the existence of the individual act or deed. Thus to Kant's demand that the law "which applies a norm to my act or deed, must be justified as capable of becoming a norm of universal conduct," Bakhtin responds: "But the question is—how will this justification be effected? Evidently, by way of purely theoretical determinations. . . . The actual deed is cast out into the theoretical world with an empty demand for legality" (p. 26).

[7]This was the "perversion" Shelley strove to undo.

[8]By contrast, an argument of the form "I ought because I exist" could obviously succumb to skeptical doubt, as one's existence cannot be "proved." Hence Bakhtin's insistence on the irreplaceability of the "I," which holds re-

from itself; it is irrevocably here to itself. Hence Bakhtin's refrain that "there is no alibi in Being": I cannot argue that *I* am not *here*, maintain that I am elsewhere right now, or that I am later on, or that I am not *here and now*. Being will not "save" me from circumstance; the ontological is no refuge from the ontic. Thus it is "this fact of *my non-alibi in Being*," Bakhtin continues, that "underlies the concrete and once-occurrent ought of the answerably performed act" (p. 40).

As Bakhtin realizes, however, the first-person position is liable to be overpowered by "fatal theoreticism (the abstracting from my unique self)" (p. 27), because the third-person position is not only an available construct but also a pervasive "technical device" (p. 49).[9] Hence he recognizes that "I can try to prove my alibi in Being, I can pretend to be someone I am not. I can abdicate from my *obligative (ought-to-be) uniqueness*" (p. 42). Such an abdication implies living in a world where everything is indifferent, and there is no principle for choice. It is a world of "contingent possibility" as opposed to that of "inescapable actuality" (p. 44). In the latter world, acting is the mode of being, and compellent as such; in the former, instead, action is only possible, and consequently impossible—for it is not easy, as we saw in previous chapters, for the subject to leave the world of mere possibility and take the step into that of

---

gardless of whether I "really" exist—of whether, for example, I am dreamt by someone else.

[9] As a device, it is central to all theoretical discourses. But it is also central to a certain type of politics. Bakhtin does not develop the relationship between this available technique and politics, but he does suggest that "abstracting from myself" is a move liable to undermine forms of political organization based on representation: "I *can* perform a political act or a religious ritual in the capacity of a representative, but . . . being a representative does not abolish but merely specializes my personal answerability. The actual acknowledgment-affirmation of the whole that I shall represent is my personally answerable act. Insofar as that act is left out and I remain only the bearer of special answerability, I become possessed, and my deed, severed from the ontological roots of personal participation, becomes fortuitous in relation to that ultimate once-occurrent unity in which it is not rooted, just as the domain that specializes my deed is not rooted for me. *Such a severing from the once-occurrent context and the loss of once-occurrent participation in the course of specialization are especially frequent in the case of political answerability*" (pp. 52–53; emphasis mine).

actuality. Bakhtin formulates this difficulty as the breaking away of theory—which world Bakhtin assimilates to the aesthetic world—from the actually performed act, which sets theory "free" to develop "according to its own immanent law" while "the performed act itself, having released theory from itself, begins to deteriorate" (p. 55).[10] While theory continues to obey its own immanent laws, the performed act will continue to deteriorate, and the first-person position on which answerable acts depend will be overpowered by the third-person, theoretical, and aesthetic position.

It is thus that Bakhtin sets out to anchor theory and aesthetics in the act again, which implies anchoring the third-person position in respect to (in relation to) the first-person position. Bakhtin calls this project "an examination of the fundamental moments [which are: I, the other, I-for-the-other] in the architectonic of the actual world of the performed act or deed." On the basis of this architectonic he announces the discussion of aesthetic activity as an actually performed act. Only after this examination does he plan to tackle a discussion of ethics and politics (p. 54). The order of his announced project suggests that before engaging ethical activity, the relationship between the first- and third-person positions that had been conflated in the aesthetic and ethical models of the Kantian tradition must be reformulated, which reformulation necessitates a "revision" of aesthetics aiming at the restitution of the aesthetic world into the world of actually performed deeds. Bakhtin undertakes this task in *Author and Hero in Aesthetic Activity*, a text to which we will turn after considering how Nietzsche contests Kant's construction of the transcendental subject and his separation of the two worlds in *The Birth of Tragedy*. That such a discussion should be framed by an account of the origins of tragedy should not be surprising, for Kant's commanding subject can be considered as an instance of the figure of the spectator, as opposed to that of the actor. This figure, as we will see, can in turn be traced to Aristotle's self-sufficient philosopher.

---

[10]One of Bakhtin's general points is, in fact, that theoretical reasoning is but a moment of practical reasoning: that for all its abstraction it is still an act, and can ground itself only in the act.

Nietzsche's philosophy of appearance

In his *Thinker on Stage: Nietzsche's Materialism*, Peter Sloterdjik argues that *The Birth of Tragedy* does away "in one stroke" with "the autonomy of the classical subject" (p. 14). According to Sloterdjik, the subject is reduced in Nietzsche's text "to an effect of antagonistic forces and the conflicting 'artistic instincts' of nature"; it "would represent merely the irreal seam" at which the antagonistic forces meet; and "subjectivity appears as the epiphenomenon within the interplay between the great subjectless cosmic forces" (p. 16). So understood, the subject is indeed done away with, but so is action: The drama of which the subject is the interplay is played out by "an unintentional natural process."

Sloterdjik's account in fact reverses the underlying narrative of Nietzsche's text. The epiphenomenal subject appears in the latter on the stage of Attic tragedy, presented by Nietzsche as an instance of participative contemplation, the possibility of which was questioned, recall, in Aristotle's *Nicomachean Ethics*. Here the activity of contemplation threatened to isolate the philosopher from the polis. In Nietzsche's text, isolation becomes the process of individuation, protagonized by Apollo, who functions in the narrative as the force of appearance, illusion, and, ultimately, of phenomena. Antagonizing this Apollonian tendency of individuation is a radical form of participation in the whole, which could in fact be called a "natural process": the Dionysian tendency of unification, or "oneness." The conflict between these two tendencies is performed in Attic tragedy, on the individuals/spectators, who thus become—indirectly, as we will see—the "actors" of the tragedy. The tragedy concludes as the Dionysian tendency of unification or oneness acquires appearance through, or in, the Apollonian tendency of individuation. It is then that phenomena incarnate oneness. Eventually, however, this movement from individuation to oneness that is the subject of Attic tragedy is disrupted, at which moment teleologically organized action takes over the stage and a new kind of spectator contemplates the scene from a distance. Nietzsche then sets the conditions for a participative subject to emerge again in the recognition and acknowledgment of the passing of time, of the ephemeral nature of appearance.[11]

Nietzsche structures his version of the conflict between individuation and oneness according to the myth of the dismemberment and re-memberment of the god Dionysus. What Nietzsche calls the Dionysian and Apollonian tendencies of Hellenic art are in fact two facets of this mythical movement of dismemberment and re-memberment of the god. The god's dismemberment and suffering correspond to the cultural process of individuation, which is consequently to be considered as "the origin and primal cause of all suffering, as something objectionable in itself" (§10, p. 73).[12] But the god's situation before dismemberment is one of individuated oneness. Thus oneness does not "precede" individuation; it is, rather, something that is done to or happens to and through individuation. This is the determinant point of Nietzsche's philosophy of appearance as developed in *The Birth of Tragedy*—that, in Heidegger's terms, the ontological is manifest in the ontic (Being is set forth only in being); that there is no such thing as abstract oneness (Being); that, as things appear *as*, they *appear* (basically, the tautology that things appear as they appear!).[13]

But what should happen to individuation in order to be re-

[11]It will become apparent that Nietzsche follows Milton's and Shelley's steps here in his confrontation of "Greek" man—not a hero, here, but the stage of the meeting of the gods—and modern man, through his analysis of the spectator in tragedy.

[12]The Apollonian principle of individuation is cultural in that it is the construct of the human that mediates between an unbounded nature and man, without which man would rejoin the ranks of nature, but without which, as well, nature is not accessible (see §1, p. 36, for a definition of the Apollonian through Schopenhauer's image of the sailor in the frail bark). The principle of individuation is thus primarily a principle of illusion, in that it founds a distinction that is not recognized by nature. It is not, in this sense, to be reduced to self-deception. Through the "gestures and eyes" of this *principium individuationis*, "all the joy and wisdom of 'illusion,' together with its beauty, speak to us" (§1, p. 36).

[13]This is, I think, what Sloterdjik means by the expression "Nietzsche's materialism," and is certainly in accordance with his observation that it is the Apollonian principle that governs the antagonism between the Apollonian and the Dionysian (see *Thinker on Stage*, p. 25).

vealed as appearance *of*, and consequently, as appearing? According to the myth, the re-memberment of the Dionysian oneness can be achieved only from the state of dismemberment, which is the state of individuations of the oneness. These should be annihilated—disappear as multiple individuations—in order to be remembered into the Dionysian oneness. The annihilation of the individual is of course not total, but rather, entitary—the individual disappears into the appearance of the god. The god, in turn, insofar as it appears, appears to the individuals it subsumes, and appears as an individual. Attic tragedy, at least at its original stages, is for Nietzsche a staging of the spectator's access to this state of de-individuated "vision" of oneness.

There are thus no "actors" in the original tragedy, and no "action" in the traditional sense of the term—the dramatic event is the advent of the spectators' vision. Accordingly there are only spectators; even the chorus, the only "actor" on stage, is to be considered a spectator, albeit of a different kind: "The chorus is the 'ideal spectator' insofar as it is the only beholder, the beholder of the visionary world of the scene" (§8, pp. 62–63).[14] The central tragic "action" is here the act of seeing, the spectator's vision of the drama. First of all, the chorus is the productive beholder of the "visionary world of the scene," a world that envisions its own visibility—the chorus sees the scene from the scene and thereby sees the spectacularity of itself and itself as appearance. The chorus is also on the scene, drawing the public's sight, so that the chorus becomes "a vision of the Dionysian mass of spectators, just as the world of the stage, in turn, is a vision of this satyr chorus." It is a vision of the spectators in that it is what they see, produced in its visibility by the fact of being envisioned; it is also a vision of the

---

[14]Nietzsche takes up the notion of the chorus as the "ideal spectator" from Scheler, but he shows that it does not make sense unless the issue of what the chorus is spectating—given that it is alone on the stage—is discussed. The suggestion is that the notion of the spectator must be reviewed in the light of the original form of Attic tragedy, and not in terms of its later development, which included actors distinct from the chorus and that the chorus could, indeed, contemplate.

spectators in that their vision of the chorus corresponds to the chorus's vision of them. The chorus here acts as the scene that stages
the spectators' spectacularity and from which they can see themselves as vision. This play of vision becomes itself the scene of a
common vision, the god, or vision of the oneness of visions.

As the spectators see themselves as a vision, their individuality
is revealed as impersonation, the "*dramatic* proto-phenomenon: to
see oneself transformed before one's own eyes and to begin to act
as if one had actually entered into another body, another character" (§8, p. 64). The spectators, in other words, see themselves as
others see them: They look at themselves with "public" eyes, they
are "transformed" in that they find themselves at the seam between their individuality (they can still see) and the participation
of their appearance in the public scene. From this new configuration of themselves, the spectators see themselves configured, in the
vision of the god, which is the individuated vision of the oneness
in individuation:

> The Dionysian reveller sees himself as a satyr, *and, as a satyr, in turn, he
> sees the god*, which means that . . . he beholds another vision outside of
> himself, as the Apollonian complement of his own state. With this new
> vision the drama is complete. (§8, p. 64)

In Nietzsche's scene of contemplation Aristotle's philosopher
would not be condemned to isolation: His appearance integrates
him with the polis, with the other spectators, and their common
appearance is completed with the appearance of the god, which
we can liken to Aristotle's temporal whole. Indeed, as a vision, the
god is seen all at once, and this all-at-onceness of the appearance
"complements" the all-at-onceness of the act of contemplation
with its semblance.[15]

[15]Thus Nietzsche puts the "device of abstraction" at the service of the creation of a "we," insofar as the "I" and the "other" are not conflated (the "other"
does not substitute for the "I"). Instead, the access to the third-person position
situates the "I" in interaction with the other, which interaction produces the vision of the god. We are far from an internalized "he" backing the autonomy of
the subject, as was the case with Locke's performative subject; here the interplay
between the two positions exteriorizes the "I," integrating it into a "oneness."

Notwithstanding its dramatic inspiration, there seems to be no place—or rather, no time—for action in Nietzsche's philosophy of appearance: "The scene, complete with the action, was originally thought of as merely a *vision*" (§8, pp. 65–66). The action completes the scene, which in turn enframes the action, so that the term "vision" refers both to the teleological construction of the action and to a further individuation of the action, through which it becomes possible to "see" it all at once, as if it happened all at once. Thus subjected to vision, action disappears from the stage. This might well be the import of the experience of the "truly aesthetic" spectator: that of wanting to "see tragedy and at the same time as wanting to get beyond all seeing" (§24, p. 141).

As soon as action "appears" on the stage the visionary nature of tragedy is forsaken, and the structure for Kant's commanding subject is prepared. Indeed, according to Nietzsche, the play between the visionary and visible (sight and vision) is disrupted when

the attempt was made to show the god as real and to represent the visionary figure together with its transfiguring frame as something visible for every eye—and thus "drama" in the narrower sense began. (§24, p. 141)

At this point the vision is represented as real, and the risk arises of taking the visionary for the visible, of confusing the teleological construction *of* what is seen with *what* is seen. This is what happens when Socrates enters the theater to see Euripides' plays, marking the new conception of drama as "action."[16] From this moment on, spectators are excluded from the stage and confined to their seats: The public is banned from the public space.

The fact that the interaction between the "I" and the "other" is incarnated in a vision, however, evacuates the process of interaction from its result, because the process itself *is* the vision, frozen, as it were, in time. In other words, while Nietzsche grounds the ontological in the ontic, what seems to interest him in this particular text is the manifestation of the former, rather than the occurrence (through time) of the latter.

[16]See Nietzsche's note in §9, 174 of *The Case of Wagner* for a discussion of drama as *pathos* as opposed to action.

Nietzsche illustrates this shift through an analysis of the explanatory function of Euripides' prologues. In accordance with tradition, which sought to avoid any missing link in the telos so as to make possible the spectators' total absorption in the play, Euripides uses the prologue to ensure a complete understanding of the play. Aristotle's famous unity of the plot follows the same principle: The point is in fact to make the plot appear as if it happened "all at once," to preserve the temporal wholeness of the play. But whereas Euripides' predecessors recur to different devices to transmit all the necessary information in the first scenes, Euripides appeals to an extraneous presence at the beginning of the play, one who explains to the spectators what happens. He introduces, in other words, another spectator, who dictates to the rest of the spectators what to see, creating a distance between the action of the stage and the spectators' vision, and preventing as a consequence the individual's access to the public vision of himself. As the spectators lose their vision of the action, they can no longer be the "actors" of the tragedy.

The spectators now relate cognitively to the action on the scene, instead of participating in it through their vision. The emphasis on knowledge ensues once the telos cannot be revealed as appearance, and it acquires the status of "reality"—although great pains are taken to preserve the status of this reality from further visionary revelations:

often some deity had to guarantee the plot of the tragedy to the public, to remove every doubt as to the reality of the myth—somewhat as Descartes could prove the reality of the empirical world only by appealing to the truthfulness of God and his inability to utter falsehood. (§12, p. 85)

The oneness that the Dionysian spectator could contemplate is here displaced to the figure of a "total" spectator who knows what happens and the truth of what happens. Hence what happens can only be "true," unless the total spectator is lying (but the total spectator is required to tell the truth). Here the possibility of illusion, or "mere appearance," is transferred solely to the instance of

individual "use" of language, and the physical world—the world
of "phenomena"—exhausts sight: It is all there is to see, and to see
all, more must be seen. The unfolding of events, of action, of time,
becomes a central concern. The spectator expects.

Socrates personifies in Nietzsche's argument the illusion that
there are no illusions, that "thought, using the thread of causality,
can penetrate the deepest abysses of being" (§15, p. 95).[17] He con-
founds the "intermediary world of the action on the stage, and the
drama in general," with the Dionysian "discharge" that it makes
manifest (§24, p. 139). In his foregrounding of the *what* of actions,
of causes and reasons, Socrates remains within this intermediate
world, where, in Sloterdijk's words, "The penultimate is perceived
as ultimate, and the tentative as conclusive," a world that "exists
because man engages in the ephemeral as if it were the permanent" (p. 42). Myth, instead, which according to Nietzsche leads
"the world of phenomena to its limits where it denies itself" (§22,
p. 131), forces upon phenomena the awareness of their phenomenality, a reflexivity that destroys them as phenomena but reveals
the "primordial One" in their destruction. In temporal terms, the
moment of "self-denial" of phenomena constitutes the all-assem-
bling moment of oneness, in relation to which "even the immediate present had to appear to [the Greeks] right away *sub specie ae-
terni* and in a certain sense timeless" (§23, p. 137). Thus myth reveals the permanent through the ephemeral, and then anchors the
ephemeral in the permanent.

Action belongs, of course, to the realm of the ephemeral; it is
only when it becomes vision that the permanent in it is revealed.
But action has no effect on the permanent, on what remains, or on
the oneness of things, the eternal. Hence Nietzsche argues that action requires the veils of illusion (§7, p. 60): The nonvisionary "ac-

[17]According to Nietzsche, however, Kant and Schopenhauer show how the
Socratic world of action "bites its own tail" in its belief in appearances, which ultimately constitutes a denial of appearance and consequently reproduces, unwittingly, the mythical denial of phenomena. He grounds his faith in a rebirth of
tragedy on this inevitable self-encirclement of science, which, he argues, transforms it into art. I do not engage this argument here.

tor" needs to believe that what he is doing will remain, that his actions *are*; the visionary observer—the aesthetic contemplator—
knows that they *are* not in themselves but knows what *is* in them.
The Socratic observer neither knows nor believes: He thinks he
knows what he sees, but he has no vision. In this sense he is like
those "soldiers painted on canvas" about whom Nietzsche says
that they are unaware that "it is only as an *aesthetic phenomenon*
that existence and the world are *justified*" (§5, p. 52).

In context, Nietzsche's famous—and infamous—statement
questions, ultimately, the justificatory powers of ethics, and, more
generally, the possibility of making sense of our actions:[18]

We may assume that we are merely images and artistic projections for
the true author, and that we have our highest dignity in our significance as works of art—for it is only as an *aesthetic phenomenon* that existence and the world are *justified*—while of course our consciousness of
our significance hardly differs from that which the soldiers painted on
canvas have of the battle represented on it. Thus all our knowledge of
art is basically quite illusory, because as knowing beings we are not one
and identical with that being which, as the sole author and spectator of
this comedy of art, prepares a perpetual entertainment for itself. Only
insofar as the genius in the act of artistic creation coalesces with this
primordial artist of the world, does he know anything of the eternal essence of art; for in this state he is, in a marvelous manner, like the weird
image of the fairy tale which can turn its eyes at will and behold itself;
he is at once subject and object, at once poet, actor, and spectator. (§5, p.
52)

We can ignore Nietzsche's appeal to the figure of the "sole author
and spectator," understanding it as the vision of Dionysus incarnated in Apollo that was the enactment of the drama in Attic trag-

[18]As will have become apparent, Nietzsche confers on aesthetics this
"exclusive" capacity to justify—ground, englobe, frame, and so on—"existence
and the world" because only participative contemplation can produce a vision of
"oneness" or give access to the permanent in the ephemeral. It can, of course, be
argued that to attempt to justify our lives with "eternal" truths is useless, insofar
as we live in the ephemeral—and Nietzsche would agree with this objection, as
his later texts suggest. The point at stake here is that, if eternal justifications are
wanted, they will be aesthetic and not ethical, as Kant wanted.

edy. The spectator of Tragic tragedy "coalesced" with this one being because he had access to the vision of himself as vision, like the "weird image" of the fairy tale (and Nietzsche's argument does sound at times like a fairy tale), and was thus transported to the all-at-onceness of eternity. The Socratic spectator, instead, having no vision of himself as vision, cannot justify—constitute sufficient grounds for—phenomena in eternity, because he cannot envision his participation in his act of knowing, in his spectating. He is, in his own eyes, as external to the "whole" of the action he is witnessing as are the soldiers with respect to the battle they are fighting. The soldiers know they are fighting, but they do not know what is happening—what appears—in their fighting; the Socratic spectator knows he is seeing, but he does not know what appears in his seeing.

Thus soldiers and Socratic spectator alike fail to recognize the ephemeral as the ephemeral, a failure that discredits, at least in Nietzsche's eyes, the significance they attribute to their actions. A "new" subject seems to be needed who could engage the permanent in the ephemeral as he engages in action.[19] This new subject

[19]This subject—who is no longer, properly speaking, a subject—appears in Nietzsche's later works, namely in the figure of the superman. Martin Heidegger discusses this figure in *What Is Called Thinking*. Man as he is now, argues Heidegger, is undetermined: "The rational man has not yet been brought into its full nature" (p. 58); he is still caught between the rational and the animal (nature and culture, the sensible and the intelligible, and so on). In Nietzsche's terms, he is the stage of the contending tendencies of the Dionysian and the Apollonian. Nietzsche's superman would be the man "who overcomes himself and so subjects himself and so first determines himself" (p. 59). Man as he is now, is a "bridge" that must be passed over; the superman "is the figure and form of man to which he who passes over is passing over" (p. 60). The nature of this "passing" is temporal, as the formulation of the "bridge" shows: The bridge is that man be delivered from revenge. Revenge, in turn, is, in Nietzsche's own words, "the will's revulsion against time and its 'It was'" (p. 93—recall Prometheus' own deliverance from revenge in Shelley's *Prometheus Unbound*). Heidegger points out that the will's revulsion is against the passing of time, which goes against the will's thrust toward the future. The will's revulsion chains it to what it revolts against, the passing of time, and thus the will surprises itself willing itself to pass. The solution to this dilemma Heidegger sees in Nietzsche's notion of

could still be a soldier, but he would have to be capable of recognizing his own partiality as actor of the battle and produce in his fragmentary experience a "oneness" granting valid significance to his actions. In order to be able to act significantly, however, this new subject would have to dwell, not only in ontological realms, but in ontic life as well.

Bakhtin's non-alibi in acting

Bakhtin's project in *Author and Hero in Aesthetic Activity* could be characterized as the dismantling of the "weird image of the fairy tale, that can turn its eyes at will and behold itself." This weird image could be considered as the subject of Kant's ethics, who is asked to be simultaneously, and toward himself, both an "ethical" and an aesthetic subject. The subject is thus in the situation where acting involves the feat, paraphrasing Bakhtin, of lifting himself up by his own hair.[20] This feat is doubtless possible in fairy tales, but it cannot be done by an actual actor and spectator. As Bakhtin points out, I *can* be an actor and a spectator at the same time, but not of the same things: I will not be the spectator of *myself* as actor—I am in fact never a witness to my acts. Were I a witness to my acts, in fact, I could not consider them mine, and I could not act.

Countering the conflation of the first- and third-person positions that was at the basis of the performative subject, Bakhtin insists on the necessity of a factual and actual spectator for the construction of aesthetic wholes. This acknowledgment foregrounds the distinction and the distance between "I" and the "other" that is elided in the theoretical thinking Bakhtin denounces.[21] Bakhtin's

---

eternal recurrence of the same: By willing the recurrence of the "It was," of the passing of time, the will is freed from revulsion.

[20]Wittgenstein formulates this impossibility through a similar image, which exposes the naiveté underlying the making of the "weird image": "Imagine someone saying: 'But I know how tall I am!' and laying his hand on top of his head to prove it" (*Philosophical Investigations*, §279).

[21]Bakhtin thus reverses the tendency of theoretical discourse to construct the spectator (and then take him for real) and to consider the whole as a given

fundamental observation is simple: The subject is "I" for himself, and "other" ("he") for the other. These two positions (which are, in fact, attitudes rather than spatial situations) are indeed conflated in aesthetic activity, but here it is the other who, "completed" by the surplus knowledge of the contemplator, can be seen to be at the same time an "I" for himself and an "other" for the contemplator, without contradiction. The contemplator is the recipient of all that is transgredient[22] to the contemplated subject—his appearance, his punctual appearance in time, his givenness—and it is from this position of outsidedness (temporal, spatial, and of meaning) that the contemplator/author consummates the subject into a hero, the center and organizing principle of the aesthetic vision. The author/contemplator confers "form" onto the subject, who is pure "content" for himself; consolidates the subject's "horizon" into an "environment"; and "finishes" him temporally.[23]

(forgetting that it is a logical construct). In the *Birth of Tragedy*, part of this reversal is already effected, in the presentation of the whole as the product of the activity (or, more specifically, of the interactivity) of contemplation. Nietzsche's scenario, however, is haunted by the "weird image of the fairy tale, that can turn its eyes at will and behold itself," even if the image is used against itself to deconstruct the autonomous subject. Indeed, in Nietzsche's account of the activity of contemplation, the movement of the spectator from himself to the other to the common vision and "back" to himself constitutes a process of deinviduation of himself, even of self-annihilation. Nietzsche does not, like Bakhtin, take the step of affirming the "I" against the subject, but rather suggests that in order for the subject to be dismantled, the "I" should disappear too. This assumption implies that for Nietzsche the "I" is in fact inseparable from the conflation he denounces.

[22]Bakhtin's translators use the term "transgredient" in the sense of "passing beyond subjective limits: objective"—the second acceptation in the *Oxford English Dictionary*. The terms "subjective" and "objective," however, do not take into account the interplay between the "I-for-myself" and the "I-for-the-other." What is transgredient for the "I" is that which is inaccessible, as a stance, to the "I-for-myself."

[23]In Bakhtin's terminology, the horizon is what the subject "sees" and perceives in general from his position of subject for himself, which is a confrontational position. What he confronts from his position of subject-for-himself becomes his environment only under the aesthetic activity of the other, for whom what the subject confronts becomes what surrounds and grounds him "reassuringly." Similarly, whereas for the "I-for-myself" the future is uncertain and

The author's/contemplator's outsidedness is thus not passive: It is an active evaluation of, and reaction to, the hero in question, manifest in the form that the hero acquires, the surroundings he is given, an so on. For this reason Bakhtin qualifies this outsidedness as axiological, as maintaining a difference in value between "I" and "the other," which is the condition for aesthetic creation:

Only the other is capable of being formed and consummated *essentially*, for all the constituents of an axiological consummation (spatial, temporal, and those of meaning) are axiologically transgredient to an active self-consciousness, that is, are not located along the line of one's own axiological relationship to oneself. (p. 188)

Insofar as the author is the "I" of the aesthetic activity, he remains himself unconsummated and transgredient, not only to himself but also to the reader, because the hero himself is not in a position to behave aesthetically, as hero, toward his author. The hero could look at the author in the eyes, but their confrontation would lose its purely aesthetic nature: The hero would look back as "I," and not as the "I" that the author completes with his aesthetic activity. The hero's unawareness of his own transgredience and of the contemplator's activity is thus a necessary aspect of his completion into an I/other by the beholder, insofar as he cannot be a hero for himself:

As long as I remain *myself* for myself, I cannot be active in the aesthetically valid and consolidated space and time; I am not present for myself axiologically in that space and time, I am not upbuilt, shaped, and determined in them. . . . I *do not yet exist* in my own axiological world as a contented and self-equivalent positive *given*. My own axiological relationship to myself is completely unproductive aesthetically: for myself, I am aesthetically unreal. I can be only the bearer of the task of artistic forming and consummating, not its object—not the hero. (p. 188)

The fact that the "I" as a complete and *whole, given* being can only be the other's aesthetic vision does not mark for Bakhtin an insufficiency in the makeup of the "I," as Nietzsche stated in his example of

---

endless—for I cannot imagine my life as being complete and finished—the author/contemplator situates his "hero" in the context of his own death, or temporal finitude, thereby "saving" him from the indeterminacy of the future.

the soldiers in the canvas. It simply marks the limits of aesthetic activity, or the limits of its consummating powers. Rephrasing Nietzsche's statement, we could say that it is only the other's existence that can be justified as an aesthetic phenomenon, insofar as "justification" is here understood, quite literally, as the provision of sufficient grounds for existence—an environment as opposed to a horizon. Part of this justification, moreover, will consist in the organizing of a world around the other, in which process the other will be the organizing principle of the world thus "given" to him. There is consequently no such thing as abstract existence or world as aesthetic phenomena:

The world of artistic vision is a world which is organized, ordered, and consummated—independently of what-is-yet-to-be-achieved and independently of meaning—*around* a given human being as *his* axiological surroundings or environment: we can see the way various objects and all relations (spatial and temporal relations, and relations of meaning) gain the validity of artistic objects *around* that human being. (p. 187)[24]

In other words, not only can my existence for myself not acquire any aesthetic validity for myself, but the world, also, is only aesthetically valid for the other. I for myself find no grounding in aesthetics.

Bakhtin's insistence on the aesthetic unreality of myself for myself—and therefore on what cannot be the "object" of aesthetic contemplation—aims at an important "corrective":

We observe in the history of philosophy a constantly recurring tendency toward a substitution of the yet-to-be-achieved unity of cognition and action by the concrete intuitive, and as it were *given*, present-on-hand *unity* of aesthetic vision.[25]

---

[24]Bakhtin alters this view in later works, particularly when he begins to work with the concept of dialogism, which implies a multiplicity of discourses acting upon each other, and therefore a more complex "view," if view at all, of the world. This present statement however retains its validity insofar as the emphasis is laid not so much on the single human being as on the arrangement of the world around him, which thereby loses its status of "natural" determination and introduces the possibility of the "existence" of as many worlds as there may be arrangements of them around human activities.

[25]"The Problem of Content, Material and Form in Verbal Art," p. 280.

The completion in the future of actions and cognition tends to be replaced by the completion in the present of appearance, givenness, and aesthetic vision, a substitution that entails that of the "I" for itself by the "I" as other for another, as if the "I" could in effect take an aesthetic approach to itself, be the contemplating other of itself. The stakes of this substitution are multiple—"protecting" the "I" from the other, as with Locke; ensuring its individuality to itself; completing the "I," which others "prove," by their presence, to be incomplete, and so forth—but they all come down to an extreme valuation (and corresponding repudiation) of the other's position, as ultimately, to covet an aesthetic approach to oneself is to want to be like the other—that is, to want to be as "I" perceive the other (provided the other does not perceive me).

But the other I perceive, in short, as finished, *as* an end and *at* an end. The other is a full person to me because I organize his temporality, his actions, his future, his goals, around his givenness:

Aesthetic creation overcomes the infinite and yet-to-be-achieved character of cognition and ethical action by referring all constituents of being and of yet-to-be-achieved meaning to a human being in his concrete givenness—as the event of his life, *as his fate*. (p. 230; my italics)

Aesthetic creation thus "concludes" action in order to constitute the givenness of the human being, a conclusion that is only possible for the other, in respect to whom the aesthetic beholder (or author) represents the present moment organizing past and future.[26] Bakhtin further argues that it is not only impossible for myself to "finish" myself (this only the other can do, and only to myself as another), but it is in fact counterproductive for me to attempt or want to do it myself, as the consciousness of myself as "finished" can only finish me to myself as well:

[26]It is in this sense that Hamlet "does not have the time (to tell)"—he certainly does not have it because he is going to die, but also because he is not in the position to "finish" himself and constitute an account of himself. Only the other can "have" "my" time, not myself—and only the other can "give" it to me, as we will see.

The consciousness of being fully consummated in time (the consciousness that what *is* constitutes *all* there is) is a consciousness with which
one can do nothing, or with which it is impossible to live; in relation to
my own, already finished life, any active axiological position is impossible. (p. 121)

The impossibility here is double: It is an axiological impossibility, in that I am determined by my future, by what is yet-to-be-
achieved, and this future is "radical" in nature. In Bakhtin's terms,
it is an absolute future because it is the future of meaning, and
consequently

it is not a future in the sense of being a temporal continuation of *the
same life*, but in the sense of being a constant possibility, a constant need
to transform my life *formally*, to put new meaning into my life (the last
word of consciousness). (p. 122)

For me the future is a constantly renewing force, whereas, for the
other, it is a principle of conclusion. As I lack such a principle for
myself, I cannot in principle consummate myself, I cannot *do* it. But
I cannot do it either, in the sense that a "perfected" me, my givenness as fully exhausting my being, can only be considered an
"impostor":

My justification is always in the future, and this prospective justification, perpetually set over against me, abolishes my past and my present
(. . . for myself), insofar as they claim to be something already on hand
in a lasting way, claim to be stilled in the given . . . and claim to be the
essential in me or the whole of me or to determine me exhaustively in
being (my givenness pretending here to be the whole of me, to be me in
truth—my givenness acting in the capacity of an impostor). (p. 122)

Thus my givenness is something I must fight against to preserve
my freedom to become myself once what is yet-to-be-achieved is
achieved, though of course, this moment will never be accessible to
me, as it is a moment of realization that is axiologically accessible
only to the other. For me, my givenness is in the absolute future, in
Bakhtin's sense, whereas for the other, my givenness is present-at-
hand.

Accordingly I believe "insanely" (and this is Bakhtin's term) in
my noncoincidence with myself as a given; "I do not accept my

factually given being. . . . I cannot count and add up all of myself, saying: this is *all* of me. . . . I cannot, axiologically, fit my whole life into time" (p. 127). I believe "in the constant possibility of the inner miracle of a new birth" (idem): I consider my factuality as ephemeral, as a condition for my yet-to-be givenness, which will have the character of permanence. Thus I resolve, when I can,[27] the noncoincidence between, in fact, my "I" for myself and my "I" for the other by spreading them in time—I set my yet-to-be givenness as a task to be accomplished, as is the world that will correspond to my future givenness:

My determination of myself is given to me (given as a task—as something yet to be achieved) not in the categories of temporal being, but in the categories of *not-yet-being*, in the categories of purpose and meaning—in the meaning-governed future, which is hostile to any factual existence of myself in the past and the present. (p. 123)

In other words, I oppose to the other's knowledge of what is transgredient to me as a given (as appearance), myself yet-to-be, which is transgredient to the other. This, however, does not constitute an interiority, but an activity—it is only insofar as I am engaged in life as a task (something to be done, including myself) that I create a *possibility* that escapes the determinateness of my appearance and appearing to the other as a given. And, conversely, it is only by positing myself as indeterminate in the present, in my givenness, that "I" can engage in the "task" of life, in action.

In Bakhtin's model, then, action is not only possible but also inevitable—only the conflation of aesthetic (for the other) and ethical (for himself) subject could obscure the fact that what is impossible is indeed not to engage in action. Once the distinction is properly made between the "I" and the "other" it becomes apparent that,

[27]For Bakhtin, I fight against my givenness, which destroys me for myself, at the same time I demand it of myself: "The demand is: live in such a way that every given moment of your life would be both the consummating, final moment and, at the same time, the initial moment of a new life. As such, this demand is in principle incapable of being fulfilled by me, for it includes an aesthetic category (a relationship *to the other*) which, although attenuated, is still alive in it" (p. 122).

for the other, I am the subject of action, in the sense that I am, for him, the organizing principle of my actions, the center of his observations, what my actions refer to, and the potential hero of a world structured around myself. For myself, instead, I am no hero; I am in action, and action is the organizing principle of myself for myself: "I act through deed, word, thought, and feeling; I live, I come-to-be through my acts" (p. 138). This coming-to-be through my acts, however, is not the coming-to-be of appearance (which, again, only "appears" for the other), as "I neither express myself nor determine myself through my acts" (p. 139).

My own determinateness (I am such as I am) is not, for me myself, part of the motivation of my act; the determinateness of the act-performer's personality is not present in the context which determines the sense of an act for the acting consciousness itself. . . . an act expressed or uttered in all its purity, i.e. without introducing any transgredient features and values alien to the act itself [such as "how the act looks to the other"], will prove to be without a hero as an essentially determinate entity. (pp. 139–40)

In other words, it is not myself-as-given that determines my acts, and not only because my determinateness is inaccessible to me, but because actions "partialize" everything except their ends. To explain this effect of actions on determination Bakhtin gives the example of someone walking on the street, who suddenly jumps to the side to avoid colliding with someone else—what the person who jumps "sees" is not the coming person as a whole, aesthetic entity, but rather as the obstacle to be avoided (p. 44). Similarly my "being-in-action" will be determined by the action I perform, while my being, in my givenness, will be undetermined (for myself) in the process.[28] And it is only so undetermined, as yet-to-be given (and therefore not apparent), that the subject *is* (for himself).

[28]My own determinateness cannot become directly the end of my actions either, insofar as I cannot, physically, make myself whole, and I can only set it as a task to be fulfilled in the realization of another task (pp. 139–40). In other words, the ontological (Being) cannot, in general, be achieved directly, but only in the ontic dimension.

From appearance to rhythm

The line separating subject from action in the scene of contemplation becomes, for Bakhtin, one dividing between, or distinguishing, the categories of "I" and "the other." In this scheme, appearance, which for Nietzsche "joined" the subject to its public instance and thus constituted the access to the "common," is replaced by the notion of rhythm, which, although it is an aesthetic category, articulates the "meeting" of the categories of "I" and "other" in action and in time, instead of outside time.[29] More specifically, with the notion of rhythm Bakhtin articulates time in function of action, rather than postulating a homogeneous flow of time through which activities are organized. Indeed, rhythm distributes—periodizes—time, organizing it according to an end-directed structure (we "follow" rhythm), which is at the same time open-ended (we expect rhythm to change, not to end). The notion of rhythm ultimately enables Bakhtin to avoid the pitfalls of a model of action structured exclusively by the temporal device of projection, and it allows him to emphasize the organization of actions through time without having to "skip" the present moment of their enactment.

We have seen that for Bakhtin the subject for himself is undetermined, "yet-to-be," immersed in life as a task to be achieved. But he is not only indeterminate in that he cannot consider his own givenness; he is also temporally indeterminate—unfinished, yet newly begun, owing nothing to the past:

In relation to myself, I experience time extra-aesthetically. The immediate givenness to me *of everything that has the validity of meaning* (outside which I cannot become actively conscious of anything as *mine*) renders impossible any positive axiological consummation of my temporality. In my living self-experience, the ideal extratemporal meaning is not indifferent to time, but is set over against it as the future of meaning—as that which *ought to be* in contrast to that which already *is*. (p. 121)

[29]For Bakhtin aesthetic activity is a specific type of activity, but it is not necessarily a "specialized" activity—not only are there inevitably aesthetic moments in our interaction with others, but, in addition, the aesthetic can in fact be defined as the reaction to the other as whole.

Whereas I experience time according to meaning and action, to the determinateness of the objects my emotions, will, and purpose are directed toward, I can consummate the other from the axiological position of the "absolute" future of meaning—I can frame the other's life in a plot, can shape its meaning teleologically, can, in short, consider his striving toward the ought-to-be as a mere moment of his givenness.[30] I can react to the other as to a whole, whereas I can only act, and partially, with relation to myself. I encompass the other temporally, but, in normal circumstances, cannot experience myself as temporally encompassed. And, as a corollary, my strivings and experiences are equally "unfinished" for me; I live them as not-yet-complete, as open-ended, inconclusive experiences and strivings: "Insofar as I find precisely *myself* in a given lived experience . . . ; as long as I am the one living in it, it does not yet exist in full. This brings us up directly to the problem of *rhythm*" (p. 117).

Rhythm is the "means," or the activity, that in Bakhtin's argument "fulfils" the experience and the striving that cannot be lived fully (as wholes, as givens) by the subject himself. It is in this sense that rhythm is an aesthetic category: It is the axiological position of the other that qualifies experience (including the experience of my actions). My involvement in meaning and in action implies that I cannot, simply, *do*—I can only do *something*. Mine is a world (or rather, a horizon) of purposes and specific actions and objects. I unlace my left boot, pull it, manage to slip out my left foot, and so on. The other can simply take his shoes off. This composition of the other's movements implies the anticipation and predetermination of the other's purposes, which neutralizes them qua purposes. Accordingly Bakhtin understands rhythm "as a purely temporal ordering" (p. 112) that comprehends the other's purposes and actions:

---

[30]I should stress that, in Bakhtin's logic, the other cannot, in principle, do all this *to* me—at least as far as I'm concerned—because I cannot, from my extra-aesthetic existence (my inner life), perceive his aesthetic activity on me. I say in principle because, as we will see, the notion of rhythm allows, to some extent, an axiological displacement of myself into the other.

Rhythm presupposes an "immanentization" of meaning to lived experience itself, an "immanentization" of purpose to striving itself; meaning and purpose must become no more than a moment in an experience/striving that is intrinsically valuable. Rhythm presupposes a certain *predeterminedness* of striving, experiencing, action (a certain hopelessness with respect to meaning). (p. 117)

Whereas I strive *for* something, which something constitutes the value of my striving, in the other's striving—insofar as it has been rhythmicized—that is, approached from the axiological position of the other—the goal is the "means" of the composition of his striving. I strive to climb the hill—the other climbs the hill as if in order to strive. Thus for Bakhtin I react to the other's striving in the other's (for himself) necessary striving *for* something:

Rhythm is not expressive in the strict sense of the term; that is, it does not express a lived experience, is not founded from within that experience; it is not an emotional-volitional reaction to an object and to meaning, but a reaction *to* that reaction. (p. 116)[31]

A rhythmicized action, then, is one that has been "encountered" by the other, that has elicited his reaction, and that thereby occurs not only in the subject's indeterminate time but also in the other's ordered, and concluded, time, partaking of the axiological attitudes—forgive the redundancy—of the "I" and the "other," without conflating them.

Let me recall, at this point, that in what I called Aristotle's model of indirect action, actions "tended" toward the temporal whole of the polis. Bakhtin in many ways reproduces this model with his notion of rhythm, insofar as rhythm represents the integration of action into the other's time, where the other is not to be understood literally as a given person but as an axiological attitude from which there are temporal wholes. Thus I can participate, consciously, in rhythm, to the extent that I do not consider myself for

[31]In his analysis of lyric poetry by Pushkin, Bakhtin explains that "rhythm represents, almost exclusively, a purely formal reaction of the *author* to the event *as a whole*, whereas intonation is for the most part the intonational reaction of the *hero* to an object *within* the whole" (pp. 215–16).

myself, but act for the other:

> Sometimes I become justifiably alienated from myself axiologically. . . .
> In my lived life, I participate in a communal mode of existence, in an
> established social order, in a nation, in a state, in mankind, in God's
> world. In all these cases, I live my life, axiologically, in the other and
> for others. . . . I experience, strive, and speak here in the *chorus* of oth-
> ers. But *in a chorus* I do not sing for myself; I am active only in relation
> to the other and I am passive in the other's relationship to me. . . .
> Wherever the purpose of a movement or an action is incarnated into
> the other or is coordinated with the action of the other—as in the case
> of joint labor—my own action enters into rhythm as well. But I do not
> *create* rhythm for myself: I join in it for the sake of the other. (pp. 120–
> 21)

Here it is clear that rhythm is the participation with the other in a
whole comprehending both, insofar as rhythm organizes a uni-
fying temporal other that inscribes my and other people's actions
in the same striving—after all, the demand of rhythm is that we
should all "follow" it, beat its time. Hence when I join in rhythm
I join in a chorus, which, this time, sings, instead of contemplating. This shift from vision to voice already announces Bakhtin's
later notion of dialogism, introducing language—discourses—as
another formulation of rhythm, in which the other's axiological
attitude constantly formulates, and "finishes," my own inner in-
determinateness. When I participate in rhythm I join in for the
other(s); similarly when I speak, whether silently to myself or out
loud to the birds, I am addressing another and thereby accepting, and adopting, his formal reaction to my words, making it
axiologically possible for myself to overcome (formally) my own
transgredience.[32] In this manner I rhythmicize my inner life—I
can recognize its givenness (though I cannot experience its giv-

[32]See Valerian N. Volosinov, *Marxism and the Philosophy of Language,* for a development of the philosophy of language of Bakhtin's Circle. Here Volosinov argues, among other things, that the notion of an internal, private space makes no
sense, because the use of language—and we cannot not use it—socializes our
every act (expression determines experience). This is of course a widely accepted
view now.

enness, of course) and believe in its formal "belonging" to the world of others.[33]

I should stress that the notion of rhythm does not permit the aestheticization of the subject for himself—I do not, at the end of Bakhtin's argument, turn my eyes inside and contemplate myself. Rhythm moves actions to the realm of the other, and therefore to the temporal realm of a community or group. But the subject "remains" a moment for himself, a moment that cannot be organized, temporally ordered, predetermined, in rhythm:

> The very moment of transition, of movement from the past and the present into the future [of meaning, the future as an *ought*, or obligation], constitutes a moment in me that has the character purely of an event, where I, from within myself, participate in the unitary and unique event of being. . . . It is precisely in this moment that rhythm has its absolute limit, for this moment does not submit to rhythm—it is in principle extrarhythmic. (p. 118)

We recognize in this extrarhythmic moment, of which Bakhtin also says that *is* and *ought* confront each other and "mutually exclude each other," the obstacle to the conceptualization of the *"passage à l'acte"* that was discussed in the previous chapter. In this moment I am—but not yet. My existence is singular—the "unitary and unique event of being"—to the extreme that I experience "being" (alive) as a one-time, unrepeatable, event. At this extreme of temporal alienation from others my existence is so singular, so radically independent from the past, that its transformation (a radical transformation) in the future is inconceivable (for me):

> It is a moment of fundamental and essential dissonance, inasmuch as what-is and what-ought-to-be, what-is-given and what-is-imposed-as-a-task, are incapable of being rhythmically bound from *within me myself*, i.e. they are incapable of being perceived on one and the same plane, incapable of becoming a moment in the development of a single positively valuable sequence of becoming. (p. 118)

[33]Skepticism would then be the impossibility of recognizing the other's axiological difference from oneself.

Ultimately my mode of existence for myself is momentary and cannot participate in a continuity, be it of meaning, or time. A way of putting it could be: For me, I am always in the same moment, the same time—time does not pass within me. I am the moment that time passes by. But it is precisely this resistance of mine to what ought-to-be, this purely temporal resistance of my "momentous" being, that enables change to occur—it is what generates, not "more of myself" but rather, to put it bluntly, the "content" that the other constitutes as a given, the actions that will submit to rhythm, the moments that the other can predetermine and arrange. Bakhtin says of the moment, "Where the ought-to-be in principle confronts me within myself as another world," that it "constitutes the highest point of my creative seriousness, of my pure productiveness" (p. 119). It is in the confrontation of the "another world" of the "ought-to-be" and myself in my momentary or momentous being that something happens, which the other will construe as the happening of the ought-to-be. "The creative act (experience, striving, action) . . . is in principle extra-rhythmic (in the course of its performance)" (ibid).[34]

[34]It is worth lingering on this extrarhythmic, "creative moment," first of all with respect to the status it has in Bakhtin's text. In the space of two pages, "this moment" appears a number of times—which is not in itself surprising, as Bakhtin tends to repeat himself—and then is never referred to directly again, although it can be inscribed at other points of his discussion. The fact that "this moment" is the moment of "creation," which immediately blends into what-already-is, might explain his sudden interest and disinterest in it—it seems to be the moment when he says to himself, "I am onto something, I am both accounting for what I am doing and doing it at the same time!" If so, Bakhtin would occasionally succumb to the illusion that he can behave like the "weird image" in the fairy tale—which illusion may well be an inevitable moment in the creative process. This author, at least, is subject to it herself.

On another front, Bakhtin's notion of an extrarhythmic creative moment can be related productively to Hannah Arendt's understanding of action as man's capacity to interrupt automatic processes, be they natural or historical (see WIF, pp. 169–71). For Arendt every act, to the extent that it does interrupt the automatism of the process within which framework it occurs, "is a miracle—that is, something which could not be expected" (p. 169). And this is precisely what extrarhythmic moments are: unexpected interruptions of the prevailing rhythm,

The confrontation of the other world of the ought-to-be is, of course, also the confrontation with the other, whom I can never quite meet in flesh, by reason of his being in another time. I may accord my actions to the other's reactions, but *we* are just never there at the same time—on the same plane. Bakhtin formulates this nonmeeting as an "axiological" contradiction:

I and the *other* [as principles] find ourselves in a relationship of absolute mutual contradiction which has the character of an event: at the point where the *other*, from within himself, negates himself, negates his own being-as-a-given, at that point *I*, from my own unique place in the event of being, affirm and validate axiologically the givenness of his being that he himself negates, and his very act of negation is, for me, no more than a moment in that givenness of his being. (p. 129)

From my moment of being, which time passes by, I can ensure the other's time in rhythm—I can consider his own momentary mode of existence as indeed a moment in the trajectory of his actions and of his whole person, as he can with respect to mine. Whereas we are, with respect to ourselves, immobile in time, and resistant to change, we are, with respect to each other, already in the process of achieving what we will achieve. In this sense, "I" and the "other" pass each other's time, and constitute for each other, as principles, the condition of possibility of action.

The other thus resurfaces as "the harness of necessity" "that impels" action, but this time it is not in the guise of an interiorized prescriptive voice. On the contrary, for Bakhtin it is because I am not the other that the *passage à l'acte* is not only possible but also happens. Although the other is integrated in my axiological makeup as "I-for-the-other," the distance and temporal difference between the first- and third-person positions are not abolished. By maintaining the "axiological contradiction" between the principles of "I" and the "other," Bakhtin is able to understand phenome-

---

which may eventually be integrated as innovations, provided they eventually develop rhythm of their own. And that is, of course, the real difficulty: Developing and sustaining such a rhythm, carrying it through until further extrarhythmic phenomena introduce factors of change.

nologically the "device of abstraction" through which theoretical thought constructs the *passage à l'acte*.

A brief recapitulation of Nietzsche's and Bakhtin's responses to Kant's ethics might be welcome at this point. Nietzsche addresses the latter's biworldly model in his staging of the embodiment of the Dionysian "oneness" in Apollonian individuation, which we formulated as the insight that what *is* must necessarily *appear* (*as*), or that the ontological is manifest in the ontic. In other words, Nietzsche's argument is that the subject necessarily appears, and is consequently anchored in, the sensible world, of which the intelligible is not only a manifestation but also the manner in which the sensible is made manifest. Nietzsche thus restores the subject to appearance and to participation in the vision that it contemplated and commanded in Kant's model. Bakhtin addresses Kant's ethical imperative as he argues that in the same way that the subject cannot but appear (*as*), it is necessarily bound to act—it appears as it acts, in its actions. He thus renders the prescriptive moment in Kant's model unnecessary and further invalidates it by considering the "ought" as a category of individual acts instead of as an order issuing from a third person, whether external to the "I" or conflated with it. As he disentangles the "I" from the "other," moreover, Bakhtin reestablishes a distance and temporal difference in the relation between the two that grounds the "I" in interaction.

The prescriptive voice of Kant's model is not, however, silenced with Nietzsche's and Bakhtin's considerations. As we will see in the next chapter, it resurges in the "misunderstanding" of the function of figures—pictures, as Wittgenstein calls them, or models—in language. This misunderstanding displaces prescription from the subject to the models it uses, and consequently, misuses. Language thus appears as the new tyrant of Shelley's pervert mechanism, ordering its users to perform impossible deeds or to actualize enterprises already achieved in the realm of eternity. Taking up the terms of the previous chapter, we could say that man here forgets the lesson of the myth of succession, which specified that the immortality of the gods was ensured by men, whose immortality as a species was, in turn, safeguarded by the gods. The equilibrium of the interdependence of men and gods and of their respective temporalities is disrupted as man overestimates the scope of his technologies of time, and "confuses" what he is responsible for—the gods' immortality—with what he is capable of. Compelled by this "confusion" to attempt to behave like a god, man is definitely in trouble, waiting for *Godot* and dressed with the "pontifical" that invests him with the power to do nothing.

6 ⌇ Certain Acts: The Tiger's Thoughtless Bound

Spirits of action

In the previous chapter we saw that Bakhtin locates the "crisis of contemporary action" in the "abyss" that theoretical thinking imposes between "the motive of the actually performed act or deed and its product."[1] This abyss between motive and product, Bakhtin goes on to argue, cannot be crossed from the latter to the former: "It is *impossible* to break through from [within the product] to the actually performed act" (my emphasis). The nature of this impossibility is of course not physical, but logical: Time is not reversible, and consequently, the conceptualization of action in terms of its product necessarily "skips" the actually performed act—what is already done cannot be envisaged as a task any more. Insofar as action is thus understood as a finished product, agents are confronted by the following predicament: I must accomplish this task (the *ought* of individual acts); but the task I must accomplish is to be already accomplished. In other words, I must accomplish the accomplished task—I must have already done it. The question of how to act thus asks, this time, how can I possibly "produce" the product directly, except by magic?[2]

[1] *Toward a Philosophy of the Act*, pp. 54–55.
[2] Or by miracle: As Hannah Arendt points out in "What Is Freedom?" all actions, to the extent that they interrupt "some natural series of events" or "some

Bakhtin counters this predicament as he insists, on the one hand, that (my) life is composed, to use his translator's terms, "as an uninterrupted deed-performance,"[3] and on the other, that it is impossible for the "I" to dwell in a "finished," or complete world. Such a finished or complete world, he argues, is the product of the aesthetic activity of the other on the "I" but can never be the world in which the "I" lives and acts. That we act whether we want to or not, and this despite the models of action that we avail ourselves of, is an argument that demystifies the power that models may have on behavior: It is not because a particular conceptualization of action suggests action is impossible that action *is* impossible; it is not, moreover, because a certain understanding of action says actions should function like magic, that they *should*. By opposing what we do to what we think we do or should do Bakhtin denounces, in short, the selfsame "pervert" mechanism that Shelley denounced in man's political behavior, that of submitting to tyrants he has himself empowered. This is not to say that Bakhtin opposes doing and thinking in the way that what is "real" can be opposed to what is only "imagined" (although doing functions in his argument, to a certain extent, as the ultimate "reality test"). On the contrary, by replacing the understanding of action as product in its valid context (that of aesthetic activity), Bakhtin acknowledges the pertinence of conceptualizations to behavior. This recognition is at the basis of Bakhtin's project (in *Toward a Philosophy of the Act*) to develop a "primal philosophy" to forestall the totalizing drive of theoretical thinking, which presents its theoretically cognized world as the whole world, and hence attempts to impose the models valid in its domain to all other domains of life.[4]

---

automatic process," "constitute the wholly unexpected" and are, in this sense, "miraculous" (p. 168). And there is, to be sure, something miraculous or magic about actions, in the sense that, as agents, we can make things happen, but we do not make what happens. Taking up the motif of magic, we can provoke their appearance, but not their existence.

[3] *Toward a Philosophy of the Act*, p. xix.

[4] "But the world as object of theoretical cognition seeks to pass itself off as the whole world, that is, not only as abstractly unitary Being, but also as concretely

In this sense Bakhtin's project joins Wittgenstein's constant dismantling, in the *Philosophical Investigations*, of the "dogmatism into which we fall so easily in doing philosophy" and which consists, mainly, in the tendency to consider models as ideas "to which reality *must* correspond" (§131).[5] This tendency is yet another form of Shelley's "pervert" mechanism: "We" give descriptions of reality, to which "we" then ascribe prescriptive power. But the agency that Shelley attributed to man, and Bakhtin to theoretical thinking, Wittgenstein locates in our use of language. Schematically, for Wittgenstein models are operative in language, which organizes itself and our spheres of activity in what he calls language-games.[6] Because language-games overlap, language users are liable to "cross" games without realizing, or transfer unawares models/descriptions from one to another. In Wittgenstein's version of Shelley's pervert mechanism, descriptions and models acquire prescriptive power when they are displaced from the motivating context of their language-games—that is, the context within which they serve one or several given purposes. In this move the question of what the model is *for* may be "forgotten," and the model may be taken as an ideal to be attained, and which, as it were, prescribes itself to *be*.[7]

One of Wittgenstein's main points throughout the *Philosophical Investigations* is that there is nothing we can *do* with such an under-

unique Being in its possible totality. In other words, theoretical cognition tries to construct a first philosophy" (p. 8).

[5]It could be said that, if Bakhtin argued against the derivation of the "ought" from necessity (as an expression of the will), Wittgenstein argues against its derivation from logical (and hence linguistic) imperatives.

[6]In §7 the notion of "language-game" is defined as "language and the actions into which it is woven."

[7]Wittgenstein speaks of a model as an "object of comparison," "a measuring-rod"—something with which we operate on "reality." The model takes on a prescriptive voice when, instead of being used to measure a given distance, the measuring-rod becomes the distance to be covered. Here the model, supposed to make an activity (an operation) possible, is taken to represent the object of the operation, its final product. In these cases the purpose of the model is forgotten; as Bakhtin puts it, an abyss separates the motive and the product of the act—the model thus becomes an ideal, something like an a priori product that should be actualized instead of being done (travel from eternity to the present time).

standing of models (or of a given model), that it does not *allow* us to do anything. An operative model, picture, or image will "guide" our behavior, give it shape, permit a certain course of action. An inoperative one—that is, one that remains unused, as if we expected it to function on its own—instead, will bind us in perplexity, captivate us,[8] and ultimately use *us*, commanding the realization of a feat for which there is no course of action to take. Therein would reside the "mystery" of ostensive gestures:

§36. And we do here what we do in a host of similar cases: because we cannot specify any *one* bodily action which we call pointing to the shape (as opposed, for example, to the colour), we say that a *spiritual* [mental, intellectual] activity corresponds to these words.

These acts cannot be performed *qua* spiritual acts, but what they represent are, most often, perfectly feasible and even daily activities—such as reading, calculating, or "meaning." Hence Wittgenstein's instigation "not to represent the matter as if there were something one *couldn't* do" (§374), which suggests, on the one hand, that we can do it, and on the other, that understood "literally," the "something" in question may well not "exist" as a possibility, and consequently, as part of any language-game. The passage continues: "As if there really were an object, from which I derive its description, but I were unable to shew it to anyone." Here, what is understood as the inability to show an object may well be an expression of the fact that there is nothing to show. Similarly, the impression that one is unable to do something may well express the fact that it is simply not feasible, that it is a "ghostly something," an insubstantial action—and that were one to attempt to perform it, one would be succumbing to the empty order to just *do*. In other words, just as "where language suggests a body, and there is none: there, we would like to say, is a *spirit*" (§36), so are there actions that no-body could enact.

Not to represent "the matter" as if it were something one could not do: Wittgenstein himself acknowledges that this is of "great

---

[8]"A picture held us captive. And we could not get outside it, for it lay in our language and language seemed to repeat it to us inexorably" (§115).

difficulty"—even *the* great difficulty. It was certainly a problem in the texts discussed in the previous chapters, formulated, we saw, as the difficulty to effect the *passage à l'acte*. We will now consider how the "captivating power of pictures" and the "imperative" model of the relationship between language (-games) and action is dramatized and explored in *Hamlet* and Beckett's *Waiting for Godot*. Then we will turn to Wittgenstein's own captivating picture of a language which, being made to "work," would be unable to paralyze its users with the enchanting repetition of "magical" figures.[9]

The pale cast of thought

Waiting for Godot is in many ways a parody of *Hamlet*, taking to the extreme its theme of inaction: Where Hamlet struggles throughout the play to finally accomplish what he has "promised" to do, Vladimir and Estragon are mainly concerned with finding something to do.[10] Beckett's treatment of Hamlet's problem is doubtless a successful effort to dedramatize through ridicule "the contemporary crisis of action," but it also analyzes the terms of the crisis, suggesting that it is the contemporaneity of action that is in itself "critical." Thus we will see that the logic that leads Vladimir and Estragon to endure the delay of being unable to set themselves to do something (which delay becomes the plot itself: waiting for Godot) is similar to, and even an extension of, that which makes Hamlet suffer from procrastination (which procrastination is also what makes *Hamlet*, the play). In *Waiting for Godot*, Hamlet's famous question, "To be, or not to be," becomes Vladimir's "What are we doing here. *That* is the question"; the former's fear of "losing the name of action" is radicalized in the latter's (and also Estragon's) fatalism: "Nothing to be done." Above all, in a typical

---

⁹Recall Faustus's enchantment with magic: "Lines, circles, letters, characters: Ay, these are those Faustus most desires" (I.i. 50–51).

¹⁰As such, it is also a parody of the model of action that would prevail among the public, which should recognize its own behaviour in Vladimir's and Estragon's—and laugh. But the laughter the play inspires is more self-conscious and critical than openly joyful.

twentieth-century move, *Waiting for Godot* features discourse (language, reason, and so on) as the organizing principle of inaction—its characters "waste [their] time in idle discourse" (they do not put language to work, as Wittgenstein would say).

For Hamlet discourse should be anything but idle—he is consequently perplexed at finding himself idling with it:

> Sure he that made us with such large discourse,
> Looking before and after, gave us not
> That capability and godlike reason
> To fust in us unused. Now, whether it be
> Bestial oblivion, or some craven scruple
> Of thinking too precisely on th'event—
> A thought which, quartered, hath but one part wisdom
> And ever three parts coward—I do not know
> Why yet I live to say, "this thing's to do,"
> Sith I have cause, and will, and strength, and means,
> To do't.
>
> (IV. iv. 32–46)

While arguing that discourse and reason are to be put to use—a notion we will consider later on in relation to Wittgenstein's *Philosophical Investigations*—Hamlet must acknowledge that his failure to act is due either to "bestial oblivion" or to discourse and reasoning themselves, the ultimate "tools" of action. The first possibility would imply, basically, that he is not a man, that he is not endowed with language and reason. The fact that he still lives to say "this thing's to do"—that is, that he can contemplate its doing, and name the thing to do—proves that he is a man, not subject to oblivion and capable of using both language and reason. It is thus the tools that are to be held responsible for Hamlet's inactivity, unless it be his being alive itself. And these are the issues under scrutiny in his famous "to be, or not to be" soliloquy.

The soliloquy is well known: Schematically, Hamlet contemplates death as an alternative to life, and concludes that it is the choice we would all make, were we not afraid of what happens after death. Then Hamlet concludes that it is thought's tendency to cast itself "after" which, in general, "makes cowards of us all," and frustrates "enterprises of great pitch and moment." Thus, whereas

above the capacity of discourse and reason to "look before and after" were signs that they were meant to be "used," here Hamlet
suggests that the selfsame capacity, particularly that of "looking
after," is to be blamed for "losing the name of action." These two
stances are not in contradiction, however, if we consider that, as it
can remain "unused," discourse can also be "misused"—which
turns out to be the case at a closer reading of this passage.

Hamlet's speech sounds so familiar that we tend to overlook
the surprising articulation of its argument. To begin with, his
opening question introduces a false option: "To be" is not an alternative to "not to be"; thus formulated the choice is unrealistic, and
the opposition asymmetrical. "To be," as we saw in the previous
chapter, is not a possibility in itself: One must be *something*, or
somewhere, or in a certain state. "To be" can not be in question; "to
be *what*?" and "to be *how*?" can be questions. To aspire to just "be"
is to aspire to the condition of absolute completion or finitude, not
just to being an end in oneself but also to being oneself the end. It
is thus that "not to be" appears as a desirable alternative to "to
be," as its "end":

> Whether 'tis nobler in the mind to suffer
> The slings and arrows of outrageous fortune,
> Or to take arms against a sea of troubles,
> And by opposing end them. To die, to sleep—
> No more; and by a sleep to say we end
> The heartache, and thousand natural shocks
> The flesh is heir to. 'Tis a consummation
> Devoutly to be wished—
> (III. i. 57–64)

Here the option "to be" is inevitably passive (insofar as the what's
and how's of being are evacuated) and consists in being the end
(the target) of events that the mind endures. The option that corresponds to "not to be" according to the symmetry announced by
the opening question of the soliloquy is, instead, a surprisingly active one, as it is here a question of "taking arms" against the ca-
lamities of life. This combativeness, however, is countered by the
figure of "a *sea* of troubles," as it is not only impossible to fight

against any sea but it is also impossible to envisage the end—resolution, conclusion, and grasp—of troubles that have been blown up to such a size.[11] Hence the shift from ending the sea of troubles to dying and sleeping: As "the mind" fails to conclude the figure of the sea, it turns its finalizing efforts toward itself—toward thinking the end of "to be." The apposition of "to die" and "to sleep," however, testifies to the mind's inability to think absolute temporal (and spatial) endings. Thought can deal only with the end *of* something, consequently an ending that refutes the possibility of an absolute counterpart *in* its particularity. Thought functions in a finite mode and can neither contemplate its own finitude nor finitude per se. In other words, from the moment finitude is posited, the notion of absolute end is excluded (we might say: completion is by definition not absolute).[12] What is perplexing is that we can still "*say* we end."

Thus Hamlet puts his remaining faith in the declaration of death, which emerges as the only definitive step to take: "a consummation / Devoutly to be wished—." Significantly, the wish for consummation becomes mandatory—to be wished—and it is "devoutly," in a devoted manner and therefore in the manner of one having vowed oneself to, that consummation is to be wished, hoped for, or expected. It is the word, then, that could achieve, by commandment, the completion "to be" requires, were it not itself cast forward with thought to "the undiscovered country" that "puzzles the will." Unfortunately the word is entangled in discourse, and looks before and after as reason does: It cannot make its own "quietus." Falling short of being the case limiting the course of discourse and thought, death cannot assume the function of limit-case of conclusive actions in general. It follows in Hamlet's argument that no actions requiring a minimal "casting" can be concluded:

[11]Indeed, to the individual mind the sea has only a "formal" ending (the horizon).

[12]We might also say: The infinite is not a "whole," it is not a perfected or more complete version of finitude.

> Thus conscience does make cowards of us all;
> And thus the native hue of resolution
> Is sicklied o'er with the pale cast of thought,
> And enterprises of great pitch and moment
> With this regard their currents turn awry
> And lose the name of action.
>
> (III. i. 83–87)

Hamlet manifestly believes that it is our capacity to think after that paralyses us, because we see no "end" to action. But here our failure to "see" the end should be related to the impossibility of putting an end to the figure of "a sea of troubles," which can be neither concluded "in the mind" nor fought by taking arms. Discourse is thus "misused," insofar as the deed it figures appears to be beyond the boundaries of performance (or of enactment) and loses "the name of action."

Hamlet's formulation of the dissolution of actions—be it their irresolution or the agent's failure to initiate them—is articulated by the term "cast," which links the registers of appearance (the agent's complexion) and of movement (action as a trajectory). The initial resolution is here presented as a physical state, an attitude manifested in and indissociable from the agent's healthy "native hue." Under the influence of thought, the agent, we gather, becomes pale (with fear). Thus to the agent's weakening resolution corresponds a physical weakening, an unfitness, that announces the disengagement of the body from action introduced by the second register, in which the term "cast" is operative. Indeed the "pale cast of thought" does not only interfere with the "native hue of resolution" but also affects the model of action as an "enterprise." The term "enterprise" anchors action firmly in the body (it is an under*taking*, a taking *in hand* of) and consequently in appearance. The term "cast," instead, disembodies action, positing action as a projectile thrown by the agent across the distance from its resolution as a project to its conclusion at the moment it reaches its "end." The process of realization thus takes place "in the air"; it is a crossing of the distance from abstraction to concretization that skips over the performance of the action. Consequently, what it skips is the doing, acting itself:

There remains nothing to be done. By attributing to discourse the magical power to "achieve" action before its enactment, enactment itself stops being a possibility, something that can be done or take place. Discourse thus obscures the courses of action and seems to impose the impossible leap from project to product.

Nothing to be done

In *Waiting for Godot*, Vladimir and Estragon find themselves caught regularly between Hamlet's nonoption of "to be, or not to be," as their repeated halfhearted attempts (they lack courage) to end their lives testify.[13] But death is not for them the most conclusive act; it is instead fully inscribed within their waiting as one among the many (im)possible occupations to *pass time*:

Vladimir *(Estragon looks attentively at the tree).* What do we do now?
Estragon Wait.
Vladimir Yes, but while waiting.
Estragon What about hanging ourselves? (p. 17)

As on other occasions, Vladimir and Estragon suffer from Hamlet's sense of the "pale cast of thought" and, "thinking too precisely on th'event"—they speculate that one of them might survive the other—they give up trying before they even start the preparations: "Let's not do anything. It's safer" (p. 18). Instead, they set out to just "wait" for Godot again, considering his arrival as the only chance of concluding anything: "Let's wait and see what he says." But they do not know what it is Godot might conclude; nowhere in the play are the reasons for their waiting specified.[14] The

---

[13]They not only contemplate the option of death but also that of sleep: Estragon constantly falls asleep and is returned from "the undiscovered country" by Vladimir, who wakes him up but refuses to listen to his dreams. Furthermore, as we will see, they both suffer from "bestial oblivion" as well as from idle discoursing.

[14]Thus to Estragon's question "What exactly did we ask him for?" they respond only with "Oh . . . nothing very definite," "A kind of prayer," "A vague supplication" (p. 18). In other words, to wait for Godot is, in Bakhtin's terms, Estragon's and Vladimir's alibi in Being, or, more to the point, it allows them to by-

reasons for Godot's absent presence, instead, are quite clear: He fulfills the function of the spectator from whose perspective Estragon and Vladimir are doing something, and for whom, consequently, there is a plot, meager as it may be. But in relation to themselves, by virtue of their waiting, Vladimir's and Estragon's doing becomes nothing. Indeed the play opens with what will be its leitmotif: "Nothing to be done."

Estragon says this as he struggles in vain to pull off his boot, a deed which, though falling short of a heroic conception of what action is (and there are definitely no Greek heroes in this play), still deserves to be called an act. In context, Estragon's words mean something like "there is nothing else I can try to do to take off my boots." Vladimir enters the stage at this point, and, ignoring the connection between Estragon's movements and his words, absolutizes his statement, thus setting the tone for the whole play:

> I'm beginning to come round to that opinion. All my life I've tried to put it from me, saying, Vladimir, be reasonable, you haven't yet tried everything. And I resumed the struggle. (*He broods, musing on the struggle.*) (p. 9)

What is lost in this gesture of abstraction is the object of the effort in question—in Estragon's case, pulling off his boot, in Vladimir's case, "everything," insofar as in his statement what counts is the trying and not what is being tried.[15] In the same stroke, the subject of the trying—Estragon—is done away with as well, substituted for in fact by Vladimir. Consequently, when Vladimir turns to Estragon to take notice of his (renewed) presence, the latter is—ironically, and most probably vindictively—uncertain of being "there":

> Vladimir   (. . . *Turning to Estragon.*) So there you are again.
> Estragon   Am I?
> Vladimir   I thought you were gone forever.
> Estragon   Me too.

---

pass the "ought" of their individual actions while functioning as a "proof" that they are "there" all the same.

[15]In Bakhtin's terms again, Vladimir is here aestheticizing himself (taking the attitude of the other toward himself).

Estragon's question emphasizes Vladimir's abstraction as "being there" becomes just "being," an abstraction further developed by their expressed belief that Estragon was gone forever: not to a definite place, but definitively.

Vladimir's initial disregard for Estragon's behavior echoes throughout the play—they will both prove unable to link word and deed again, a discursive failure apparent in their lack of memory: Estragon is regularly beat up but cannot tell whether by the "same" people or not; they come every night to the same place but are unsure it is the place they have come to the night before; they meet Pozzo and Lucky and either fail to recognize them or pretend they do not; they themselves are recognized by neither the Boy nor Pozzo and Lucky. . . . What is past seems (especially for Estragon) to be gone forever too. But this inability to "bind" time is not just a shortcoming of their discourse. It is in fact presented as an effect of it, and even more, its *doing*, in accordance with the use to which Estragon and Vladimir put it. Thus, asked by Vladimir what they did the evening before, Estragon answers that they "blathered"; asked about what, he remembers they "spent" the evening "blathering about nothing in particular" (p. 66). Here Vladimir and Estragon spend the evening talking, their blathering consumes, rather than passes, time, as it passes. It is not surprising, then, that "nothing in particular" should be left behind—or that in Estragon's and Vladimir's world there is, as the former puts it, "no lack of void" (ibid.).

In a soliloquy that conflates references to Hamlet's two soliloquies, Vladimir further demonstrates that discourse cannot only fail to "look behind" but can also close its eyes to "after." Vladimir and Estragon have been contemplating the possibility of helping Pozzo to get up, which Vladimir considers favorably:

Let us not waste time in idle discourse! (*Pause. Vehemently*). Let us do something, while we have the chance! It is not every day that we are needed. Not indeed that we personally are needed. Others would meet the case equally well, if not better. To all mankind they were addressed, those cries for help still ringing in our ears! But at this place, at this moment of time, all mankind is us, whether we like it or not. Let us make the most of it, before it is too late! Let us represent worthily for once the foul brood to which a cruel fate consigned us! What do you say? (*Estragon says nothing.*) It is true that when with folded arms we weigh the pros and cons we are no less a credit to our species. The tiger bounds to the help of his congeners without the least reflection, or else he slinks away into the depths of the thickets. But that is not the question. What are we doing here. *That* is the question. And we are blessed in this, that we happen to know the answer. Yes, in this immense confusion one thing alone is clear. We are waiting for Godot to come— (p. 80)

The length of Vladimir's speech is telling enough: Here discourse replaces or at least postpones action while it becomes "about" action, idling to the point of turning action itself idle, a waiting. In the process, the prospect of doing something (in the near future) vanishes, and becomes the question of what Vladimir and Estragon are doing here. The shift from prospection to inspection, as it were, is emphasized in the remainder of Vladimir's speech: "Or for night to fall. (*Pause.*) We have kept our appointment, and that's an end to that." Thus the future is absorbed in the "past present" of Estragon's and Vladimir's kept appointment, to which even Godot becomes irrelevant. Once again time is "consumed" before it passes—"a consummation devoutly to be wished."[16]

As it takes the place of action, discourse is asked to take the subject through the time "separating" a project and its embodied, concrete counterpart. It is asked to skip over the time that it takes to do things, and consequently their doing. To ask this of discourse is of course to ask too much of it, to attribute to it magic powers that could effect an immediate realization of a project, to make it "appear" at once from its formulation—for this only God's words (and not Godot's) can do. Thus discourse fails time and again to

[16]The kept appointment also functions in Vladimir's discourse as a gesture of definition (it's the end of the question) enclosing both him and Estragon within completion. We can almost imagine Estragon and Vladimir pointing at themselves as they answer the question "What are we doing here?" with "We are here"—becoming as it were the outcome of their "doing here," the finished product of an unspecified activity that no longer needs to be determined. Vladimir's discourse, in short, appoints him to inaction, ordering him with the invisible finger of abstraction to "just be there."

pull rabbits out of Vladimir's hat or Estragon's boots; it masters only the trick of making things *dis*appear:

> *Estragon* Why don't you help me?
> *Vladimir* Sometimes I feel it coming all the same. Then I go all queer. (*He takes off his hat, peers inside it, feels about inside it, shakes it, puts it on again.*) How shall I say? Relieved and at the same time . . . (*he searches for the word*) . . . appalled. (*With emphasis.*) AP-PALLED. (*He takes off his hat again, peers inside it.*) Funny. (*He knocks on the crown as though to dislodge a foreign body, peers into it again, puts it on again.*) Nothing to be done. (pp. 10–11)[17]

Here Estragon has already asked Vladimir for help, in vain—Vladimir is moved only to speak by his request. Consequently Estragon is forced to change registers, and ask, not for help, but a question about his call for help. The "reasons" that Vladimir invokes for his failure to react should hold our attention. His answer refers not only to Estragon's cry for help but also to their previous replicas, which inform us that Vladimir has a tendency to postpone urinating until "the last moment," and that they both missed a chance to commit suicide from the Eiffel Tower, long ago. Thus what Vladimir "feels coming" at times is the moment to urinate, the last moment of death, or the moment of the *passage à l'acte*—which, in the logic of his discourse, is the moment of the immediate passage from the realm of projects to that of realization. The only moment he seems to be able to "control," and this by making it last, is that of the realization of his bodily functions, which, by virtue of his postponing them, become in a sense "actions." As for death, it can only be anticipated, which requires the moment of the *passage à l'acte*: but this passing into action is neutralized in the anticipation of the concluded deed. Once the act is "accomplished," it cannot be done anymore, and it consequently "disappears" as an act that can be "named" and done. Vladimir expresses this fact as "Nothing to be done." And indeed, once he says this, Estragon manages to pull off his boot—and it is done.

[17]Recall how Hamlet's agents lose the name of action under the "pale cast of thought": Here Vladimir is AP-PALLED, etymologically, "pale," or "dismayed," and has already "abstracted" his body from action in the opening lines of the play.

Pozzo is the only character in the play to come close to being a magician, through the intermediary of his obedient Lucky, who, following his monosyllabic orders (much in the same way as Wittgenstein's characters play their primitive language games), hands over objects and effects gestures as if moved directly by Pozzo's words. Vladimir and Estragon, however, are no magicians.[18] Though they recur frequently to the imperative mode to attempt to initiate actions, they usually fail miserably, uncovering a wide gap between word and deed that they are incapable of fulfilling. The play closes with a common instance of it:

> *Vladimir* Well? Shall we go?
> *Estragon* Yes, let's go.
> *They do not move.*
> CURTAIN

It might have helped Vladimir and Estragon to be able to formulate where they would go, so as to know how to get there—that is, how to go about going. But from the very beginning of the play they lack the most basic savoir faire, they do not know how to behave:

> *Vladimir* Together again at last! We'll have to celebrate this. But how? (*He reflects.*) Get up till I embrace you.
> *Estragon* (*irritably.*) Not now, not now.

Here Vladimir knows what the word "celebration" means but does not immediately know what to do with it—he must reflect about what makes a celebration, what are the gestures, words, circumstances that would make us say, "They are celebrating." When he comes upon a way of celebrating—embracing—he still fails to understand how *they* can do it and prepares Estragon for its "magical" realization with the request that Estragon get up *till* he embraces him, instead of "in order that" he can embrace him. The formulation

---

[18]Except when it comes to pure being (p. 69):

> *Estragon* We always find something, eh Didi, to give us the impression we exist?
> *Vladimir* (*impatiently*) Yes yes, we're magicians . . .

suggests that Vladimir expects his act of embracing Estragon to "arrive" with the chariot of time—to happen "spontaneously," without his or Estragon's participation. As for Estragon, his reaction to Vladimir's appeal is coherent with their lack of savoir faire, although it is, to say the least, impolite: He misbehaves (and disobeys).

Their faith in orders—in the power of discourse to do things in their stead—also interferes with Estragon's and Vladimir's behavior retrospectively: They intervene upon each other every time a conversation or some kind of an "event" is taking place, to objectify their behavior and transform it into "something to do" (which should be done). Thus Estragon interrupts an exchange of insults with Vladimir to both name and prescribe it—"That's the idea, let's abuse each other" (p. 75)—and intervenes again in order to anticipate its formal conclusion—"Now let's make it up." This conversion of *is* into *ought* gives the illusion that they have forecast their behavior, as if it were a question not of ordinary (everyday, common, shared) interaction but of "enterprises of great pitch and moment." But the selfsame recasting of behavior into such enterprises subjects it to the "pale cast of thought," leaving Vladimir and Estragon with nothing in their hands, gesturing in the air. In the end there are no more stones to throw (p. 74):

> Estragon   . . . Tell me what to do.
> Vladimir   There's nothing to do.

As he replaces the formulation "nothing to be done" by "there's nothing to do" Vladimir is on the brink of acknowledging that "pure doing" is not possible and that his and Estragon's use of language has bound them to the "ghosts" of action, demanding to be "avenged" of their murder by abstraction. He is also confirming what the public, spectator of their "idleness," knew all along: that both he and Estragon have been performing their "nothing to be done," actively constructing the "nothing" and acting out the "to be done." Accordingly it is only at the end of the play, when there is indeed no more to perform, that it can be said that there is, truly, and in the present tense, "nothing to do." Until then Vladimir and Estragon counter-act the model of action they openly profess, for they cannot not act, nor not do *something*. But what they do, they think they do not do: And what they do not do, they think it is impossible to do. Their lives are thus completely chimerical, and they are themselves strangely quixotic characters with respect to the world as well as each other.[19] But the giants Don Quixote saw in windmills, Vladimir and Estragon see in action—and these may well be more difficult to dispel, because they can invade the "dispelling" itself.

Putting language to work

The feat of Nietzsche's figure in the fairy tale and Bakhtin's individual trying to pull himself up by the hair are both examples of actions "demanded" by the models that captivate language users. In the *Philosophical Investigations* examples of this kind abound, often accompanied by Wittgenstein's challenge to his staged interlocutor to actually perform the act he supposes must be performed. In the context of a "dialogue" on the act of meaning, for instance, Wittgenstein's reader or character is asked to mean "Scot" first as proper name and then as a common name, or to say cold and mean warm. This, of course, neither character nor reader can do, not because they are incapable of meaning in general—they (we) do it all the time—but because, conceived as a separate act, we would not know how to do it, or what it would be like to do it. In other words, insofar as the question "what does saying something and meaning another consist in?" cannot be answered, or imagined, there is nothing for us to do. The corollary to the difficulty of not "representing the matter as if there were something one *couldn't* do" is thus the difficulty of resisting the sense that one must do it (because a "captivating picture" presents the act in question as done, hence as a possibility, and "consequently" as something to do).

 Given Wittgenstein's constant efforts to dismantle the impossible tasks that language seems to impose on its users, it may come

---

[19]They are, in the image of the mythical couple of Don Quixote and Sancho Panza, the other of each other, mutually bound in interaction.

as a surprise that the characters of the *Philosophical Investigations* are very successful at obeying orders—witness for instance the protagonists of the first "primitive" language game (§2: at A's call "slab" B brings a slab, and so on). Their ease, however, is not due to the force of the orders they follow; they are not moved by them as Lucky is by Pozzo's commands. Against this understanding of orders (of prescription), Wittgenstein makes from the outset a distinction that he maintains and develops throughout the rest of the text, first formulated as a parody of St. Augustine's "picture of language."[20]

Now think of the following use of language: I send someone shopping. I give him a slip marked "five red apples." He takes the slip to the shopkeeper, who opens the drawer marked "apples"; then he looks up the word "red" in a table and finds a colour sample opposite it; then he says the series of cardinal numbers . . . up to the word "five" and for each number he takes an apple of the same colour as the sample out of the drawer.—It is in this and similar ways that one operates with words.—"But how does he know where and how he is to look up the word 'red' and what he is to do with the word 'five'?"—Well, I assume that he *acts* as I have described. Explanations come to an end somewhere. (§1)

There is, doubtless, a prescriptive moment in this "use" of language, the moment the "I" sends someone shopping (in his stead). The straightforward order, however, does not exhaust the operation with words. The "I" accompanies his order with instructions for the shopkeeper—a slip of paper—that do not tell him only what to give the go-between but also how to reassemble the desired merchandise. The order as prescription and the order as instruction could obviously have been delivered "together"—the "I" could have ordered his messenger to "go and buy five red apples."

---

[20]The picture is: "Every word has a meaning. This meaning is correlated with the word. It is the object for which the word stands"(§1). Wittgenstein's critique of such a metaphysical notion of language will not be directly discussed here. For a thorough discussion of it, and in particular of Wittgenstein's critique of "the body of meaning" and its correlated "body of rules," see Jacques Bouveresse, *La Force de la Règle*.

That they are clearly separated in this example expresses Wittgenstein's concern to distinguish between these two "orders" of orders, to emphasize the fact that they do not fulfill the same function, that they do not accomplish the same "work."

In addition to distinguishing between prescription and instruction, Wittgenstein roots the former in the latter in his notion of language-games ("language and the actions into which it is woven," §7): The rules of a game do not "cause" the players to play the game; rather, they "tell" the players what the game is as they tell them how to play it (how to do it).[21] The players know what game they are playing if they know how to play it: What the players do, *that* is the game, and what they do is how it is played. This emphasis on the actual playing of the game, moreover, does not confer a privileged status on the players' personal or "subjective" knowledge of the game (this attitude would easily lead to the belief in the players' "private" knowledge of the game), for the simple reason that games have rules—they *are* rules. The options of surplus or private knowledge are possible within the distinction "outside" and "inside" of the game, a distinction that is clearly at work in St. Augustine's "picture of language," as the term "picture" itself suggests. Indeed, in his account of how he learned language, St. Augustine is first an outsider, observing the adults speak and behave, seeming to enter the scene only once he has "trained [his] mouth to form [the] signs" he has come to understand through observation. This postulate of an external position allows him to suppose that one can know language before one actually speaks or writes it—thus St. Augustine first acquires a passive knowledge of his native language, and then it is sufficient for him to learn how to pronounce the words he already

[21]This approach to games and to action in general does not involve the aesthetic moment of surplus vision and knowledge to which Nietzsche appealed in his comments on the soldiers painted on the canvas. Indeed, Wittgenstein's language-games are not painted, although they do produce pictures—these, however, are not "detachable" from the game from which they issue; they are forms of instruction within the game, or part of the game. When these "pictures" are displaced from the "game" within which they serve a purpose, they take on the prescriptive "voice" discussed above.

knows to be immediately able to "use" it properly to express his already existing desires. But then the question arises, as with the *passage à l'acte*, of how he could effectively "enter" the scene.

The term "language-game" instead articulates different options: Either one knows how to play it or one does not know how to play (and is consequently unable to play *it*). Here the distinction outside / inside gives way to that of doing / not doing, participating (or being able to) or not. Thus Wittgenstein's shopkeeper is able to heed the order "five red apples" because he knows the particular language-game corresponding to his profession—he knows that it is an order, that someone wants to buy these items; he knows how to react to the words on the paper. More important, however, he is able to satisfy his customer because he can read the instructions in the command: "Five" is what he should count up to, "red" is the color for which he should find a sample, "apples" is the name he must look for among his drawers. Significantly, the shopkeeper does not need to know what the different words "mean," and he obviously does not imagine five red apples in his mind. In other words, he does not need to know in advance what it is that he will finally hand over the counter: He knows only how to proceed to satisfy his client. There is no "casting" involved in the process of materializing his order, no magical transition from project to realization, no already finished deed to translate from abstraction to concretization.

There are no instructions to read the instructions either: The "I" assumes the shopkeeper acts the way he does. Like the children of the tribe in §6, the shopkeeper has been "brought up to perform *these* actions, to use *these* words as [he does so], and to react in *this* way to the words of others." He has learned to speak and to behave at the same time, or, more precisely, knowing how to speak— what to do with words—is part of his behavior. The term behavior here is important, even though Wittgenstein does not use it himself systematically. It denotes a particular way of acting, a way defined in interaction and recognizable by others, a way moreover that permits such interaction. In this sense it bears a "family resemblance" to games as Wittgenstein uses the term. Behavior refers to the *how* of action rather than to its object, which is fully integrated in the formulation of the manner of its being acted upon. To talk about behavior instead of actions is to pay attention to the process of enactment, as a determined *parcours*, but by no means as predetermined one.[22] Thus, returning to our shopkeeper, it is significant that the "I" assumes he acts as described, suggesting that the shopkeeper could have behaved differently—that there is no necessary relationship between the order and his reaction to it. Orders do not, in short, prescribe, predict, or foreshadow the future: "In what sense does an order anticipate its execution? By ordering *just that* which later on is carried out?—But one would have to say 'which later on is carried out, or again is not carried out.' And that is to say nothing" (§461).

Recall Vladimir's tiger, who "bounds to the help of his congeners without the least reflection, or else . . . slinks away into the depths of the thickets" (p. 80). Vladimir opposes—or rather, apposes—the tiger's behavior to his own, proper to his species, that of weighing the pros and cons with folded arms. He concludes that "That is not the question" ("What are we doing here. *That* is the question"), but we are obviously not supposed to believe him, given his and Estragon's tendency to disaccord with their words. The tiger, in short, responds readily (he bounds) to the "call" for help, or hides away from presumably the same danger that would have required his intervention. But either way he reacts to the situation, responds to its characteristics and characteristically—his response is his behavior. Because he reacts without previous reflection, his decision-making is simply equivalent to what he does. He does not contemplate two possible courses of action and their probable outcomes to then choose between them. Simple as it sounds, and difficult as it is to understand, the tiger either bounds or slinks away—with this description his behavior is fully analyzed.

[22]Bakhtin's term for act, postupok, comes to our minds here: Recall that it means, literally, "the taking of a step," suggesting a procedure, a process, as well as a parcours.

Vladimir and his "congeners," instead, are capable of deliberation—because they are endowed with language and reason, or because that is just one of the things this particular species does.
While they deliberate, they are certainly responding to a situation,
and their response might even be apparent in their gestures:
Vladimir, for example, might look back and forth to the thickets,
and Pozzo scratch his head, and so on. But deliberation does not
replace the kind of response that the tiger has; it does not even
necessarily "prepare" it.[23] Ultimately, Vladimir would also, in the
tiger's place, either bound to help or slink away. And this kind of
description in fact applies to his own case: His considerations do
not alter the fact that he does not bound to help Pozzo, and consequently does not help Pozzo. Thus his and the tiger's behavior *can*
be compared; the asymmetry posited in Vladimir's apposition of
their respective behavior—one deliberates, the other either helps
or does not help and runs away—is misleading. Vladimir's "decision" is made as he deliberates, his choice is made before he can
project his response—he does not help Pozzo, until he does, and
deliberation is the way in which he does not help Pozzo.

Discourse, then, need not create a discontinuity between the tiger's and Vladimir's behavior, as the example of the shopkeeper
shows. That it does in *Waiting for Godot* can be explained by the
confusion (to use one of Wittgenstein's favorite terms) between the
two orders of orders: Whereas Vladimir waits for something to ensue from his words—for his acts to be "obedient"—the shopkeeper
makes use of the words on the slip of paper to interpret (perform)
his customer's order. Vladimir's attitude toward discourse dissoci-
ates language from action, whereas the shopkeeper's enacts their
continuity in behavior.[24] The latter may well not serve his customer

[23]Although it can, in the sense that Prometheus' providence prepares him for
what is to come, and fashions his response/reaction.

[24]It is important to note here that the kind of continuity between language
and action that there is in behavior is not one of correspondence: The shopkeeper's words do not describe his actions, and they do not prescribe them either (description and prescription as standard ways to understand the relationship between one's words and acts). If it were the former, we would have to

after all, as Wittgenstein points out, but whatever he does, he will not attempt to respond to his client's order with a full description of five red apples, or with a project for the obtaining of five red apples. And that he does what he does needs no further explanation than that he does it given his know-how of language. Hence Wittgenstein answers the voice demanding how the shopkeeper knows how to use language this way: that he acts as described—or not. Then he adds what has become a slogan for many Wittgensteinians: "Explanations come to an end somewhere."

The statement can certainly be read as an empirical observation: We simply have to stop speculating at some point, because we are only mortals, or because there are things beyond human knowledge. It also expresses, in its sheer violence, the arbitrariness of grammar and language. It is tantamount to the mother's response in Beckett's short story *The End* (p. 2377):

A small boy, stretching out his hands and looking up at the blue sky, asked his mother how such a thing was possible. Fuck off, she said.

But Wittgenstein's example suggests that his is more than a comment on the necessary violence of socialization. The objecting voice asked for explanations concerning the origin of the shopkeeper's behavior, or at least this can be one reading of the question "How does he know . . . what he is to do with the word 'five'?" A possible answer to this question would be to recount the story of the shopkeeper's mastery of the word "five" (the story of his learning its use). Another possible—but impossible—answer would attempt to situate the origins of the shopkeeper's knowledge of the use of the word in nature or language (depending on the "philosophical" orientation of the questioner), independently of the shopkeeper's actual use of it. The point that Wittgenstein seems to be making, however, is that explanations do not have to

---

imagine that what we say when we run, for example, would be a description of running; if it were the latter, Vladimir and Estragon would have no problem going when they announce they will. Moreover, in both cases we would have to assume that our words anticipate our acts, whereas, as is well known, they always come too late, after the event.

pertain to origins. If we take the present tense of the question "How does he know how to do this?" literally, then the answer can only be that "he knows how to do it"—he is doing it, and the way he does it is the way he knows how to do it. Here explanations do not just end, they end somewhere—in the shopkeeper's acts, in the present time.

With his emphasis on behavior Wittgenstein returns in a sense to a philosophy of ends that takes into account action as a process, and underlines the function of this accounting in either enabling or disabling action. This is apparent throughout his discussion of rules, in which he rejects the notion that rules predetermine actual behavior in favor of an understanding of rules as instructions to be applied (performed, interpreted). The first notion is closely linked to the understanding of orders as enacting beforehand what they order, "prophesying" themselves, as it were:

§187. "But I already knew, at the time when I gave the order, that he ought to write 1002 after 1000"—Certainly; and you can also say that you *meant* it then; only you should not let yourself be misled by the grammar of the words "know" and "mean." For you don't want to say that you thought of the step from 1000 to 1002 at that time—and even if you did think of this step, still you did not think of other ones. When you said "I already knew at the time" that meant something like: "If I had then been asked what numbers should be written after 1000, I should have replied '1002'." And that I don't doubt. This assumption is rather of the same kind as: "If he had fallen into the water, I should have jumped in after him."—Now what was wrong with your idea?

Before I quote the answer to this question, let me consider briefly Wittgenstein's treatment of the two ways of "knowing already." As he himself points out, there is no inherent problem with the expression; the formulation is correct and "usable." But he is discussing the belief that understanding, meaning, and knowing are something that happens all at once, a belief that he obviously attributes to his interlocutor. In order to dismantle this belief, Wittgenstein first takes the sentence literally: Did the speaker, when he uttered his order, have the whole series in mind at once? Did he think of all the steps, without taking the time to think them? The answer being no, Wittgenstein has shown that there is no "literal" justification for the belief in the all-at-onceness of thought, understanding, orders, and so on, and suggests instead that "knowing already" is akin to "doing it when the occasion arises." In other words, the adverb "already" does not indicate that the speaker has completed the series in his mind and that the full "unfolded" series exists in an aspatial and atemporal realm, but rather that the speaker knows how to operate with the rule in question and is consequently confident that he would do it or would have done it if . . .

The conditional here neutralizes the futuristic impulses of the past tense:

§188. Your idea was that the act of meaning the order had in its own way already traversed all those steps: that when you meant it your mind as it were flew ahead and took all the steps before you physically arrived at this or that one.

Thus you were inclined to use such expressions as: "The steps are *really* already taken, even before I take them in writing or orally or in thought." And it seemed as if they were in some *unique* way pre-determined, anticipated—as only the act of meaning can anticipate reality.

Hamlet had already denounced the consequences of this idea in his condemnation of "the pale cast of thought." In this example, Wittgenstein locates the casting in the act of meaning, but the principle allowing the image of the casting is also at work in the image of *doing* as having no volume of experience, as "an extensionless point, the point of a needle" §620. "This point," Wittgenstein continues, "seems to be the real agent. And the phenomenal happenings only to be consequences of this acting. 'I *do* . . .' seems to have a definite sense, separate from all experience" (§620).[25] Here the doing and the something done seem to be causally related by an

---

[25]Wittgenstein makes a similar point about the will: "One imagines the willing subject here as something without any mass (without any inertia); as a motor which has no inertia in itself to overcome. And so it is only the mover, not moved. That is: One can say 'I will, but my body does not obey me'—but not: 'My will does not obey me.' (St. Augustine.) But in the sense in which I cannot fail to will, I cannot try to will either" (§618).

"act of completion" that takes place in the pure doing itself, before, however, the something even begins to be done. Thus doing is reduced to performativity; it becomes a speech act—"I *do*"—that, as an act of predetermination, will either succumb to or overcome the passing of time and the test of incarnation.

The problem, as Jacques Bouveresse suggests in his conclusion to *La Force de la Règle*, is that we often fail to distinguish between the temporality of a model or a proposition and that of actions, facts, and experience. Thus, he argues, "We are not to think a timeless (*intemporel*) fact, but rather to understand how a proposition can be used in a timeless manner, and not as a proposition of what Wittgenstein calls 'natural history'" (p. 174). Similarly, and to understand how a proposition can be used atemporally, we should also understand how a proposition, and discourse in general (or language-games), are used in a temporal manner. For Wittgenstein this implies the realization that discourse is figurative, although he does not, given his background, use this term himself. He does, instead, remind us constantly that discourse draws pictures for us, or that we construct images with it. Wittgenstein is not the only one to have noticed this, of course—the figure of Nietzsche is the first to come to mind when the figural, and more specifically, metaphorical nature of language is evoked. But whereas Nietzsche was still denouncing this fact, Wittgenstein recalls it in order to remind us that the figures we invoke work for us. Furthermore, they work against us if we do not put them to use as figures:

§426. A picture is conjured up which seems to fix the sense *unambiguously*. The actual use, compared with that suggested by the picture, seems like something muddied. Here again we get the same thing as in set theory: the form of the expression we use seems to have been designed for a god, who knows what we cannot know; he sees the whole of each of those infinite series and he sees into human consciousness. For us, of course, these forms of expression are like pontificals which we may put on, but cannot do much with, since we lack the effective power that would give these vestments meaning and purpose.

As Bouveresse remarks, Wittgenstein is here pointing out that we use images to represent the simultaneous co-presence of the ulterior usages of the meaning that we understand—of propositions, of rules. But these images are of no use to us, because they presuppose a "user" capable of seeing through time all at once (a super-agent)—a user, moreover, who would have access to precisely that to which we, as humans, do not have access. In other words, only a god, in possession of the surplus vision and knowledge that eternity grants, would be capable of making those images function.

Pictures—and figurative language understood as pictorial—induce us into this kind of dead end if we let ourselves be taken in by their apparent atemporality—that is, if we consider them as static because we are under the impression that they can be seen all at once. This is of course true, if we compare seeing pictures with watching a long train pass. But we neglect in this belief the fact that pictures can be inspected from close up and from far away, and that not only will not the same things be noticed in both instances but that in addition we certainly cannot see them from both positions at once.[26] We also neglect the fact that seeing is an activity organized through time—seeing itself, in short, takes time, as does the actual production of pictures, which are not made all at once. Hence Wittgenstein opposes the perspective of a "straight highway" that expressions offer us to the "sideroads" we actually take in using them: "In the actual use of expressions we make detours, we go by sideroads. We see the straight highway before us, but of course we cannot use it, because it is permanently closed." The figure of the road is significant here: It emphasizes that we take courses of action, that we behave in certain ways, and that both courses and ways have to be trod, and traced—"with a particular end in view" (§132). Forms of expression present us with the prospect of a highway, leading directly to the end in view (and

[26]Compare to Wittgentein's comments on analysed and unanalysed sentences: "We think: If you have only the unanalysed form you miss the analysis; but if you know the analysed form that gives you everything.—But can I not say that an aspect of the matter is lost on you in the latter case as well as the former?" (§63).

hence often identifiable with the end in view), but this highway is not open to use. Although we need to have the end in view to find the detours leading to "it," to make our way, the prospected end will not coincide with the attained end.[27] Hence forms of expression "guide" our actions if we use them to trace the detours and courses leading to a particular end, but block our way to it if we attempt to take the "closed highway" of their apparent all-at-onceness. Thus we can make pictures, images, and rules "work" for us only if we follow their in-directions, which requires that we dismantle their apparent all-at-onceness and unfold them in time.[28] Such a dismantling requires further figuration—in the *Philosophical Investigations* it is never a question of reaching the literal level of discourse to relate directly to action. On the contrary, it is when we take images literally—such as the expression "Now I know!" understood as "I grasped it (all) in a moment" (§151)—that we lose sight of action and can be at a loss as to how we behave.

Let us consider an example similar to that of §187, the example of the expression "Now I know! / Now I can go on!" which B utters when he succeeds in finding a law for the sequence of numbers A is writing down. The idea that Wittgenstein works to dispel is that B's understanding "makes its appearance in a moment," which suggests that understanding is a mental process, accompanied by a certain behavior, and that it is "felt" as a particular experience. His procedure is double: On the one hand he develops the expression literally until it reaches its dead end; on the other hand he devel-

[27]Here Wittgenstein is very Aristotelian. Recall that for Aristotle it was "desirable" to have knowledge of the good in order to better "aim" our actions—the image he used was that of a target, which could not be attained directly (for the good does not "exist," it is not a particular entity), but without which we could not be "archers." Similarly, the "end" that expressions formulate cannot itself be attained, but it allows for the "aiming" that will lead to the particular target.

[28]The image of the closed highway of forms of expression could be developed thus: Forms of expression fulfil the function of orientating our courses of action, as the sun will guide our course through a desert. The sun "directs" our course in that it tells us where we are with respect to where we want to go; it is not the place where we want to go, and it does not trace a straight line from where we are to our destination (indeed both we and the sun move all the time).

ops the figure of the expression into behavior—how we behave with this figure, how the figure behaves (figures). Hence the notion that understanding is a particular experience can be treated in the same way as Wittgenstein responds to the notion that "being guided" is a particular experience: "The answer to this is: you are now *thinking* about a particular experience of being guided" (§173). And indeed when Wittgenstein considers what it might be like to "know it now," he does so with particular examples (§151):

A has written down the numbers 1, 5, 11, 19, 29; at this point B says he knows how to go on. What happened here? Various things may have happened; for example, while A was slowly putting one number after another, B was occupied with trying various algebraic formulae on the numbers which had been written down. After A had written the number 19 B tried the formula $a_n = n^2 + n - 1$; and the next number confirmed his hypothesis.

Or again, B does not think of formulae. He watches A writing his numbers down with a certain feeling of tension, and all sorts of vague thoughts go through his head. Finally he asks himself: "What is the series of differences?" He finds the series 4, 6, 8, 10 and says: Now I can go on.

The rest of the example suggests other possibilities for B to have understood. All of them have in common the fact that B tries to understand, and consequently does a number of things (like calculating silently) to come to the realization that the series goes on like this. In this sense B can go on when he sees how to go on—when he has envisaged a way of doing it. The "Now" of his expression, however, does not refer to the moment of sudden understanding (to his grasping the series all at once), but to his readiness to continue the series, regardless of whether he continues it right or wrong: "*Now* I can *go on*," and I will do it, or not (not: I have just acquired miraculously the potential to go on, and this I have, regardless of whether I do go on or not).[29]

The problem of the "now" in the above example is taken up

[29]"Or he says nothing at all and just continues the series": Would this be more problematic than his saying, right before he continues it, that he can now do it?

again in Part II, ii, of the *Investigations*, where it is formulated, on the one hand, as the difficulty of grasping the relation of the use of a word at a given moment to its "general" usage, and on the other, to the similar difficulty of understanding the relation between a given moment in a course of action and the course of action (through time):

> In saying "When I heard this word, it meant . . . to me" one refers to a *point of time* and to a *way of using the word*. (Of course, it is this combination we fail to grasp).
>   And the expression "I was then going to say . . . " refers to a *point of time* and to an *action*. (p. 175)

From the temporal stance of the speaker of these two exemplary sentences, the meaning of the word and the action in question are already accomplished. This suggests that it is once more the "picture" of a full-blown usage independent of actual use, and of a completed action before enactment that blocks our understanding. What it blocks our understanding of is the "now" of action (or behavior), which appears as either preceding or announcing action. Hence the speaker's articulation of the relation between his hearing and his understanding in two stages—when I heard it, it meant—and his isolation of a moment previous to his saying that anticipates it—I was *then, going* to. In both cases the "now" of understanding and saying is formulated as a gap or a pause in the *durée* (continuance) of the activity, in which nothing happens (the speaker does nothing between hearing and understanding, and between "then" and "saying"). The question thus seems to be: How can I know now what something means, or what I am saying? This, Wittgenstein tells us, we fail to grasp: He does not suggest, however, that we should grasp it, or even that it can be grasped. Instead he insists throughout the *Investigations* that we do understand as we hear, and "say" numerous things as well. In other words, we do fine without grasping the combination of a point of time and an action, which suggests that grasping this combination does not fulfill a function in our acting, that "knowing now what I am doing," or "knowing now that I will have done it," are, if not irrelevant to what I do, at least not what make me do it. I know, for example, how I will move my arm, because it is a voluntary movement, and as Wittgenstein points out in §629, voluntary movements are "predictable." But if I know that I will so move my arm, it is not because I "see" the movement ahead in time, but because I will move it—or not.[30]

Let us return to Hamlet once again. In the soliloquy in which he wonders at his misuse of discourse and reason, he remarks: "Examples gross as earth exhort me" (IV. iv. 46). He is thinking of Fortinbras, of course, who is capable of "stirring without great argument," whereas Hamlet himself, who has numerous reasons to stir (he lists them) as well as reason and discourse to do so, does not budge. This opposition obviously suggests that Fortinbras stirs because he has no great argument, while Hamlet remains inactive under the weight of too many reasons / too much reason. We have already seen in what sense this can be said of Hamlet—as for Fortinbras, it is crucial to his exemplarity that his reasons do not account fully for his actions, that they fail to "measure" them. Questioned closely, Fortinbras may have answered like the "I" in §211 of the *Investigations*:

How can he *know* how he is to continue a pattern by himself—whatever instructions you give him?—Well, how do I know?—If that means, "Have I reasons?" the answer is: my reasons will soon give out. And then I shall act, without reasons.

Though in this example it is a question, once again, of following a rule (and of how one avails oneself of the instructions to read the instructions, and so on), the statement of the finality of action with regard to the reasons that should lie at its origin applies to Fortinbras's case. The assimilation of the third person of whom the question is asked—"How can he know?"—with the first person answering in its stead is significant in itself, as it posits a similar "relationship" between my view of someone else's acts and my

---

[30]Taking up the terms of previous chapters, foresight does not "harness" actions, it is not its "ought": Rather it is because I can do something that I am subject to the ought of actions, and not because I anticipate what I will do.

view of mine. I do not know how the other knows how to do it, but I can certainly see that he knows how to do it. Similarly, in my own case I am bound to fail to find an explanation that can account fully for what I do, that can "measure" or "match" my acts, beyond the statement "this is how I do it—this I what I do." Reasons do not account for my acts if what I understand by reasons is an absolute origin that would predetermine them, or an "original" model, in the form of a projection, that I would copy as if with carbon paper. If I am looking for a determination of my acts, then it is in my acts themselves—in my acting—that I will find it. And that is "where" my reasons ultimately reside.

Wittgenstein's laconic "my reasons will soon give out. And then I shall act without reasons" thus implies, not only that reasons are sometimes dispensable, but also that they are not (pre-) determinant when it comes to acting. To think of our acts as behavior clarifies this point, for in the notion of behavior projects, justifications, foreknowledge, and reasons are not at stake. Behavior denotes a manner of doing something, which could be different, but is not, because we can act only in a certain way, which certainty does not derive from knowledge but from specificity.[31] The certainty of acts is thus neither a priori nor a posteriori, and even provides the ethical grounds—the justification—that Nietzsche and Bakhtin denied to Kant's ethics. Consider in this respect Wlad Godzich's reading of Bakhtin's understanding of a properly ethical act:

When we are faced with a given situation for which we do not have a predetermined theory, we do not then surrender to the resulting aporia or proclaim undecidability but act. In fact, [Bakhtin] insists, the proper meaning of an ethical act is one that is undertaken when the understanding is no longer a guide to our behaviour, and the act that we then perform . . . restores cognitive possibility. This act that takes place at the

[31]In other words, behaviour is defined as much by circumstance as by the models—not ideals—of which we avail ourselves to guide our acts. These models, moreover, are only predetermined in the sense that they are "shared," in common, and even constitute the conditions of commonality of a community—they indicate how to play (social) games.

extreme end of the faculty of the understanding's cognitive ability, then extends the boundaries of the understanding, since it creates a practical sphere, that is, a sphere resulting from human actions that is analogous to the sphere of nature upon which the understanding has been exercising its theoretic watchfulness and effecting its differentiations.[32]

Even though neither Bakhtin's nor Godzich's terminology is in tune with Wittgenstein's, this passage accords substantially with the views developed in the *Investigations*—witness for example Wittgenstein's reference to our behavior as "facts of our natural history," and his regular insistence on the role of examples in teaching and learning, as well as his constant use of them in his arguments.[33] The main point of agreement between all three authors is that acts can have epistemological import, a point that Wittgenstein seems to formulate more forcefully. Indeed in the *Philosophical Investigations* reason always gives out to behavior and acts. We find a representative instance of this repeated surrender of reason to action in Wittgenstein's discussion of rules: Even when one knows how to follow a rule, one does not know how one knows how to follow a rule—one knows in the fact that one knows how to follow it. In this sense for Wittgenstein all our acts would be "properly ethical acts" because they all create a practical sphere, but this sphere is created and consequently "new" only insofar as every instance of use of a rule, for example, is new.[34] Furthermore, as we have seen, Wittgenstein refuses to treat understanding independently from behavior—hence there is, properly speaking, no "when" for him in which under-

[32]Wlad Godzich, "Correcting Kant: Bakhtin and Intercultural Interactions," p. 11. The literary texts I have discussed could be said to stage precisely the surrender to aporia and undecidability that results, theoretically, from the concept of understanding, and which confines it to representation.

[33]In fact he argues through examples rather than illustrating (the utilitarian understanding of "use") his points with them.

[34]Godzich discusses Bakhtin's ethical acts through the example of a European who meets for the first time a or several non-Europeans—"the encounter with an Otherness that could be brought under the control of his or her representational powers" (p. 10). In the *Philosophical Investigations*, otherness does not reside in the other but in the next moment (and, of course, to use language is to interact with the other's otherness).

standing would "guide" our behavior, beyond the time of our be-having.[35]

Let us return one last time to Fortinbras's behavior: It is exemplary in that it shows an enterprise in the making and consequently anchors reason and discourse in particular acts—in this sense, his acts have "epistemological import." Fortinbras's insufficient justification for his acts highlights them in the eyes of Hamlet as a process, suggesting that there is a way of using reason and discourse that does not just look before and after actions but that looks behind and after in action—I do not stop before each step I take in order to think about the step I will take next; I do however look ahead to avoid puddles, and maybe look behind to check I am on the right way. Thus Fortinbras's example exhorts—it is not an order—Hamlet in that it shows him that there is a way to act, this is it, and he can follow it—not copy it—if he follows it.

But should he?

Fortinbras's thoughtless bound could almost conclude this book, were it not conducive to such a questionable deed. Insofar as his "exemplary" behavior implies a war—a war, moreover, for "a little patch of ground / That hath in it no profit but the name" (IV. iv. 18–19). The more "traditional" ethical and political question of whether Fortinbras's is in fact a "good" example cannot be easily avoided. Is his act right, just, politically sound? Is it reprehensible? Should he have done it, whether for a patch of land or more? We may of course apply Wittgenstein's observations on rules to his "thoughtless" decision to go to war: had he "good" reasons to fight the Poles, they would give out too, as would, ultimately, his reasons not to fight them. Wittgenstein's reasons, however, pertain to the manner of following a rule, and not to the motivation to follow a rule, or to the rule one follows (instead of another rule). Once it is established that it is, logically speaking, not only possible but also inevitable to act—

[35]For Bouveresse this means that philosophers should be ready to discover at every moment that reality behaves in a way corresponding to the very way they refused to contemplate by sheer lack of imagination (my paraphrase, p. 150).

that we are bound to act—the issue of the evaluation of our actions, whether individual or collective, remains open to discussion.

I do not address this issue here, not only because it would exceed the original scope of the book but also because an abstract discussion of "ethics" or "politics"—that is, abstracted from a specific context, and about abstract actions—risks being inconsequential or going the prescriptive way of Kant's considerations on "how to act." It seems to me crucial, however, to keep open the possibility of discussing the questions raised by Fortinbras's decision to go to war, because asking these questions and attempting to act according to the criteria that sustains them is in itself a response to the question of "why to act." Is it worth it? Do our acts count? Are they to any avail? Can they have consequences, and if not, why bother even thinking about them? In other words, it does not suffice to say that we cannot not act; it still seems necessary to have some kind of motivation to qualify our acts. And it seems necessary, to keep any motivation alive, to believe that our acts will have some effects, that there is *something* to do.

7 ⌒ After Wars

Acts of war

The paralyzing models of action under scrutiny in previous chapters do not, to be sure, prevent us from taking off our boots—this even Estragon could achieve, affected as he was by the giants of action. It is in the realm of the political, as I anticipated in the introduction, that they are most pervasive and most difficult to disprove with the sheer evidence of a successful enterprise: In this realm, it seems, there really is "nothing to be done." To the "crisis of contemporary action" corresponds, inevitably, a crisis of political action, as much an effect of a concrete historical situation as of the models with which it and politics in general are understood. One of the models that is very clearly in "crisis" is the traditional understanding of politics as being fundamentally oppositional, and of political action as being fundamentally confrontational. In this "traditional" model, war—and, more generally, armed struggles—constitute not only the last resort of political action but also the actual grounds for it, according to the logic that what is last is what remains, unconditionally, after other (mere) possibilities are exhausted.[1] Although this seems to be an outdated view of politics, it will become apparent throughout the discussion of Jean Bau-

---

[1] See, for example, Clausewitz's "formula," as quoted in Baudrillard's text (*La Guerre du Golfe n'a pas eu lieu*, p. 21), that "war is politics pursued by other means."

drillard's and Jean-François Lyotard's analysis of the 1990–91 Gulf conflict that wars are still widely understood as something like "naked" political action, as politics at its extreme.

Such a view is in accordance with the status of wars and combats as paradigmatic scenes of action implicit in many of the texts discussed in previous chapters. When the chorus announces the shift from deed as act to deed as compact in the Prologue to *Doctor Faustus*, the first example it gives of the kind of action the audience should not expect is war, in the specific guise of a combat:

> Not marching in the fields of Trasimene
> Where Mars did mate the warlike Carthagens . . .
> Intends our muse to vaunt his heavenly verse.[2]

The combat between the two kings is again the exemplary deed as act in *Hamlet*, contained from the outset, however successfully, by the "sealed compact" stipulating its definitive closure; Fortinbras's war against the Poles is the example "exhorting" Hamlet to effect the *passage à l'acte* of revenge. War is also the "state" that individuals rule out when they agree to give up their right to self-defense and join a civil society as performative subjects in Locke's *Two Treatises of Government*; war against the Philistines is what Milton's Samson strives to continue without abandoning his newly acquired performative status; it is what Shelley's Prometheus, having liberated himself from the chains of performativity, contemplates from the atemporal and intersubjective realm of his "cave." It is with a scene of war, again, that Nietzsche "disproves" Kant's transcendental subject—recall the soldiers painted on a canvas, who cannot look at themselves. In other words, wars and combats seem to be paradigmatic of what action is at its "most" active and interactive.

It is clear, however, that the act of combat cannot be considered as paradigmatic in the same sense that the act of contemplation

---

[2]The next examples are "sporting in the dalliance of love," politics ("courts of kings where state is o'erturned") and "proud audacious deeds." All these examples are related in one way or another to the first, war: Hence the term "mate" suggests a kinship between war and love in the second line, whereas the court is the proper stage of love, both of which are "o'erturn'd" with the state.

was paradigmatic in Aristotle's *Nicomachean Ethics*. In fact "fighting" and contemplating seem to be hardly comparable acts, if only because combat, in Aristotle's terms, is by definition directed toward the achievement of an aim other than the activity of combat itself. What makes contemplation a paradigm of whole actions, its self-sufficiency, does not seem to apply to combat. There is, however, a similar temporal structure in both acts: namely their concentration, as events, in the (present) moment. A combat, one could say, is "whole" at all moments of its duration, at least according to the model of a combat as an agonistic confrontation. It may not be over, but it is never "incomplete" or lacking in something, as a combat. Thus the scene of a combat shares, with the scene of contemplation, the paradigmatic quality of temporal wholeness, of an all-enclosing here and now.

What cancels out the "lack" that the end-directed nature of combat should produce is the unpredictability of the expected outcome. In the confrontational setup of a combat, the other constitutes an element of uncertainty that confers cognitive value on the acts of both parties. As we saw at the end of the previous chapter, in situations in which what will happen cannot be anticipated or be made to conform to a "predetermined theory," and in which the understanding is "blocked," acts take over reason and open the field of cognition.[3] Similarly, in the confrontational situation of a combat, acts constitute the only field of certainty: The tiger bounds, or not, but does it *certainly* in either case. Hence the other paradigmatic quality of the act of combat resides in its collapsing of reason and action—deliberation, decision, and action are all one,

---

[3] See pp. 217–19. It is worth noting that the example Godzich gives of a situation in which the understanding is "blocked" and can no longer "guide" our behavior is that of the first encounter between a European and a non-European. Confronted by the other's irreducible alterity, which has not yet been made to conform to preexisting concepts, and which excludes any preexisting commonality from which the imagination could create a concept to comprehend it, the European, Godzich argues, eventually has to act—and it will be on the (cognitive) ground opened by this act that a commonality will be created or imposed. This "opening" act may well be, as has too often been the case, a combat.

an act. In this sense, once the combat has begun, the *passage à l'acte* is not an issue. And beginnings are not a problem for wars, because they are characteristically triggered by an act that cannot be categorically attributed to a single subject, and that is, moreover, usually attributed to the other "side." Indeed, a common situation in the staging of confrontations, whether of war or mere fights, is a moment in which the adversaries accuse each other of having "begun" the affair. Thus the problematic moment of the *passage à l'acte* is avoided, as it is always the other, from the perspective of the combating subjects, who has motivated its necessity.

The paradigmatic aspects of wars and combats that justify their status as action par excellence can all, finally, be formulated in terms of their confrontational structure: Confrontations define a "complete" here and now, within which stage deliberation, decision, and action collapse in each single act and moment, while the necessary interaction that confrontations imply does not allow the question of an impossible *passage à l'acte* to be raised. It should be kept in mind, however, that if war can be understood as a best case of action, it is with respect to the models of "impossible" action discussed in previous chapters.[4] Indeed, for Aristotle contemplation was a paradigmatic act in contrast to those acts done for the sake of something else (and hence, incomplete); similarly, war acquires paradigmatic value because, as opposed to the threat of inaction, it appears as an action already in course, which course is ensured in an "immediate" interaction that short-circuits anticipatory and procrastinating moves. There is, of course, the time and the space in a combat for the kind of anticipation required by strategy, but it is an anticipation that remains within the time of the combat. Thus what is (theoretically) preserved in the confrontational setup of wars and combats is, ultimately, a stage of action—a place and time for action to happen—as opposed to the *non-lieu* in which the performative (and the transcendental) subject's actions had to take place, or the timelessness of

[4]And also with respect to the "lonely" subject, retrieved from interaction, for the confrontational nature of combat can become a paradigm of interaction when other models of interaction are either lacking or lacking social force.

the models of action that Wittgenstein discusses in the *Philosophical Investigations*. In the context of this contrast, if the stage of war founders, as is the case in Baudrillard's account of the Gulf War, the stage for political action follows its collapse.

Staged wars, stageless politics

The three essays published as *The Gulf War Did Not Take Place (La Guerre du Golfe n'a pas eu lieu)* are all variations of the theme of a play by Jean Giraudoux, *The Trojan War Will Not Take Place*, written after and as a commentary on the vacuity and insensateness of World War I.[5] In Giraudoux's play, Hector, Andromach, and other Trojan women attempt to prevent the Trojan War, and in effect succeed in dismantling all the reasons for the war to take place.[6] But in the last scene, the Trojan poet Demokos, who defends the ideal of war, lies about his own death, attributing it to the Greek messenger, who is then killed by the Trojans. The conditions for the war are thus set with the poet's lie, and the play ends as Hector announces that the war will take place. This announced war, however, recalls the unidentified war from which Hector returns at the beginning of the play, of which he says that it "sounded fake":

Before those I was going to kill seemed to me the opposite of myself. This time I was kneeling on a mirror. This life I was going to take was a small suicide (*Cette mort que j'allais donner, c'était un petit suicide*). . . . I continued. But of this minute nothing remained of the perfect resonance. The spear that slid over my shield suddenly sounded fake, and the impact of the dead against the ground, and, some hours later, the collapse of palaces. . . . The cries of the dying sounded fake. . . . That's where I stand (*J'en suis là*). (I. iii. p. 23)

[5]Baudrillard's essays are entitled in French "La guerre du Golfe n'aura pas lieu"; "La guerre du Golfe a-t-elle vraiment lieu?"; "La guerre du Golfe n'as pas eu lieu." As for Jean Giraudoux's play, the original title is *La Guerre de Troie n'aura pas lieu.*

[6]Helen is ready to go back to Melenaus; Paris agrees to let her go; Ulysses agrees to take her back to Melenaus and to convince the latter that there has been no violation of her body/his territory; and Busiris, the jurist, agrees to interpret international law in favor of peace instead of war between Greeks and Trojans.

As the confrontational structure of the war collapses for Hector into identification, the war loses its genuineness, to the point that it takes on the character, according to his description, of a poorly performed play—even the screams of the dying sound "fake," as do the screams on a stage, when they are badly faked. When this happens, the audience is reminded that what is being performed on stage has been predetermined—written—and the immediacy of the perform-ance fails to appear as the immediacy of what is being performed. Instead, the nonimmediacy of what is being performed intrudes in the immediacy of the performance, so that the latter appears as "already done." Thus, in Hector's war, the "perfect resonance" be-tween what happens and its happening is disrupted, as if the course of events had been decided in advance, and as if, consequently, the war were being badly played by unconvinced actors, instead of taking place.

The Trojan war-to-be in Giraudoux's play shares with its prec-edent the same character of predetermination, as if it were the plot to which its characters' plotting is subject. First of all, confrontation fails to set between the "enemies." The Trojans are ready to fight for Helen's face, and to give the war her face, but hers is not the face they will fight against. Ulysses himself, from the offended party, confesses himself to be no enemy. There is, in short, no stake to oppose the parties. It is, however, this selfsame lack of involve-ment in the war-to-be, the lack of reasons and of a confrontational setup, that ultimately puts the war out of its participants' hands.[7] The war, Ulysses argues, is not for him and Hector to decree or impede; they can only try to elude it by outwitting Fate. Thus the war somehow appears, before it even starts, as already played out—and remains, accordingly, only announced in Giraudoux's play. Cassandra tells us that the Greek poets will give its account—

[7]Helen explains to Hector that she is not unwilling to go back to Greece, but she does not see the ship that should take her back: Non-war simply does not appear as a possible event in her eyes. Similarly, Ulysses tells Hector that he is not unwilling to avoid the war, but that the situation is set for it to happen—among other things, Troy is rich, and the Greeks feel cramped (à l'étroit) on their rocky island.

an account which, needless to say, is now bound to sound "fake" as the "perfect resonance" of the war is shaken by the revelation of its fragile foundations (no inimical confrontation, no reasons to fight, no stakes in the fighting). The taking place of the Trojan War thus appears to be doubly "faked": On the one hand it seems to have already taken place, and on the other, it seems like a farce—it promises to be an unconvincing performance of a war.

Baudrillard's essays, which discuss the Gulf War respectively before, during, and after its "advent," basically take up Giraudoux's war scenario, developing the non sequitur of the closing announcement of the Trojan War as well as the "fakeness" of its sounds. The audience is under siege before the television screens, waiting for the announced war to finally take place. But the war, as a concept and as an event, Baudrillard argues, is in a crisis, and the different powers involved in this war are in fact striving to save it: Like Demokos, the Trojan poet, who improvises lines on Helen to give the war a semblance (a face), the media give this war a face in the hostages. With a certain nostalgia, Baudrillard denounces this "hostage" war as the symbol of a "weak war," a "degenerate" war in which representation replaces confrontation; where there are no warriors, only inactive hostages; where the *passage à l'acte* emerges as an impossibility, submerged in the sheer virtuality of the announced, commented on, and anticipated, war (pp. 11–12).

Even in the two essays written "during" and "after" the war, Baudrillard maintains his view of the Gulf War as a "non-war," a nonevent that the media strives to present as the "real" thing when it is but a simulacrum of war, a film of war without images of war (p. 45). Taking the position of the cheated audience who wants to get its money's worth, Baudrillard even compares the war to a "long strip-tease" (p. 86) that eventually dissolves, in its suspense, the desire for the naked body, which then appears, in the light of the audience's disappointment, as itself deceptive and unreal. At other moments the frustration of the audience to this war is compared to that caused by a "failed copulation" (p. 25) or to making love with a condom (p. 13), while the war itself becomes akin to an in vitro fertilization (p. 64) in which the sexual act has been skipped over. And in the same way that babies born from in vitro fertilization are not a proof that the sexual act has taken place, the 100,000 dead Iraqis fail to prove that the Gulf War was a war. Instead the war remains, in spite of the dead, "a shameful and useless fraud, a programmed, melodramatic version of what was the drama of war."[8]

The images with which Baudrillard expresses his frustration and indignation at the Gulf War suggest that he has been taken in himself by the "melodramatic version" of the conflict offered on the screens that he so fiercely denounces. For it is hard to imagine that for the dead Iraqis no war, in whatever form, took place. Similarly, the body of the stripteaser is no fake for the stripteaser; a failed copulation for one partner may be a great success for the other; and the baby born of an in vitro fertilization might argue that some kind of a sexual act must have taken place, if only an act of "sexuation." Moreover, the pleasure of the parents is irrelevant to the birth of the baby, as is the satisfaction of the Western audience to the death of the Iraqis. Baudrillard seems to believe that the war, staged by the media for the audience's sake, was in itself fought for the audience. In this sense, confusing the accounts of the war with the war, he seems to have accepted the version of a "clean" and "surgical" war that the Western media were so eager to convey.

What justifies his statement that there was no *passage à l'acte* in this war—the deaths, as it were, took place by magic—is the discourse of dissuasion that political powers have developed since the Cold War. According to Baudrillard, the Gulf War follows a logic of dissuasion (p. 13), within which the virtual does not give way to the actual, but to more virtuality:

The most widespread belief is that of a logical linking (*enchaînement*) from the virtual to the actual, according to which all available weapons

---

[8] It is worth quoting the whole passage: "The worst is that these deaths still serve as alibis for those who do not want to have gotten themselves worked up (*s'être excités*) for nothing, or to have been taken in for nothing: the dead, at least, could prove that this war was really a war, and not a shameful and useless fraud, a programmed and melodramatic version of what was the drama of war" (p. 79).

can but be used one day, and such a concentration of forces but lead to
a conflict. But this is an Aristotelian logic which is not at all ours anymore. Our virtuality definitively prevails over actuality, and we shall
have to content ourselves with this extreme virtuality which, as opposed to Aristotle's, dissuades the *passage à l'acte*. (p. 15)

What impedes the transition from the virtual to the actual in this
logic of dissuasion is the formulation of the potentiality (and possibility) of war in terms of its programming: "It is the problem of anticipation. Does something that has been meticulously programmed
still have a chance of occurring?" (p. 28). The war has been anticipated in all its details; it is as if it had already taken place: How can it
then take place? As we saw in the previous chapter, to conceive of
something as already done or as capable of being done all at once is
to close off the courses of action that actually allow for its realization.
In this sense, Baudrillard is right to point out that the logic within
which the Gulf War was presented by the media led to the logical
impossibility of the advent of the war, an impossibility that held,
logically, even while the war was being presented as actually taking
place. The logical, however, does not rule the phenomenological: It
so happened that some, if not all, of the available weapons were
used, whether according to Aristotle's logic or not. Ultimately, if the
logic of dissuasion had any effect, it seems to have been on the audience, dissuaded from acknowledging that the war was taking place
in the realm of the actual instead of in the ethereal realm of the virtual.

Baudrillard himself acknowledges the effect of the "total machine of dissuasion" (p. 73) on the audience, which would have
been fascinated by the evidence of the simulacrum (and montage)
of the war, itself aimed at "abolishing all understanding of the
event" (p. 74). But what the obvious simulacrum of the war would
confuse, according to Baudrillard, is the fact of its nonadvent: The
Gulf War would be the "living illustration of an implacable logic
that makes us incapable of considering another hypothesis than
that of its real advent" (p. 71). The "implacable logic" in question,
however, is that of an operative total machine that could in fact
program the war and ensure that its course follow the program—

this logic does indeed pretend that the war has taken place as fore-
seen. But to deny the possibility of such programming, to resist the
model of the war according to which it has already taken place
and is simply being "delivered" by the war machine, is not the
same as denying the advent of the war itself. Baudrillard, however, develops the myth of the "ready-made" war to the extreme:
"There have been no accidents in this war, everything took place
in accordance with a programmatic order, without passionate
disturbances. Nothing occurred that could have metamorphosed
things into a duel" (p. 80). If the above is granted, then it can be
granted that the war was no "real" event, that it must have
sounded "fake" even to those who cried out dying (the war having
been already written, and badly performed). But to grant the possibility of a functioning "total machine" is to grant that either
things can happen without taking place—a possibility Baudrillard
refuses—or that they simply do not happen, and do not take
place—the argument he seems to be defending.

The nostalgic reference to a duel, which would have reintro-
duced the "event" in the war, the stakes of the war, the stage to the
war, and an issue (resolution) of war, functions in Baudrillard's
argument as the proof that the war neither happened nor took
place. That is, had it taken place, and consequently happened, it
would have been in the form of a duel, of a confrontation defining
boundaries within which a political issue was being decided. That
it did not take place that way, at least according to the media, is
the sign that the war did not happen either—that it was a nonwar,
as Baudrillard calls it, a nonevent. The notion of the war as a nonevent is thus asserted, on the one hand, by the imagery of the "total machine" and the fully programmed war, and reinforced on the
other with the comparison to the "traditional" model of war—that
is, the confrontational setup, stylized in the "duel."

But Baudrillard himself explains the nonevent of this war, as
well as that of all that passes as "the actuality" in the information
networks, as the "involution of real time, an involution of the event
in the instantaneity of the all-at-once" (p. 46). The event disappears
in the construction of an instantaneous "real time" (NOW!), in which

it could simultaneously take place and be described. The construction of this real time of the event could be performed as follows: The actor moves, and describes his/her movements at the same time. In this context, what the actor is playing cannot be deployed, unless, of course, it were understood that what is being performed is the myth of the real time of the event.[9] In this "utopic time," of course, the event cannot be significantly constructed as an ongoing event: "War implodes in real time, history implodes in real time, all communication, all meaning, implode in real time" (p. 48). The term "implode" points to the replacement of a place by a moment: The "mass" of the event—a term that Baudrillard himself uses, with reference to the Gulf War's failing to reach a "critical mass"—disappears, and with it its staging, its context, duration, and so on. We are left with an abstract event, or even the "being" of the event, which "being" can be called, with Baudrillard, a nonevent. In this sense, I think we can say that the Gulf War became, in its representation, a nonevent, as do all events reported according to the construction of a "real time." It does not follow, however, that the war did not take place, nor that it was a nonevent. Thus when Baudrillard argues that "in the Gulf, the event was, as it were, devoured in advance by the parasite virus, the retro-virus of history" (p. 66), his analysis seems correct with regard to the Gulf War on the screens, but unrealistic as an analysis of what happened in the Gulf.

To return to the comparison of the Gulf War and the "duel": It is clear that the Gulf War does not seem to correspond to the confrontational setup of a "combat," and consequently it does not correspond to the model of a combat as action par excellence. But if we cannot analyze the event of the Gulf War according to such a model, it does not follow that the model of the machine of war applies. In other words, it may well be that the Gulf War is an event for which there are no "instructions for analysis" available yet. Baudrillard, however, does not contemplate this possibility. He acknowledges the tension between the two competing models of

[9]Another way of putting this is that in "real" or "clock-time," all we do is move our bodies. . . .

the war, implying respectively that the war takes place and that it does not take place, but concludes that both are operative at the same time: "The war and the non-war are taking place at the same time" (p. 49). What allows him to reach such a paradoxical conclusion is once again the myth of the application of the implacable course of logic to the course of events. Thus the "apocalyptic escalation" and "intensification" of the war preparations will, according to the Aristotelian model of the transition from the virtual to the actual, inevitably lead to a catastrophic war, while the inexorable logic of dissuasion will inevitably keep the war in the realm of the virtual. The fact that these two "hypotheses" would be "taking place" at the same time is a sign, for Baudrillard, that "the space of the event has become a hyperspace of multiple refraction, that the *space of war has definitively become non euclidean*" (p. 49). As a result, the war will reach no resolution: "We will remain within the undecidable of the war."

Leaving aside the question of what a "hyperspace of multiple refraction" is exactly, Baudrillard's hypothesis that the Gulf War will not, has not, or does not take place is here literalized. His argument now becomes: There is no single place/space to which we can assign the event of the Gulf War; an event without a place is not an event; the war is a nonevent. Although it can be easily granted that there is a sense in which the event of the war was "refracted" by the media—in which case it can be said that the war consists of a series of events, happening at different places, of which the stakes are multiple—the "strong" sense of Baudrillard's hypothesis still seems naive, insofar as it relies on the myth of total programming, of the war machine, and of the ruling of phenomena by the inexorable course of logic. Indeed, the motor of his argument is the suspension of the war in the nonspace, and in fact the nontime, of dissuasion, functioning according to mechanisms of anticipation and programming. There can be no events outside of time and space, whether Euclidean or not: The question is, where, outside a model, is there such a thing as a nonspace/place, and a nontime? Hence either the war remained at the stage of being modeled, or it "fired"—and did not become a copy of its model but an event subject to, among other things, accidents.

Baudrillard's despatialization of the war has a series of theoretical consequences, the first of which is to remove the war definitely from the reach of human agency. The myth of the fully programmed war already introduces a strong element of disempowerment, as it is indeed hard to conceptualize the changing of the course of already established events—it is hard to go against Fate, or to revolt against the plot in which one is a character. But as Ulysses suggests to Hector in Giraudoux's play, Fate can be "tricked," convinced, persuaded, or simply misled. As long as the events are in the hands of agents required for their enactment, there is the possibility of influencing their "course." But if events are "placed" outside of the realm of the physical, in a nonspatial and atemporal realm, even this possibility dissolves. We become the "targets" of the consequences of something that is happening, as it were, elsewhere. And there is no possibility of intervening in an event that unfolds in an absolute "elsewhere."

The second consequence of Baudrillard's hypothesis is closely linked to the first. If nothing can be done with respect to an event that does not take (a) place, no politics can be envisaged for such an event either. If the stage of war, considered as the "last" stage for political action, disappears, then the stage for political action, and indeed for politics, crumbles into thin air as well. Thus Baudrillard asserts that this war "does not correspond anymore to the 'clausewitzean' formula of politics pursued by other means; it would respond rather to the *absence of politics pursued by other means.*" And, again:

Variant of Clausewitz: *the non-war is the absence of politics pursued by other means. . . .* It does not proceed any longer from a political will to dominate, from a vital impulse, from an antagonistic violence, but from the will to impose a general consensus by means of dissuasion (*par la dissuassion*). (p. 95)

Here the notion of war as the last recourse of politics, the last stage of politics where negotiation and dialogue give way to violence and conflicts are resolved through "direct action," is clearly displayed against the putative nonwar, which becomes the sign of a nonpolitics. Politics thus appears as the term englobing forms of action, the paradigm of which is the confrontational setup of a combat, whereas nonpolitics emerges as the term englobing, as it were, performative action, motivated by the will to cancel out "real" action in the establishment of a general (global) consensus (Locke's model applied to an international "civil society"). Consensus, thus opposed to confrontation, would not allow for any course of action other than agreement, so that politics becomes a nonevent, already decided and determined in advance, and consequently a nonpolitics of subjection, once again, to a global plot.

According to Baudrillard's analysis, the real stake of the Gulf War is the final abolishment of the possibility of confronting the global network of consensus:

> The Gulf War is the first consensual war (*guerre consensuelle*), the first war carried on legally, throughout the world, in view of putting an end to war, in view of eliminating all confrontation liable to threaten the world control system, henceforth unified. (p. 96)[10]

Here, again, even if it made sense to suppose that it would be beneficial for the "world control system" not to be contested at all, it would still remain to be seen whether the aim of the war was reached, and whether it can be reached. The fact that the war did not take place in the ethereal realm of programming already speaks against the possibility of a purely consensual, and worldwide, order. This possibility, moreover, is grounded in Baudrillard's argument on the definition of an entity, "the world-control system," against which there

---

[10]The fact that as of March 1998 there is still an ongoing crisis in the Gulf, and precisely around the issue of Iraq's possessions of weapons with which it could defy the Western system, certainly questions Baudrillard's version of the successful programming of the war. But it also seems to question the view that the "system"—granting its existence—desires the abolition of armed confrontations. Indeed, as we will see with Lyotard, the Western system should in principle benefit from confrontations, for they are liable not only to help consolidate it politically and economically but also to reactualize the issue (if not the fiction) of its hegemony (see, for example, the articles on the "new" Gulf crisis in *Le Monde Diplomatique* of March 1998, where the United States is discussed in its unquestioned, if not uncontested, role of world leadership).

cannot be, logically speaking, any kind of confrontation: Indeed, how could a system be confronted? Whether confrontation must be considered as the ultimate form of political action or not is, I think, an important and debatable issue. And to dispel its possibility, and with it that of political action, by transforming the parties of a failed confrontation into programs or systems is, I think, a highly debatable move. The stakes of such a move are not so much the "existence" of the war or its status as an event, but rather the implications of the conclusion that the Gulf War is, in Baudrillard's words, "a site of collapse" (*un lieu d'effondrement*, p. 76) rather than a "historical" event, which entails, as I have tried to show, *l'effondrement du lieu*— the collapse of sites or places that could be the stage of political action. Without such places or stages for action, we are bound to remain waiting for the consensual order to collapse under its own weight, a possibility that Baudrillard considers at the end of his third essay as he lets the German poet Hölderlin speak: "There where the danger grows, also grows that which saves us" (p. 100). More prudent than Hector, Baudrillard concludes his trilogy on the nonwar with the announcement of the growing possibility of such a collapse: "Hence, the more the hegemony of the world-consensus is reinforced, the higher are the risks, or chances, of its collapse" (ibid.). According to Baudrillard's own logic, however, what is announced too early arrives too late to take place.

We could say, using Wittgenstein's words, that "a picture held Baudrillard captive," the picture of a "surgical," completely programmed, and consequently uneventful war, presented by the media as a direct account of the war. Indeed, although Baudrillard recognizes throughout his three essays the constructedness of the "live" report of the war, and denounces it accordingly, he concludes that the war cannot, properly speaking, be said to have taken place. This, we have seen, is not only in total accordance with the logic of the model he criticizes but is also a statement with heavy consequences, as it leaves no theoretical space for human intervention in human affairs. Assuming that there is a relationship between the analysis and the description of a given situation and the courses of action that may be envisaged either to change or participate in it, Baudrillard's analysis can propose only, as a response to the New World Order, a resigned waiting.

Staging the system

If Baudrillard's treatment of the "picture" of the war can be dismantled and criticized, the question of how to respond to the political model it figures still obtains. Indeed, the image of a programmed world order seems to captivate not only him but also Western societies in general, and it is powerful enough to block reflection on political action, if not so acts themselves. This is what Lyotard shows in "The Wall, the Gulf, and the Sun: A Fable," in which he develops an even more dissuasive version of Baudrillard's programmed world order that overpowers—as a framework—the liberal and Marxist frameworks of analysis, traditionally thought to provide the means to intervene in political affairs. Lyotard "tests" the validity of these two "traditional" frameworks on the events of the fall of the Berlin wall and the Persian Gulf crisis, concluding that neither of them is capable of accounting for these events.[11] Accordingly they also fail to propose effective means of intervention on the current historical situation, and, in fact, to "follow" the models of action they propose is, according to Lyotard, to participate in the situation they oppose. The framework of analysis with which Lyotard disqualifies liberalism and Marxism, and that proves to be comprehensive to the extent of ac-

[11] Lyotard's treatment of these two events as the "limit" cases of liberal and Marxist analysis suggests that, after these two events, politics is not "the same." In this he adopts the joint-classification of the fall of the Berlin wall and the Gulf War, which Baudrillard considers throughout his three essays as "sites of collapse" (*lieux d'effondrements*, p. 76), and hence as two instances of the noneventfulness of politics today, or of the nonpolitics of contemporary events.

I should stress that Lyotard's analysis should not be taken at face value: His position cannot be determined from what he says, but can be surmised only from what he does. Accordingly in my discussion I treat the views Lyotard presents in his article as retellings of pervasive contemporary accounts of current historical situations, to which Lyotard himself may, or may not, adhere.

counting even for the future of "life" in post–solar system time, suggests that political struggle, as it has been understood, is bound to further the functioning of the world (and even cosmic) order. Thus neither analysis nor actions seem capable of altering significantly the historical situation that the stronger version of Baudrillard's programmed world order describes and prescribes.

What disqualifies liberal accounts of current historical situations in Lyotard's "fable" is the fact that they still posit confrontational scenarios in which a party having right on its side measures its force to a second party that must consequently have "wrong" on its side. The fall of the Berlin wall demonstrates that no such parties can be defined, while in the Persian Gulf crisis none of the conflicting parties can be honestly said to be "right." Marxism, in turn, which posits the proletariat as the protagonist of history, is proved inadequate in a situation such as the Persian Gulf War, where the "Arab masses" cannot be identified as the proletariat. It is even more directly questioned by the fall of the Berlin wall, which Lyotard qualifies as the "practical critique of communism" (p. 114).[12] The more appropriate account of the current historical situation that Lyotard offers avoids the pitfalls of liberalism and Marxism by postulating the efficiency of systems instead of the agency of either the proletariat or of opposed parties, and cancels out confrontational stakes by positing conflicts in terms of the (evolutionary) adaptation of systems to their historical "environment." Thus the fall of the Berlin wall would provide the evidence

[12]My reductive version of Lyotard's analysis is supported by the formulation of his own summary. Thus he says of the Gulf crisis, one of the two events marking the "current political situation" and the failure of the liberal and Marxist readings to account for it, that "the good conscience of the West appears impoverished in the assertions that Saddam Hussein is a tyrant, that Arab people are hysterical and fanatical, that international rights are being violated, and so on, as if the West was exempt from the same sins, even recently. On the other hand, if the Marxist reading could legitimate its own discourse, it wouldn't have to confuse the Third World, the South, or the masses of the Middle East who have been made wretched by imperialism with the figure of the proletariat—a confusion that is absurd in theoretical and practical terms and shameful with regard to the responsibility for thinking" (p. 119).

that "the more open the system, the more efficient it is," showing that "closed and isolated systems are doomed to disappear, either by competition or merely by entropy" (p. 119). According to these criteria for analysis, the issues of the Gulf crisis "are predictable": (The system of) Islam "cannot match the concrete performances achieved by the Western system and is therefore obliged either to change its positioning . . . or to disappear" (p. 119).[13]

Given this "description" of the historical situation, militancy appears as a quixotic enterprise, not because forms of action are practically impossible but rather because theoretically they are predictably ineffective with respect to the really determinant "historical" factor: "the openness (or looseness) of systems competing with each other" (p. 119). Thus Lyotard opens his "fable" with the explanation of how the practice of the "risky exercise" called situation analysis, which he himself used to undertake as a member of the theory and practice institute "Socialism or Barbarism," finds a dead end in the systemic framework of analysis. The exercise in question consisted in the formulation of the current historical situation, in view of formulating "practices to enable the goal" of helping "exploited and alienated peoples to emancipate themselves from exploitation and alienation" (p. 112). These practices, Lyotard observes, are now encouraged and required in Western societies, for the sake of improving the functioning and development of "the system as a whole" (p. 113). Opposition and criticism function as correctives to the efficiency of this system, which assimilates them to achieve its self-emancipation. Indeed, according to this view, the goal of emancipation has itself become a goal promoted by the system, "an ideal that the system endeavors to actualize in most of the areas it covers" (p. 113), and implicitly understood to be in charge of the system by those instances that denounce it. For the system, however, emancipation cannot be emancipation from the system: By virtue of its openness, all conflicts become means to further implement its own emancipation. And, as the goal of emancipation motivating political

[13]Adapt or die: This would be the evolutionist expression of Baudrillard's "consensual world order" (agree or die).

struggle becomes the system's goal, exploitation and alienation become the signs of the inefficiency of systems that fail to achieve their own emancipation.[14]

The argument that all political action can be shown to further the system's development can be countered, with, for example, Wittgenstein's "answer" to the paradox discussed in §201 of the *Philosophical Investigations*:

> This was our paradox: no course of action could be determined by a rule, because every course of action can be made out to accord with the rule. The answer was: if everything can be made out to accord with the rule, then it can also be made out to conflict with it. And so there would be neither accord nor conflict here.

Similarly, if all actions can be made out to further the system, then they can also be made out to hinder it. If the notion of system has any use, then it might well be in the same sense that rules do: "'obeying a rule' is a practice" (§202)—so is "furthering the system," whose subversion is therefore as possible as disobeying a rule. But if, as Lyotard argues in different essays, the systemic framework of analysis has become the predominant interpretive framework for the realms of the political and the historical, it cannot be simply dismissed with the logical proof of its inadequacy. It seems necessary, rather, to find a way of responding to it other than an outright rejection of it, a full acquiescence to it (political cynicism), or a disinterested abdication.[15] The main problem it presents to those unwilling to accept the picture of "natural exploitation" it offers is that of finding practices that do

[14]In other words, the fight for emancipation—which may well comprehend the fight for the emancipation of peoples participating in "other" systems—contributes to the emancipation of "the system," which, in turn, competes with other systems for "survival," and consequently thrives on their "non-emancipation," which in old-fashioned political terms consists in the exploitation and alienation of peoples.

[15]See, for example, "Le temps aujourd'hui" (in *L'inhumain: Causeries sur le temps*), where Lyotard argues that this systemic framework of analysis is operative in different ways today—mainly in the attempts to synthesize time through the global memory networks—and hence that it is being accredited and "followed" by important decisional instances in Western democracies—mainly, again, via policies of scientific research.

not aim to achieve the goal of emancipation the system is capable of assimilating. Toward the end of his article, Lyotard seems to suggest that one such practice might be "imagination," in the form, "for example," of "a story freely told" (p. 120).[16] He then goes on to tell the story of "the unavowed dream that the postmodern world dreams about itself," which turns out to be a post-Darwinian evolutionary tale sustaining the systemic framework of analysis previously deployed in his discussion of the fall of the Berlin wall and the Gulf crisis.

Very briefly, Lyotard's "freely told" story, which takes the perspective of the system, tells the "improbable" advent of systems of life on earth, the most successful of which turned out to be those called "liberal democracies," the openness of which not only enabled them to capture all forms of energy—including human energy—particularly well, but also to control events (and consequently, to "stock" time and "synthesize" it in a permanent present):

It happened that systems called liberal democracies *came to be recognized* as the most appropriate for the task of controlling events in whatever field they might occur. By leaving the programs of control open to debate and by providing free access to the decision-making roles, they maximized the amount of human energy available to the system. The effectiveness of this realistic flexibility *has shown itself* to be superior to the exclusively ideological (linguistic) mobilization of forces that rigidly regulated the closed totalitarian systems. In liberal democratic systems, everybody could believe what they liked, that is, could organize language according to whatever system they liked, provided that they contributed to the system as energetically as they could.

Given the increased self-control of the open system, it was likely that it would be the winner in the competition among the systems all over the Earth. (p. 123; my emphasis)

[16]In his foreword to *L'inhumain*, Lyotard suggests that a way to resist the "inhumanity" of the system is through the "inhumanity" of our humanity—that is, childhood. Without going into a discussion of what he means by these two inhumanities, it is interesting to note that for him to recall our "debt towards childhood" is a (even *the*) form of resistance. He assigns the task of remembering such a debt to writing, thinking, literature, and the arts ("C'est la tâche de l'écriture, pensée, littérature, arts, de s'aventurer à en porter témoignage," p. 14).

The story goes on to announce the difficulty the victorious system is already preparing itself to overcome: "the unavoidable collapse of the solar system." The only chance for the system to survive after the death of the sun is exodus and adaptation to cosmic conditions of life. This is what "all the research that was in progress at the time this story was told" would already be preparing. This happy ending, however, is overshadowed by the uncertainty of what "Man" will have to become in order to adapt to the cosmos: "What Man and 'its' brain, or better, the Brain and its man would look like in the days of this final terrestrial challenge, the story did not say" (p. 123).

Lyotard's "freely told story" highlights the implication of "Man" in the development of the system, not only because it links the survival of the latter to the self-induced evolution of mankind, but also because it is, after all, "Man" himself who must do the "recognizing" of the superiority of liberal democracies, as well as that of their "realistic flexibility." In this sense Lyotard himself, through whose computer "the system" speaks, presents himself as taking part in the realization or frustration of the system's migratory impetus. Thus the tale could be considered as a warning, denouncing the consequences and limitations (the end of mankind) of the operativeness of the fable.[17] It is also certainly a joke, insofar as it uncovers the fabulous basis of the systemic framework of analysis, telling it for what it is: a tall tale. But either way its spreading is ambiguous, for there is certainly no possibility of action within the fable itself: To resist the migration of the system is to condemn mankind to extinction, whereas to participate in its programming is to renounce mankind as we know it, mortal and terrestrial.

What, then, is "free" in this "freely told" tale? For it does not offer an alternative to the system it tells; it does not announce better times

---

[17]Lyotard argues that the "fable" is not only told and "accredited in the very serious milieus that the communities of physicists, biologists, and economists represent" (p. 120) but also suggested by "the convergence of tendencies animating all the sub-sets of contemporary activity" (Foreword to L'Inhumain, p. 13). It is, in other words, an operative fable.

to come, or console us with a critique of the model it deploys. Neither could these activities create a "free" space within the system, according to the logic that the story deploys. In fact, as the speculations that "Lyotard's purpose" in telling this tale give rise to, if the tale has an end(ing), its telling does not seem to have a specific objective. This might well be one of the senses in which the story is "freely told"—the telling of the story is free from ends.[18] But a more immediate—to the article—way in which Lyotard's telling is "free" is that the telling of the story enacts the difference between the system and those to whom the story is addressed—the former, after all, has no ears. This differentiation is not a negligible act, as it recalls the reader or listener to his/her place, here and now, in the act of attention all stories call for, thus addressing the reader/listener's activity and capacity to act. Insofar as the system is differentiated from the reader/listener, the possibility of a differentiation of the reader/listener's acts from the activity of the system is also raised, and consequently, a certain "freedom" to act is asserted—a freedom, that is, from the system. As a corollary, the possibility is also raised of political action that would not succumb to the assimilatory mechanism of the system, and hence that would not posit "emancipation" as its goal.[19]

---

[18]This conjecture is consistent with the view, developed by Bill Readings in his foreword to Lyotard's *Political Writings*, that Lyotard argues for an "endless politics"—a politics that would not function to end conflicts once and for all, and that would not presuppose a time in which politics would be "obsolete," because everything would be fine. In such an "endless politics," conflicts would never be overcome once and for all, but they would be given the space for their enactment.

[19]It is, again, tempting to dismiss the notion of "system" altogether, on both historical and political grounds. Historically, it can be argued that it is precisely a notion that characterizes a postmodern discourse on history, rather than the events that become the subject matter of such a discourse. When I say "postmodern" I have in mind Hannah Arendt's argument, in "The Concept of History," that it is the notion of process that most profoundly marks the difference between the modern age and the past:

To our modern way of thinking nothing is meaningful in and by itself, not even history or nature taken each as a whole, and certainly not particular oc-

It is, however, difficult to imagine political action that would not be motivated, or sustained, by the principle of "emancipation"—it would seem that to give it up is tantamount to giving up the notion of "political action" itself. "Emancipation," however, need not be understood solely in narrative terms—that which occurs at the end of the story. It can also be understood in terms of what is achievable now, through this specific act. This understanding of emancipation roots it in the act of differentiation discussed above. In this sense, Lyotard's fable could suggest that the only viable "form" of emancipation is "differentiation," a notion that could replace the political goal of emancipation understood as that which occurs at the end— after—politics. Indeed, "differentiation," if a goal, is enacted constantly and punctually—at the now-oriented "end" of actions. In contrast to "narrative" emancipation, differentiation is exempted, as it were, from the dangers that a long path of realization represents:

currences in the physical order or specific historical events. There is a fateful enormity in this state of affairs. Invisible processes have engulfed every tangible thing, every individual entity that is visible to us, degrading them into functions of an over-all process. (p. 63)

Similarly, it could be argued that it is the notion of system that separates modern thought from our contemporary thought, whatever that could be called. But this historical perspective does not do away with systems, however conceptual they may be.

Politically, it can be argued that systemic frameworks of analysis are disempowering, and consequently, useless—that is, that they are antipolitical, and this much more so than modern frameworks of analysis dominated by the notion of process. Indeed, as Arendt herself shows, the notion of process, in spite of its voracity, leaves open the possibility of human action. In "What Is Freedom?" she argues that all human life, including the political, "takes place in the midst of processes," that "automatism [is] inherent to all processes," and that all automatic processes "spell ruin to human life"—but it is precisely proper to humans to assert themselves against processes and through action, and precisely proper to action to interrupt (albeit not always) automatic processes (p. 168). In other words, processes can be acted upon, and they are, at least to the modern mind, what there is to act upon. The system, however, cannot be "interrupted," as it cannot be "infiltrated," "opposed," or "escaped from"—and in this sense it is a particularly inapt concept on which to ground political analysis. But how do dominant notions give way to others? How are we agents of conceptual reconfigurations?

In Giraudoux's play, for instance, Ulysses has 461 steps to take to reach his ship and ensure peace between the Trojans and the Greeks, a large enough number to let the "plot" (Fate) redirect his steps toward war. It would thus seem that the "practice of imagination" that Lyotard engages in with his "freely told tale"—free from the goals of the system—would consist, mainly, in the practice of differentiation, which would open a theoretical space for action "within" the system that would not participate "in" the system.

To consider "differentiation" as a form of political action raises, however, a number of debatable issues. One of the attributes of political action in its ordinary, everyday sense, is that a state of affairs of public or general concern is affected by means of some kind of concertedness, whether the concertedness resides in the understanding of the state of affairs or consists in collective, organized action. It seems, however, difficult to conceive differentiation as a principle of political action to the extent that neither collective action—requiring a certain adaptation of analysis, ends, and means—nor agreement, concertation, nor convergence toward a desired state of things is "covered" by the notion of differentiation. Instead, Lyotard's fable suggests that differentiation is an act that bypasses models and ends, and that it is because it does so that it can be a significant act with respect to the all-comprehensive, systemic model that turned all actions in its favor. Differentiation, however, need not exclude the principle of political ends altogether. If we see it as creating the conditions for political action, and more specifically, for political action which opens, innovates, or disrupts existing models of action and definitions of ends, differentiation can be understood as allowing ends to be constantly renewed, displaced, and redefined.[20] For, whether political "ends" are formulated as utopias, models, or simply as punctual objec-

[20]It is obvious that distinguishing between the system and the people, the model and the act, logic and phenomenology, is crucial to envisaging action. It is because this distinction cannot be made from the perspective of the system or from that of a model—and neither can it be made by logic, although logic states it—that differentiation is an act. In this sense differentiation is akin to the tiger's thoughtless bound, which, in the previous chapter, opened the field of cognition.

tives, they function as the "mark" which, like Aristotle's "good," guides behavior and courses of action without being itself directly or permanently achievable. In other words, ends are not absolute and need not be so treated—it all depends on how "ends," models, and objectives are understood to function with respect to courses of action.

Political action will certainly not be rescued from the paws of the system by any "idle" concept, including that of "differentiation." If it is effective, it must be already at work. And it is, if we consider that all the paralyzing models of action discussed throughout this book are not only impracticable but also refuted by practice—"certain" acts invariably breach the limits imposed by models; acts of differentiation constantly recall that there is such a breach for action to have effects on models, and to produce further models. This, of course, is not news: According to Eduardo Galeano's anecdotal history of Latin America, Puerto Rican Indians experienced it themselves as early as 1511 and used it against the Spanish invaders.[21] The story, which could be the counterpart to Lyotard's fable, recounts how Puerto Rican Indians realized that the invaders were not gods and acted accordingly, for the better or the worse.

It is 1511, and the soldier Salcedo—alone—reaches the Guauravo River. The Indians offer him their shoulders to cross it. Halfway, they let the soldier fall and crush him against the bed of the river. Then they lay him on the grass. After three days, the body rots and stinks. In case he were still alive, the Indians had been begging his pardon, but now they realize that it is not necessary. The drums spread the good news: *The invaders are not immortal.*

Galeano is careful not to attribute the intention to drown the soldier to the Indians—their act is not introduced by a process of deliberation; neither is it explained a posteriori. As a result of this act, however, the enemies are shown not to be immortal, and the Indians can envisage a collectively organized course of action against them—they prepare a revolt. The revolt could not be a possibility as long as the belief in the enemies' immortality pre-

[21]Eduardo Galeano, "Agüeynaba," pp. 65–66.

vailed, but it was not necessary that the belief be questioned for the Indians to crush the soldier against the bed of the river. In the story, it is the "thoughtless" act that breaches an existing descriptive framework, thus opening the possibility of courses of action that could not, before, be envisaged (at least as strategies). As long as the belief in the invaders' immortality, or at least the unawareness of their mortality, persisted, the Indian chief Agüeynaba treated captain Ponce de Léon with great honors. After the enactment of the soldier's mortality, new prospects for action opened.

In the next story of the volume, "Becerrillo," we learn that the Indians' revolt was crushed—as they have been, repeatedly, until the present time. Thus the question arises of whether the course of action that followed upon the realization of the invaders' mortality was the "best" possible one—whether "revolt" was an effective response to invasion, or whether, even, the presupposition of the invaders' immortality would not have allowed better means of preservation of the Indian communities. But although the question is worth debating, it does not annul the "goodness" of the news spread by the drums. The drums spread the news that something can and has been done. The situation is not foreclosed, the dead end has been shown to be no end. This book, I hope, conveys a similar kind of "news"—which is not news, but remains good: that models are not inviolable. They may not be atemporal, but they are certainly not immortal.

☞ Afterword

The Subject Is an Akrates

Translated as either "weakness of the will" or "incontinence," *akrasia* has received particular attention at least since Socrates in view of the problems it presents for models of rational action, and, more generally, for the understanding of man "in his role of Rational Animal," to use Donald Davidson's expression.[1] In contemporary discussions of incontinence, it is generally assumed that it is manifested in or consists of the agent's taking an alternative and even contrary course of action to that judged by him to be the best.[2] We have seen, however, that this is precisely the behavior that marks the formation of a willful subject, author and origin of his actions: For St. Paul, recall, it is the norm for the "inward man" to do what he would not, and not do what he would; while Samson discovers his will as he acts contrary to his prediction; and Hamlet, Vladimir, and Estragon tend to do anything except that which they announce they will do. There seems to be a sense, then, in which incontinence is constitutive of the

[1]Donald Davidson, "Actions, Reasons and Causes" (henceforth referred to as ARC), p. 8. The expression "Rational Animal" is, I think, Aristotle's.

[2]Here is Davidson's working definition of an action that "reveals weakness of the will or incontinence": "In doing x an agent acts incontinently if and only if: (*a*) the agent does x intentionally; (*b*) the agent believes there is an alternative action y open to him; and (*c*) the agent judges that, all things considered, it would be better to do y than to do x" ("How Is Weakness of the Will Possible?"—henceforth referred to as WWP—p. 22).

subject as defined within a philosophy of origins. And in this sense it is also, as we will now see, a structural trait of Davidson's "Rational Animal."

This similarity is not surprising if we consider that for Davidson reasons cause actions, in much the same way that the will, or the interiorized "principle of necessity," was supposed to cause the performative subject's deeds. As Davidson himself announces in his introduction to his *Essays on Actions & Events*, the general thesis of the collection is that

the ordinary notion of cause which enters into scientific or common-sense accounts of non-psychological affairs is essential also to the understanding of what it is to act with a reason, to have a certain intention in acting, to be an agent, to act counter to one's own best judgment, or to act freely. Cause is the cement of the universe. (p. i)

For Davidson, to be sure, reasons are not "within" agents—he does not appeal to the metaphor of interiority to elaborate on the relation between agents and actions. But reasons are for him at once proper to the agent and what ultimately cause his behavior.[3] Thus, although they may sometimes remain unexplained, intentional actions are always explainable in terms of the reasons that cause them, at least in the sense in which it is said of an agent that he "performed the action *because* he had the reason" (ARC, p. 9):[4]

When we know some action is intentional, it is easy to answer the question, "Why did you do it?" with, "For no reason," meaning *not that there is no reason* but that there is no *further* reason, no reason that cannot be *inferred* from the fact that the action was done intentionally: no reason, in other words, besides wanting to do it. This last point . . . defends the possibility of defining an intentional action as one done for a reason. (ARC, p. 6; first emphasis mine)

---

[3]By "proper to the agent" I mean that my actions, for instance, cannot be caused by someone else's reasons; or, the reasons causing my actions would not necessarily have caused someone else's.

[4]For Davidson, to provide a reason for an action, which can then be said to be caused by that action, is to rationalize it. Thus "rationalization . . . is a species of causal explanation" (p. 9).

Here reasons are not causes retrospectively, for the agent does not provide an a posteriori explanation of his action other than referring the questioner to the fact that he performed it. It is not, moreover, what the agent did, but that he did it, which constitutes the point of "no further reason," a point from which other reasons, such as justifications (which are not causes) are elaborated. It is from the coincidence, as it were, of the point of no further reason and the fact that the agent did it that Davidson can infer that there is a reason that caused the agent's action, which reason, in turn, can be presupposed because the agent acted, and must consequently have had a cause for his action.[5] This causing reason may well have taken place in the "real time" of the action, without deliberation or actual rationalization on behalf of the agent, but it is still a distinct moment of the agent's act, which logically precedes it in that it is its moving principle.

Man, then, is "the Rational Animal" because reasons have, as it were, executive power over his actions. This model of rational action, however, is not at all challenged by incontinent actions, because although these are enacted against or in spite of the agent's best judgment, they can still be said to have been caused by a reason—albeit not by that the agent himself reasoned. Indeed, the problem that incontinent acts present is that the agent has good reasons to do x, which should cause x, but what is ultimately caused is another action, y. But, Davidson argues, "if reasons are causes, it is *natural* to suppose that the *strongest reasons are the strongest causes*" (p. xii; my emphasis). The reasons that cause the incontinent act can then be measured against those that fail to cause what would have been the continent act, and the incontinent act can thus be explained in terms of its causal strength. To the extent that Davidson's "naturalist(ic)" slippage from reason to cause does not work the other way

[5]This point might recall Wittgenstein's "Explanations come to an end somewhere" (*Philosophical Investigations*, §1) but is in fact significantly different. As I argued in chapter 6, the fact that explanations end somewhere suggests that they do not, in fact, have to pertain to origins—accordingly they end, and precisely in the action in question.

around—it is not *natural* to suppose that the best reasons are the strongest causes—he can defend the causal view of action "by arguing that a reason that is causally the strongest need not be a reason deemed by the actor to provide the strongest (*best*) grounds for acting" (p. xii; my emphasis). Thus, in their causal role, reasons participate in actions, determining them rather independently of the agent's reasoning: "For a person can have a reason for an action, and perform the action, and yet this reason not be the reason why he did it" (p. 9). The fact that the agent's reasoned reasons do not necessarily function as the cause of his actions, even though they may coincide with the reasons that in *deed* cause them, does not imply that reasons are not reasons anymore. On the contrary, the assimilation of reasons to causes reinforces their protagonism with respect to actions by freeing them from the contingency of thinking. Thus action can only be (supposed to be) rational, although the agent may himself be irrational.

In view of the above, it is clear that the postulate of an alternative course of action to that not taken by the incontinent agent—that is, alternative to what should have been the "continent" action—is crucial to preserving the executive role of reasons in actions and to maintaining the reputation of man as a "rational" animal. For, were there no "other" action, there would be no stronger cause to deflect the "best" reasons' causal power. It is hard to imagine, however, that there could be no other course of action, if only because, according to Davidson's own understanding of action, agents engage in it constantly—we are always doing something intentionally, whether according to our best judgment, against it, in spite of it, or in partial oblivion of what we are doing. From this perspective, Davidson's point sounds banal—for what is there to be explained, in fact, if the incontinent counterpart of the unrealized continent action of, say, going jogging in the morning, were an action such as brushing one's teeth?[6] In other words, if we are unable to establish a connection

---

[6] The matter does not change substantially by postulating more consequent actions, for, as Davidson himself shows, incontinence is not a problem exclusively for moral philosophy—the incontinent action is not necessarily evil or

between the reasons for going jogging and those for brushing one's
teeth, the "problem" of incontinence seems to dissolve into thin air,
for, without a tension between the two sets of reasons, there is no
conflict other than that of the agent's inability to do what he thinks
best to do. And in this case, the formulation, and the stakes, of incontinence, change significantly: For the problem then is that reasons fail to act as causes, which failure clearly questions their executive power over actions. The incontinent act thus seems to be a cover
for what fundamentally challenges the causal role of reason—that
continent acts fail to occur, or, in the terms of this book, that the *passage à l'acte* does not take place.

In Aristotle's *Nicomachean Ethics*, in fact, incontinence is most
broadly characterized in terms of the would-be continent act: As
opposed to the man who has "practical wisdom not by knowing
only but by being able to act," the incontinent man is ultimately
"unable to act" (1152a8–9). A more literal translation would be: "The
incontinent man [is] not practical" (*o akrates ou praktikos*)—and a
more elegant one, "the incontinent man is not *prone* to act."[7] With

---

wrong; it can be as harmless, or "good," as the envisaged but not enacted continent act. Thus one of the examples Davidson gives of an incontinent act is that of
brushing one's teeth instead of staying in bed. It is worth noting in this respect
that Aristotle, who discusses incontinence at length in Book VII of *The Nicomachean Ethics*, and who is certainly an unavoidable reference on the subject, is
indulgent toward the incontinent man, who is not as bad as the self-indulgent
man, can be cured (because he repents), and so on. The incontinent act is not
necessarily a "social" problem either, for, though Davidson brushes his teeth incontinently in his example, he does not do it in a beastly manner—he most
probably does it with "calm, and even with finesse," like J. L. Austin, who, in "A
Plea for Excuses," helps himself incontinently to two segments of a bomb (a des-
sert) at High Table and does not raven, snatch the morsels from the dish, and
wolf them down. He does not, in short, "lose control of himself," which would
be a more socially unacceptable behavior than succumbing to the temptation of
taking two servings instead of one. In other words, once they are removed from
the field of morality, there is simply nothing in incontinent actions themselves to
justify the amount of attention they have received as a type of action.

    [7]Davidson is in fact well aware of these and similar formulations of inconti-
nence in Aristotle's text, but ignores them—legitimately, but significantly—in
favor of those that coincide with his: "Aristotle sometimes characterizes the incontinent man (the akrates) as 'abandoning his choice' (*Nic. Eth.* 1151a) or

this definition Aristotle does not exclude the possibility of there being an alternative course of action, but he significantly shifts the emphasis from the incontinent to the nonenacted continent act, which is
the act that not only resists explanation but that also seems unex-
plainable to a rational model of action. Davidson himself acknowledges—indirectly—that, while the agent has a reason to undertake
his incontinent action, "he lacks . . . a reason for not letting his better
reason for not doing [it] prevail" (p. 42, note 25). Another way of
phrasing this remark is to say that the agent's incontinent action is
not the reason for which he refrains from enacting his continent action, so that the agent has no reason, not only for doing what he
eventually does, but also for not doing what he does not do. Davidson's incontinent man might thus speak like Hamlet, who, assuming
that the "godlike capabilities" of speaking, "looking before and after," and reasoning cannot have been God-given to men "to fust in
us unused" (IV. iv. 36–39), wonders: "I do not know / Why yet I live
to say 'This thing's to do', / Sith I have cause, and will, and strength,
and means / To do't" (ibid. 43–46).

Hamlet's words could also have been uttered by Aristotle's incontinent man, likened at one point to "a city which passes all the
right decrees and has good laws, but makes no use of them"
(1152a19–21). In this image, there is no causal relation between reasons and actions—it is not enough for the city to have good laws for
them to be executed. Thus to the extent that reasons are themselves
unimpaired, it would seem that the defective piece in the artifact of
action is causality itself. Unless, of course, Aristotle's city had laws
that decreed (and executed) their own nonexecution.[8] And this is in-

---

'abandoning the conclusion he has reached' (1145b); but also often along the
lines suggested here: 'he does the thing he knows to be evil'; (1134b) or 'he is
convinced he ought to do one thing and nevertheless does another thing'
(1146b)" (WWP, pp. 25–26, note 7).

[8]Davidson's defense of the view that there is a causal relation between reasons and actions (that reasons are causes) leads him, in "Actions, Reasons and
Causes," to discuss the necessity of finding a law governing this relation. His position is that there may well be laws governing each instance of this relation—in
his terms, "a law to back each singular causal statement" (p. 17). But, he adds, "it

deed the view that Davidson defends toward the end of his essay on incontinence:

There is no paradox in supposing a person sometimes holds that all he believes and values supports a certain course of action, when at the same time those same beliefs and values cause him to reject that course of action. (WWP, p. 41)

Here Davidson addresses an instance of incontinence without recurring to an alternative course of action, and consequently, to the notion of the causal strength of reasons: The agent has one set of reasons that supports in his view the course of action that the selfsame reasons ultimately "cause him to reject." His behavior cannot in this case be explained by appealing to the superior strength of one set of reasons over another. This time the agent's best reasons to do x actually cause him not to do x. In other words, what he holds as good reasons to undertake a certain course of action, hold him from enacting that selfsame course of action. Reason is thus saved from disuse, for it is still operative as a cause, but, instead of conducing to action, it actively impedes it. Hence Davidson is able to say, with a hint of relief, that the "fault in incontinence" is not that "the akrates . . . [holds] logically contradictory beliefs": "What is wrong is that the incontinent man acts, and judges, irrationally" (p. 41)—the problem is the man, not the model. But whereas contradiction is a favorite device of comedies, that agents counteract themselves is instead the favorite subject matter of tragedies, as the plays discussed throughout this book show.[9]

---

does not follow that there is a law connecting events classified as reasons with events classified as actions" (p. 17). Formulated in the terms of my argument, this might mean that the causal and the rational functions of reasons are not governed by laws. Taking up Aristotle's image of the incontinent man, we could say that in the case of the man whose reasons hold him from acting, the causal (executive) function of reasons has taken over and suspended its rational (legislative) function, in what sounds like a *coup d'état*. The man is under curfew.

[9]*Waiting for Godot* is not an exception to this "rule," because although it is most certainly a funny play, it is far from being a straightforward comedy—the laughs it provokes are not exactly lighthearted—and it has clear tragic elements in it.

Ultimately, then, the phenomenon of "intentional actions that are *contrary* to the actor's best judgment" (p. xii; my emphasis) is, at its most literal instance (inaction, or inability to act) also a necessary postulate for defending what I have called the executive power of reasons. It is, moreover, a fundamental postulate, for if reasons are to have any causal strength at all, then they must be responsible for cases in which the agent does what he would, those where he does not do what he would, and those where he does what he would not. But in this sense, it would seem that instead of considering that incontinence is a problem for rationality, the latter could be considered as a problem for action, at least within a causal model of the relationship between reasons and actions. More specifically, the problem within such a model is that reasons should be directly conducive to actions, skipping, as it were, the agent's agency—the laws of Aristotle's city should execute themselves. In Aristotle's image, however, the laws are not executed because the city makes no use of them: Their execution is thus conditional on their application, and, we could add, on their applicability. And for this, the agent's agency is required, as long as it is not understood in causal terms—for the laws must be interpreted, situations evaluated, and so on.

The case of the agent whose reasons to do something ultimately "cause" him not to do it could thus be compared to that of a city that does not apply its laws. This is what happens to Hamlet in his famous "To be, or not to be" soliloquy, where he blames "the pale cast of thought" for weakening "the native hue of resolution" and making "enterprises of great pitch and moment / . . . lose the name of action" (III. i. 84–88). Hamlet, recall, demonstrates the intervention of thought in this slippage from action to inaction in the same speech, as he stages mortals confronted with the choice of either suffering "the slings and arrows of outrageous fortune" or of taking "arms against a sea of troubles / And by opposing end them" (III. i. 57–60). Insofar as taking arms against a *sea* of troubles is an impossible task, the two options concur: From the moment that he conceives his troubles as a sea, and then dramatizes himself brandishing his sword against it, Hamlet vows himself to inaction. Here "thought" is to blame in its choice of the image to envisage the enterprise to accomplish—not, to be sure, because it is an image, and even less because it causes his inaction, but because it cannot be "used." Had Hamlet imagined himself sailing across a sea of troubles, or taking arms against dragons of troubles, he may have been able to act accordingly. As it is, however, the image is useless, for it proposes a course of action that cannot be taken, further blinding Hamlet to the possibility of a feasible alternative. In this sense, Hamlet might seem more akin to a city that avails itself of inappropriate laws, which can either be never applicable or inapplicable in given circumstances. But if Hamlet's image is inadequate, it is because he holds on to the belief that it is enough to have, in his words, "cause, and will, and strength, and means / To do't," for *it* to be done. In other words, the choice of an inappropriate image is in itself symptomatic of the agent's misunderstanding of how the will, reason, and causes are actually involved in action.

Incontinence thus appears as a shortcoming of reason, which would basically fail to be practical, because the agent misses out a stage, as it were, of practical reasoning. Accordingly in Aristotle's image the city does not avail itself of inappropriate laws: These are good, but are not applied—the incontinent man makes no use of them. More precisely, the man in an incontinent state fails to accord universal and particular premises, and is as a result unable to exercise his (better) knowledge even when both premises are correct. He may be using only the universal premise, in which case he is bound to act "against his knowledge," because "it is particular acts that have to be done" (1147a2–4). Or his particular premise may be untimely activated by the senses, as in the case of the man who eats sweets in spite of the universal opinion refraining him from tasting them: Here the man holds the correct opinion that "everything sweet is pleasant," and that "this is sweet," and acts accordingly, following his appetite. In all cases, however, action will be determined by the particular premise, for acts are necessarily singular—in Aristotle's terms, "It is the opinion that is active" (1147a32–34)—and this whether they are incontinent or not. Incontinence consequently expresses the man's failure to contain or grasp the particular with the universal, and the incontinent man's words (and thoughts) are accordingly comparable to those spoken by actors on a stage (ibid.): The latter's use of language is not meant to apprehend particulars or to lead to action; what he says and reasons in his role is not what makes him play his role.[10]

The incontinent man, then, abandons "the result of his calculations" (1145b10–12), because he fails to relate the universal to the particular. To insist on the term "universal," however, may be misleading, unless it is understood in terms of its temporal implications. For it is apparent that for Aristotle the incontinent man has a special relationship not only to his reasoning but also to time. He is compared, for example, to the self-indulgent man, because they both pursue "the present pleasure" (1146b22–24); he is also said to be "impetuous"; the fact that he is led by his passions instead of by deliberation is also a sign of precipitation. Most important, the incontinent man is subject to regret, or repentance, and this as opposed to the self-indulgent man. Now regret or repentance apply to what has already been done, and is therefore achieved, concluded in time, temporally "complete" as opposed to what has yet to be done. All these are indications that the incontinent man does not relate the temporal whole of his projected action to the moment of its enactment—he does not relate the course of action that his reasoning achieves to the achievement of it in action. In this sense, he temporarily—Aristotle insists that incontinence is a passing state—"falls out" of the relationship between the whole of the moment and the temporal whole of the action, and, concentrating on the former, misses out the time of the latter.[11]

[10]Aristotle in fact relates the use of language to incontinence more generally as he specifies that animals "are not incontinent, . . . because they have no universal judgment" (ibid. p. 167)—which lack of judgment of course implies that of language.

[11]This fall might be qualified as a moment of reversal of the model of action according to which it is the end of actions which is their cause. Instead, the incontinent man, because he relies on the wholeness of the moment, could be said to lapse into a model according to which the cause of actions is their "beginning"—in other words, the displacement of the temporal whole of the action to the temporal whole of the moment originates, for a while, a philosophy of origins. In this sense, it seems to me that incontinence, understood as the phe-

This is indeed what seems to happen to Hamlet as he stages himself in arms against a sea of troubles. For in his conceit the evacuation of possible procedures or ways of doing is reinforced by the suppression of the duration of action: His troubles, unified in the image of the sea, should be solved all at once, in one single mortal blow, and in no time at all. Hamlet thus makes the *passage à l'acte* impossible for himself, for there is practically no time in which the deed to be done could take place—no moment he could seize to "step" into action, and no occasion that could offer it to him. And, as we have seen, it is ultimately an occasion forced upon him that precipitates him into action—until then, and paraphrasing him, although "all occasions" "inform against" him and "spur" his "dull revenge" (IV. iv. 32–33), he is bound to inaction by the paralyzing logic of having to do what he has to do without doing it, and hence of having to have already done it. It is ultimately this "temporal defect" in Hamlet's conceptualization of action that, imposing on him the impossible task of having to solve his troubles without solving them (in time and in a specific manner), prevents his reasoning from being practical and wise—for, recall, only agents that effectively act can be said to have practical wisdom.

The "temporal defect" interfering with Hamlet's *passage à l'acte* is not only inherent to the particular image of himself battling with the sea. It is more generally proper to models of "direct" action, whether they are inflected in terms of the causal role of reasons or in terms of the subject/author. And what the "defect" reflects is precisely the understanding of action as ensuing from either agent (the will) or reason, rather than as a process requiring specific skills—a central one of which is to know what to do with concepts, reasons, and models, and, more generally, with language. According to Wittgen-

nomenon of not being prone to act, has had a fate similar to that of Aristotle's philosopher, whose activity of contemplation isolates him from the temporal whole of the polis in the course of the history of philosophy—it is the shift from a philosophy of ends to one of origins, or from a model of indirect action to one of direct action, which eventually makes it the norm to be unable to act—although this is a norm, I should stress, that, in contrast to St. Paul's divine laws, can be followed only in the letter.

stein, we tend to treat models, rules, and conceptualizations as ideals that should be concretized, directly brought from the atemporal realm of universals to the temporal realm of particulars. We forget, in short, that models are not directly applied, but that they have to be used—and that it is *use* that operates the transition from the atemporal to the temporal, which use, moreover, is primarily linguistic. To take up a biblical topos, or, indeed, the performative subject's dream, actions do "begin" in the word, but only in the sense that courses of action, ways of behaving, and procedures in general are imbedded in language. In this sense, language is much more than performative—it is part of the performance. But this is precisely what, according to Wittgenstein, we "forget" under the enchantment of language: We forget that we are ultimately playing language-games—which we are certainly in no position to take lightly, if only because we risk being taken in by them. And that we are playing in and with language means, simply, that it is inextricably woven into action, and that action implies a use or practice of language—a constant interpretation and adaptation of concepts, of models, and of reason itself, which is a crucial aspect of the agent's actual agency. In other words, Aristotle's "practical man" is also practical with language—*he acts with it.*[12]

In this work I suggest a way—and only one—of accounting for the spell language puts on agents, which account begins precisely with Faustus's fascination with "lines, circles and characters," following his dismissal of Aristotle's model of indirect action, and partial integration of the Christian figure of the "inward man." In my account, Faustus's desire for magic powers is inextricably linked to what I characterize as a shift from a philosophy of ends to one of origins, and more specifically as the transition from an understanding of deeds as acts to one of deeds as pacts. Locke, recall, relies on this transition to ensure a better conceptual control of events and, most

[12]If he is a "rational man," moreover, it is not because in addition to being able to act he has reasons to act, and still less because his reasons control or determine his acts, but because he acts with reasons.

important, to provide the necessary criteria to distinguish individuals from each other. Locke's agents first acquire singularity with their status of authors, but they must still be ensured against losing it through time. For this, they must refrain from engaging in action "again": Indeed, to act would imply plunging into a hectic present in which agents would once again be marked and determined by their actions and consequently by interaction. Thus Locke ultimately distinguishes agents by their speech acts, which allow them to be both at the origin of and disengaged from their actions, thereby maintaining their singularity through time and out of it. With this move, I argue, Locke's agents become "proper" subjects; they are formally independent from each other and remain agents only within the scope of their performativity. But, ideally, these subjects do not act: They predict their actions.[13] Accordingly, it is characteristic of performative subjects to succumb to the illusion that their actions will "arrive" already accomplished from the future, as if brought back by the boomerang effect of their predictions.

More generally, I argue that it is the category of the subject that induces a "temporal defect" in models of action and turns them into models of inaction, because this category imposes a temporal order incompatible with that of action. This hypothesis implies that the categories of subject and action are themselves incompatible, and that it is the effort to harmonize them that renders action problematic. Let us picture this hypothesis with the help of Hamlet again, considering how he stages himself alone against the sea instead of, in accordance with what preoccupies him, in duel with his uncle. He is thus following the demands of the performative subject: He gets rid of both the other of interaction and the time of action, and situates himself at the origin of his revenge, without engaging in it. But the fact that he retains the interactive setup of the duel (he is confronting the sea), instead of imagining himself flying over it with magic wings, suggests that he cannot quite renounce the "traditional" model of action—he cannot *not* envisage it. He is thus trying to be a subject and to act at the same time: And that is the really impossible

---

[13]This is why I call them performative, as opposed to autonomous subjects.

feat, according to Hamlet's own mise-en-scène, in which subject and action fail to be conceptualized at the same time, or even in the same time. The real choice underlying Hamlet's "To be, or not to be" is thus "To be (a subject), or to act." A more sober but rather more extreme formulation of Hamlet's choice can be found in Davidson's essay on "Agency," where he demonstrates that, if the agent is maintained at the origin of his actions, and the latter are defined only with respect to the agent, then it follows that only "mere movements of the body" can be considered as actions—"these are all the actions there are." But then the category of action becomes, from the agent's perspective, inconsequential, for not only do acts have their origin in himself, but they also end there.

Needless to say, "mere movements of the body" can have enormous—and disastrous—consequences, and all the more so if the agent can conceive them only in these terms. But the performative subject has no trouble apprehending the actions of others as a whole: On the contrary, as conceived by Locke and as confirmed by history, the performative subject relies on others to conclude things in his stead, for him and for his profit. It is with the attempt to stage the "I" as it acts—that is, "me" acting and watching myself act—that difficulties arise. These are akin to those the man in Bakhtin's example is bound to encounter as he tries to pull himself up by the hair. And yet, the performative subject ignores such obvious impossibilities: He is like the man in Wittgenstein's example, who lays his hand on top of his head to prove that he knows his height. Here the man is not just "mistaken"; he has "forgotten" that he is playing the game of knowing, and more generally, that language games cannot be played alone. He is thus unaware of the role he can play as an "I" in it, and attempts to play the others' part with respect to himself—in some instances he even plays with ghosts. But ultimately the man cannot fill in the other's role properly, and this lack is made apparent in the prescriptive turn he gives to language, which ends up ordering him to perform impossible tasks, and to disconnect himself, like Aristotle's incontinent man, from his fundamentally circumstantial condition.

In Bakhtin's terms, the obtuseness of the "I" is due to his need to be subject to the aesthetic activity of others, who have, however, been expelled from the scene of the subject. The "I" then tries, and fails, to follow the aesthetic imperative himself—he looks into thin air and hopes it will reflect back his image. What he needs, of course, is a mirror: the mirror of interaction. And this the "I" needs to give some form to the present, so as to permit his experience of it (experience cannot be abstract). Indeed, in Bakhtin's argument, the present takes shape as it is addressed to someone in interaction, be it the tacit other of language, the "other" inherent to the future, or concrete, personalized others for whom the "I" can be, at least temporarily, a "hero." For, as was the case with all the heroes discussed in this book, it is only under the other's aesthetic activity that the "I" can be heroic and do something—as opposed to just moving his body. It is also only in doing something that the "I" can be responsible for his actions, which he cannot be with respect to "mere movements of the body." And, finally, it is by assuming this responsibility that the "I" assumes that he is here, in time, and with the time others have produced for him. In short, if interaction is done away with, so is action, the time of action, and time itself.

This is not to say that interaction can effectively be done away with: Once again, as with action, and indeed, the others, it cannot be evacuated from actuality. But it can be—and is—evacuated from interpretive frameworks, with rather serious implications. Individuals, once again, will always manage to tie their boot laces; the problem arises when political action is associated, whether argumentatively or metaphorically, with the impossible feat of lifting oneself up by the hair. This is serious because, taking up Hannah Arendt's reflections on the contemporary man of action, it is clear that his capacity to act continues to be the "most dangerous of all human abilities and possibilities," and that it requires that we act upon it in turn–thoughtfully, to be sure, but not under "the pale cast of thought." In other words, to keep actions within human dimensions—meaning, the dimension of peoples, as opposed to abstracts like "the Economy," "the System," or even "the Nation"—it is crucial to avoid "losing the name of action." As we saw in the discussion of Baudrillard's stageless war and of Lyotard's equally stageless politics, however, this is precisely what seems to be happening, or to have already happened. Indeed, in both cases political discourse and the political imaginary are haunted by the ghost of Hamlet, alone and in arms against the system, striking useless blows. This is the image that this study purports to dissipate, to clear the way for more productive models of (inter)action.

Such models can of course be neither invented nor imposed—this is not how models can be made to function or to prevail. If we are to look for inspiration anywhere, however, it seems clear that those models featuring the *akratic* subject will not provide it. It is worth keeping in mind, then, that this figure predominates in Western tradition and that it is predominantly male—Aristotle goes as far as to discard the possibility of attributing incontinence in its "extended sense" to women, "because of the passive part they play in copulation" (1148b29–33). Even if we disregard this comment, there are in fact enough reasons to discard the incontinence not only of the female figure but also of all the "marginal" figures of Western history. Indeed, reputed for their kinship to animals and considered to be deprived of both reason and will, neither women, slaves, nor colonized peoples could be candidates for *akrasia*, which requires the specifically human attributes of, precisely, Reason and Will. To the extent that they were not, then, as figures, invited to participate on equal terms in the incontinent subject's drama of inaction, it can be expected that they have not assimilated his characteristics, and that they are, as figures, liable to feature in models of action significantly different from that of the *akratic* subject. As such they are promising figures in the search for interactive models of action.

☞ Works Cited

◌ Works Cited

Aeschylus. *The Oresteia*. Translated by Robert Fagles. New York: Penguin Books, 1979.

———. *The Oresteian Trilogy*. Translated by Philip Vellacott. London: Penguin Classics, 1959.

———. *Prometheus Bound*. In *Prometheus Bound and Other Plays*, translated by Philip Vellacott. Middlesex: Penguin Classics, 1961.

———. *Prometheus Bound*. Translated by J. Scully and C. J. Herington. New York: Oxford University Press, 1975.

———. *Prometheus Bound*. In *Seven Against Thebes and Prometheus Bound*, translated by P. Arnott. New York: Macmillan, 1968.

Arendt, Hannah. "The Concept of History"; "What Is Freedom?" In *Between Past and Future*. 1954. Reprint, New York: Penguin Books, 1977.

———. "Labor, trabajo, acción: Una conferencia" ("Labor, work, action: A lecture.") 1957. In *De la historia a la acción*. Translated by Fina Birulés. Barcelona: Paidós, 1995.

Aristotle. *Éthique de Nicomaque*. Traduction, préface, et notes par Jean Voilquin. Paris: GF Flammarion, 1965.

———. *The Nicomachean Ethics*. Translated by H. Rackham (bilingual edition). London: Harvard University Press, 1934.

———. *The Nicomachean Ethics*. Translated by David Ross. Oxford: Oxford University Press, 1980.

———. *Poetics*. Translated by I. Bywater. New York: Modern Library, 1984.

———. *La Poétique*. Textes, traduction, et notes par Roselyne Dupont-Roc et Jean Lallot. Paris: Éditions du Seuil, 1980.

Austin J. L. "Performative Utterances"; "Plea for Excuses." In *Philosophical Papers*. Edited by J. O. Urmson and G. J. Warnock. Oxford: Oxford University Press, 1979.

Bakhtin, M. M. "Author and Hero in Aesthetic Activity"; "The Problem of Content, Material and Form in Verbal Art." In *Art and Answerability:*

Early Philosophical Essays. Translated by M. Holquist and V. Liapunov. Austin: University of Texas Press, 1990.

———. *Toward a Philosophy of the Act*. Translated by V. Liapunov. Edited by V. Liapunov and M. Holquist. Austin: University of Texas Press, 1993.

Baudrillard, Jean. *La Guerre du Golfe n'a pas eu lieu*. Paris: Ed. Galilée, 1991.

Beckett, Samuel. "The End." In *The Norton Anthology of English Literature*. 4th ed. Vol. 2. New York: Norton & Company, 1979.

———. *Waiting for Godot*. London: Faber & Faber, 1975.

Benveniste, Émile. "La nature des pronoms." In *Problèmes de linguistique générale*, vol.1. Saint-Amand, Cher: Gallimard, 1966.

Bouveresse, Jacques. *La Force de la Règle: Wittgenstein et l'invention de la nécessité*. Paris: Les Ed. de Minuit, 1987.

Bradshaw, Graham. *Shakespeare's Skepticism*. Brighton: Harverster Press, 1987.

Cavell, Stanley. "Hamlet's Burden of Proof." In *Disowning Knowledge*. Cambridge: Cambridge University Press, 1987.

Davidson, Donald. "Actions, Reasons and Causes"; "How Is Weakness of the Will Possible?"; "Agency"; "Intending." In *Essays on Actions & Events*. Oxford: Clarendon Press, 1980.

Eliot, T. S. "Hamlet." In *Selected Essays*. London: Faber & Faber, 1969.

Gadamer, Hans-Georg. *Truth and Method*. Translated by Sheed and Ward. London: Sheed & Ward Ltd., 1975.

Galeano, Eduardo. "Agüeynaba." In *Memoria del fuego. I. Los nacimientos*. Mexico D.F.: Siglo Veintiuno Editores, 1991.

Giraudoux, Jean. *La Guerre de Troie n'aura pas lieu*. Paris: Bernard Grasset, 1935.

Godzich, Wlad. "Correcting Kant: Bakhtin and Intercultural Interactions." *Boundary 2* 18, no. 1 (1991): 5–17.

———. "Foreword" to *The Resistance to Theory* by Paul de Man. Minneapolis: University of Minnesota Press, 1986.

———. "The Time Machine." Foreword to *Narrative as Communication* by Didier Coste. Minneapolis: University of Minnesota Press, 1989.

Heidegger, Martin. *What Is Called Thinking*. Translated by J. Glenn Gray. New York: Harper & Row, 1968.

Hesiod. *Theogony*. Edited by M. L. West. Oxford: Clarendon Press, 1966.

Holy Bible. Authorized King James Version. Grand Rapids, Mich.: Zondervan Corporation, 1962.

Kant, Immanuel. *Fundamental Principles of the Metaphysic of Morals*. Translated by T. K. Abbott. Buffalo, N.Y.: Prometheus Books, 1988.

Laslett, Peter, ed. "Introduction" to *Two Treatises on Government* by John Locke. Cambridge: Cambridge University Press, 1988.

Locke, John. *Two Treatises on Government*. Edited by Peter Laslett. Cambridge: Cambridge University Press, 1988.

Lyotard, Jean-François. *L'Inhumain: Causeries sur le temps*. Paris: Ed. Galilée, 1988.

———. "The Wall, the Gulf and the Sun: A Fable." In *Political Writings*. Translated by Bill Readings and Kevin P. Geiman. Minneapolis: University of Minnesota Press, 1993.

Macpherson, C. B. *The Political Theory of Possessive Individualism: Hobbes to Locke*. Oxford: Clarendon Press, 1962.

Marlowe, Christopher. *Doctor Faustus*. Edited by John D. Jump. New York: Methuen Educational Ltd., 1965.

Milton, John. *Samson Agonistes*. Edited by F. T. Prince. London: Oxford University Press, 1957.

Nietzsche, Friedrich. "The Birth of Tragedy." In *The Birth of Tragedy and the Case of Wagner*. Translated by Walter Kaufmann. New York: Vintage Books, 1967.

———. "Homer's Contest." In *The Portable Nietzsche*. Translated by Walter Kaufmann. New York: Viking Press, 1968.

———. *On the Genealogy of Morality*. Edited by Keith Ansell-Pearson. Translated by Carol Diethe. Cambridge: Cambridge University Press, 1994.

Oxford English Dictionary, the Compact Edition. Oxford: Oxford University Press, 1971.

Readings, Bill. "Foreword" to *Political Writings* by Jean François Lyotard. Translated by Bill Readings and Kevin P. Geiman. Minneapolis: University of Minnesota Press, 1993.

Shakespeare, William. *Hamlet*. Edited by J. B. Spencer. New York: Penguin Books, 1987.

Shelley, P. B. "Prometheus Unbound." In *Alastor and Other Poems; Prometheus Unbound with Other Poems; Adonais*. Edited by P. H. Butter. Estover, Plymouth: Macdonald & Evans, 1970.

Sloterdijk, Peter. *Thinker on Stage: Nietzsche's Materialism*. Translated by Jamie O. Daniel. Minneapolis: University of Minnesota Press, 1989.

Soucher, Emmanuel, and Yves Jeanneret. "Manipuler les idées et les désirs. Publicité et politique: Le mélange des genres doit être clairement dénoncé." In *Le Monde Diplomatique*, December 1994.

Strawson, P. F. "Intention and Convention in Speech Acts." In *Logico-Linguistic Papers*. London: Methuen & Co., 1971.

Telford, Kenneth A. "Preface" to *Aristotle's Poetics: Translation and Analysis*. Chicago: Henry Regnery, 1970.

Tully, James. *A Discourse on Property: John Locke and His Adversaries*. Cambridge: Cambridge University Press, 1980.

Volosinov, Valerian N. *Marxism and the Philosophy of Language.* Translated by Ladislav Matejka and I. T. Titunik. New York: Seminar Press, 1973.

Waswo, Richard. "Damnation, Protestant Style: Macbeth, Faustus, and Christian Tragedy." *Journal of Medieval and Renaissance Studies* 4 (1974): 63–99.

Webster's New Collegiate Dictionary. Springfield, Mass.: G. C. Merriam Co., 1979.

Weigel, Alexander. "Hamlet o La Intrusió del Temps en l'Acció." In *Commissió internacional de difusió de la cultura catalana. Art, Ciéncia: Medi Natural.* Barcelona: Departament de Cultura de la Generalitat de Catalunya, 1994.

Wiggins, Martin. "*Hamlet* within the Prince." In *New Essays on Hamlet.* New York: AMS Press, 1994.

Wittgenstein, Ludwig. *Philosophical Investigations.* Translated by G. E. M. Anscombe. Oxford: Basil Blackwell, 1968.

Index

In this index an "f" after a number indicates a separate reference on the next page, and an "ff" indicates a separate reference on the next two pages. A continuous discussion over two or more pages is indicated by a span of page numbers, e.g., "57–59." *Passim* is used for a cluster of references in close but not consecutive sequence.

Library of Congress Cataloging-in-Publication Data

Wagner, Valeria
    Bound to act : models of action, dramas of inaction / Valeria
Wagner.
        p.   cm.
    Includes bibliographical references (p.   ) and index.
    ISBN 0-8047-3330-9 (cloth : alk. paper).
    1. Act (Philosophy).   I. Title.

B105.A35W33   1999
128.4—dc21   99-17526

This book is printed on acid-free, archival quality paper.

Original printing 1999
Last figure below indicates year of this printing:
08   07   06   05   04   03   02   01   00   99

Designed and typeset by John Feneron

Typeset in 10/13 Palatino